Disco Divas

Disco Divas

Women and Popular Culture in the 1970s

EDITED BY SHERRIE A. INNESS

PENN

University of Pennsylvania Press

Philadelphia

Copyright © 2003 University of Pennsylvania Press
All rights reserved
Printed in the United States of America on acid-free paper

10 9 8 7 6 5 4 3 2 1

Published by
University of Pennsylvania Press
Philadelphia, Pennsylvania 19104-4011

Library of Congress Cataloging-in-Publication Data

Disco divas : women and popular culture in the 1970s / edited by Sherrie A. Inness.
    p.   cm.
    ISBN 0-8122-3707-2 (cloth : alk. paper). —ISBN 0-8122-1841-8 (pbk. : alk. paper)
    Includes bibliographical references and index.
    1. Feminism—United States—History. 2. Women—United States—Public opinion.
3. Women in popular culture—United States. 4. Sex role—United States. 5. Public
opinion—United States. 6. Social change—United States. 7. Nineteen seventies.
8. United States—Social conditions—20th century. I. Inness, Sherrie A.
HQ1421 .D57   2003
305.42'097—dc21   2002040861

For Hallie Bourne

Contents

Introduction

"Strange Feverish Years"

The 1970s and Women's Changing Roles

SHERRIE A. INNESS

Bell-bottoms. Lava lamps. Platform shoes. Mood rings. There is no doubt about it: the 1970s are back with a vengeance, and the decade's influence crops up everywhere in popular culture.[1] The pages of *Vogue, Glamour, Seventeen,* and *Mademoiselle* are crammed with retro fashions. In interior design, '70s style is trendy and hip; Naugahyde sofas, suede furniture, and disco balls decorate households across the United States. In music, whole radio stations are devoted solely to that decade's music, and musicians, including ABBA, Earth Wind and Fire, Fleetwood Mac, Bee Gees, Bay City Rollers, Peter Frampton, Chicago, Roberta Flack, Donna Summer, and Gloria Gaynor. These icons have gained a new audience of young fans. Themes from the 1970s have become a staple in television shows, including *Freaks and Geeks* and *That '70s Show,* and films, among them *The Brady Bunch Movie, The Last Days of Disco, Austin Powers, Velvet Goldmine, Boogie Nights, The Ice Storm,* and *Outside Providence.*

Sometimes it seems as though it is impossible to go anywhere without 1970s iconography cropping up. Visit a movie theater, shop for clothing or furniture, or turn on a radio station, and you are apt to encounter what historian David Frum refers to as those "strange feverish years."[2] Recently, I was sitting in a coffeehouse and saw a young woman stroll by wearing hip-hugger bell-bottoms and a fringed suede jacket with a Day-Glo yellow smiley face plastered on its back. She was walking with another teenager in platform shoes. On the radio the Bee Gees were wailing "Staying Alive" from the *Saturday Night Fever* soundtrack. After my coffee, I walked to a furniture and home décor store where I could buy everything for the fashionable retro home, including lava lamps, suede rugs, and beanbag chairs. I couldn't escape the 1970s. How different this was from the 1980s, when no one with any fashion sense would have decorated a house in '70s style or worn '70s clothing; the just-concluded period drew sneers or, at best, dubious head shakes because of its excesses. No one wanted to be associated with this time; it seemed too frivolous, especially after the 1960s. Who wanted anything to do with an era famous for polyester leisure suits?

This fascination is the result of many factors. People in their thirties and forties grew up in this era and now are nostalgically looking back to their youth, perhaps because they no longer can keep up with the super speed of the new millennium. Carla Power writes in *Newsweek* about the current interest in the 1970s, "With the speed of computers doubling every eighteen months, and the net doubling in size in about half that, no wonder we're aching for familiar surroundings. Since the cornerstone of the Information Age is change, anything enduring becomes precious."[3] One of the eras we view as enduring is the 1970s. Through everything from fashion to film, we try to recall it. We look back at a time when we didn't have to worry about clocking in at work or downsizing, a time when our biggest concern was whether Mom would let us watch *The Bionic Woman* on television.

It's not only adults who look back at the 1970s with nostalgia. Even young people who weren't alive then look at it as a more innocent time. With the debacle of Watergate and the end of the Vietnam War, it might be difficult for some people who were alive in the era to view it in such a light, but many young people who have grown up with AIDS and mass murders in schools understand the decade differently, as a time when teenagers' major concerns were where to buy a lava lamp or what to wear at the disco. Adults and youth long to recapture, if only fleetingly, a time that has little to do with the reality of the 1970s. However unrealistic it is, this fantasy attracts many, whether they're watching *That '70s Show* on television, decorating their homes with beanbag chairs and shag rugs, or collecting '70s kitsch—puka-shell necklaces, platform shoes, Pez dispensers, and polyester leisure suits.

Why is our society fixated on the 1970s? As I mentioned earlier, many people long for a simpler time, so they turn to periods that view as more innocent than our own. The 1950s is also such a decade. In the American cultural imagination, this era has become so mythologized that it now has little to do with the actuality of the time. We are left with a fantasy, but one that has had a strong impact on the United States. The 1970s, similarly, has been distorted into a time supposedly less complicated than the current one. But how is this possible? After all, that was an era of *Charlie's Angels* fame, with the trio slinking around in skimpy outfits and getting kidnapped by bad guys every time they wandered to the local 7–11 for a six-pack of Tab. The 1970s was definitely a very different time from the 1950s, but both have been idealized in America's popular imagination. We long for a '70s defined by smiley faces, lava lamps, and rainbow suspenders. Perhaps that is why we shy away from social critique when it comes to this period; we do not want to acknowledge that our fantasy has little to do with reality.

This nostalgic attitude toward the decade threatens to turn it into one composed of nothing but its trivia. Between the activism of the 1960s and the greed of the 1980s, the 1970s can easily slip into obscurity, notable only for its excesses, whether in clothing, drug use, or sexual freedom. Because of its association with everything frivolous and excessive, the era seems suspect in the academy. Few scholars have tackled it—perhaps in part because it seems too close, too personal, at least for many who lived through it. Those who have essayed cultural analysis often make scathing observations about those years. Pagan Kennedy writes, "The seventies have the worst reputation of any decade in the twentieth century."[4] Scott Matthews is more critical: "The era that we look back on with the misty fond nostalgia of childhood . . . is a cultural wasteland devoid of any and all redeeming qualities. We are a generation of blunted wits dulled at the hands of Mike and Carol Brady. We are societal mutants weaned on *Zoom*, the Fonz, and Pop Rocks."[5] Kennedy and Matthews are not alone in their criticism; others express similar views.

In spite of such reactions, the 1970s deserve closer scrutiny, and I hope that *Disco Divas: Women, Gender, and Popular Culture* will play a part in this. The book's contributors examine how 1970s popular culture shaped women's (and men's) lives in this period and beyond. They suggest that the decade, far from being an era of cultural stasis, was actually one of social change. The great cultural shifts of the 1960s were still reverberating loudly, and American society had to come to terms with them. One of the arenas in which these shifts were negotiated was popular culture.[6] The 70s provided a venue for exploring gender roles that had shifted radically from earlier years. Charlie's Angels were definitely not the Beaver's mom.

Born in 1965, I grew up in the 1970s. I watched *The Bionic Woman* and *Charlie's Angels* on television. My mother frowned at such programs and would ask me, with exasperation clear in her voice, "What do you see in them?" Despite her displeasure, I was glued in front of the TV set when these shows aired. I was mesmerized because I saw them as different, particularly for women. The Bionic Woman got to rip a telephone book apart with her bare hands and run sixty miles an hour. The Angels solved mysteries and traveled to exotic places. But even more important, the Bionic Woman and the Angels were free to do what they wanted without men bossing them around (the Angels' boss Charlie and helper Bosley always seemed ineffectual).

This personal involvement with the 1970s has made me interested in how others reacted to popular culture. It also has made me curious about the resurgence of interest in '70s popular culture over the last decade. How did popular culture shape women's (and men's) roles in the '70s? How did it address the changes in women's roles that resulted from second-wave feminism, a movement that swept the United States and had a broad impact on women's lives? What messages did it convey to women of different races, ethnicities, and social classes? How did it create new role models for women? *Disco Divas* explores these questions.

The 1970s has been stereotyped as an era when few important historical or social changes occurred. It was a period, the stereotype goes, when people were so caught up with everything banal and empty that few had time or energy to devote to social issues. Who had time to worry about social change when the biggest priority was dancing until dawn at the disco or getting high with your friends?

But was the 1970s as devoid of change as it has been stereotyped? It was actually a time of great change, although it has not always been viewed that way. Andrew J. Edelstein and Kevin McDonough write, "The idea that the Seventies was merely a lull after the frenetic Sixties is simply not true."[7] Similarly, Herbert Muschamp comments, "In hindsight it is obvious that something big was going on beneath the decade's beige Ultrasuede surface, a cultural shift we have yet to fully comprehend."[8] After all, many of the social movements of the 1960s—including the youth movement and the movements for gay rights, civil rights, and women's rights—were alive and thriving in the 1970s. Many argue that it was in this era that these movements had their broadest impact.

It was also a time of change in other arenas. Watergate permanently altered the way Americans perceived their government. The end of the Vietnam War changed the way Americans understood warfare. The oil crisis and soaring inflation challenged many people's notions about the United States as a land of endless plenty. The high unemployment rate altered many Americans' assumption that anyone who wanted to work could find a job. In 1973, American Indian Movement members took over the village of Wounded Knee on the Pine Ridge Reservation in South Dakota, an act that transformed many people's views of Native Americans. These are a few of the myriad social changes that marked 70s United States.

For women, too, the decade was a time of change.[9] Women's liberation was everywhere, it sometimes appeared. The National Organization for Women (NOW), founded in 1966 by Betty Friedan and others, was highly visible in the 1970s, picketing media events that NOW members considered sexist. Gloria Steinem and others started *Ms.* magazine as a one-time insert in *New York* magazine; it proved to be so popular that it became a full-fledged magazine in July 1972, creating an important forum for feminism and becoming the first feminist magazine with a mainstream national audience. Consciousness-raising groups gave many women a place to discuss feminist ideas. Across America, second-wave feminism was a visible and influential movement that demanded changes for women.

And changes did happen. In the 1970s, women made great strides toward equality. In politics, Shirley Chisholm, a black U.S. representative from New York, was nominated for the presidency in 1972. In the same year, Anne Armstrong became co-chair of the Republican National Committee. Through the decade, women's agitation for the Equal Rights Amendment (ERA), which ultimately failed in the early 1980s, was an important part of the political scene. In education, millions of college women demanded equal treatment in programs ranging from law to medicine. In 1972, President Richard Nixon signed Title IX of the Education Act, which stated that no person would be discriminated against on the basis of sex from pursuing any educational program receiving federal aid; this law had a major impact on women's participation in sports programs. Women's studies became an established discipline in the academy, and the National Women's Studies Association was founded in 1977. In the area of women's reproductive rights, the Supreme Court decision to legalize abortion in 1973 had wide-ranging effects. The birth control pill began to spread in the 1960s and was an established part of American culture in the 1970s, giving women greater autonomy over their sexual lives.

With the changing environment for women, it comes as little surprise that popular culture changed as well. Popular culture came to terms in a variety of ways with second-wave feminism and the impact it had in many areas. Some forms of popular culture addressed feminism by subverting and undermining it, showing that feminism was a threat to America's traditional values. Other forms celebrated feminism and embraced the New Woman. *The Mary Tyler Moore Show* was a huge hit. Successful career girl Mary lived alone, loved her independent life, and was on the pill, as we learned in one memorable episode. Yet other forms of popular culture had a multivalent response to women's changing roles, embracing some while rejecting others. For example, *Charlie's Angels* featured a group of independent women detectives who rarely needed male help, but they also were traditional sex symbols who appealed to male viewers; the Angels were trapped between old and new visions of womanhood.

Disco Divas examines how 1970s popular culture reacted to second-wave feminism and women's changing roles. With its mass audience, popular culture, whether in the form of movies, television shows, or magazines, reveals important lessons about how feminist ideas were made palatable to a large audience. The popular media played a part in disseminating changing gender ideology. But the media did not only convey changing women's roles; they also altered those roles and created new ones. For example, the concept for *Charlie's Angels* stemmed, at least partially, from the increasing number of women in nontraditional jobs, including the police force; what emerged was a show that had its own impact on how women created and led their lives. Thus, examining the popular media is vital for understanding social change in the 1970s.

The essays in Part I of *Disco Divas* focus on how the 1970s media depicted second-wave feminism, a movement born approximately a half century after the end of the first wave, which had essentially ended after passage of the Nineteenth Amendment, granting women the right to vote. Because of second-wave feminism's centrality, the popular media had to address it as well as the issues it raised. Some media sources helped advance feminist issues, while others sought to limit their impact. Studying the depiction of second-wave feminism reveals the importance of the media in conveying these ideas to a mass audience. We also discover how the media were involved in watering down and diminishing feminist ideas.

The first two chapters analyze ways the popular media reacted to second-wave feminism. In Chapter 1, Steve Craig examines the advertising industry, which was at first reluctant to embrace feminist demands but then did so because it made good business sense. "The New Woman," as she was called, represented a powerful audience, and advertisers found ways to use New Woman imagery to attract a larger market share. Craig argues that second-wave feminism played a role in changing advertising, especially altering how women were depicted. Chapter 2 moves from advertisements to film. Through an analysis of *The Stepford Wives*, Elyce Rae Helford shows how the media sought to contain the perceived threat posed by feminism and its followers. *The Stepford Wives* addresses but trivializes a variety of second-wave feminist issues, defusing the threat of two feminist rallying cries: "Sisterhood Is Powerful" and "The Personal is Political." Helford discusses the history and meanings of these central tropes while exploring their exploitation in this popular film.

The next two chapters explore in more detail how second-wave feminists used the popular media to achieve their goals. In Chapter 3, Carrie N. Baker analyzes the ways feminists used the media to spread ideas about sexual harassment. Although sexual harassment has always existed, it was only in the 1970s that the term was coined and discussion about the issue burst into the mainstream media. In the press, sexual harassment was not always depicted as a serious sociopolitical issue; it was mocked or presented as primarily a minor personal concern. The feminist media addressed sexual harassment more seriously. Chapter 4 draws seemingly unlikely connections between second-wave feminists and cheerleaders and the depiction of both in the popular media. After discussing the development of cheerleading in the early twentieth century as a typically male activity, Molly Engelhardt examines how it was feminized after World War II. She then analyzes the transformation of the 1950s image of the All-American cheerleader into the 1970s image of the sexual, promiscuous cheerleader. This new figure, Engelhardt argues, had some similarities with a surprising character: the radical feminist.

The chapters in Part II take a broader look at the depiction of women in 1970s popular culture. A host of cultural forms ranging from television shows to films to magazines grappled with women's changing roles in this era and also helped create them. Studying representations of women in everything from blaxploitation films to disco songs, this section examines the complex and sometimes contradictory ideas about women's roles found in popular culture. We will find that these sources used a variety of different strategies to address women's changing place in society.

Part II begins with two analyses of the depiction of black women in the 1970s media. In Chapter 4, Stephane Dunn focuses on actress Pam Grier in the popular film, *Foxy Brown* (1974). This blaxploitation work reveals important lessons about black women's changing lives. On one hand, Foxy is an independent, fearless, tough hero, a major shift from times when the hero was more likely to be a white man, not a black woman. On the other hand, Foxy exemplifies racist ideas about the black female as dangerous and sexual. Dunn argues that *Foxy Brown* offered a new vision of black womanhood but also capitulated to many stereotypical cultural assumptions about the black woman. In Chapter 5, Toni C. King views *Ebony* magazine similarly, as changing black women's roles but also as adhering to some stereotypes about black career women. Although these women were sometimes stereotyped, they played a positive role in helping black women envision themselves in a variety of different careers that were opening up to them. This was a particularly important service because much of the booming self-help literature for working women was aimed at white women. Thus, *Ebony*'s depictions of working women were vital for black female readers to gain a better understanding of the special challenges faced by African-American working women.

Focusing on cookbooks and soap operas, the next two chapters address how these stereotypical female genres changed in the 1970s. In Chapter 7 I discuss swinging singles' cookbooks and suggest that they offer important insights into changing gender roles both in and out of the kitchen. The large number of cookbooks that catered to the needs of the growing singles population did more than transmit messages about how to broil a steak; they also conveyed lessons about how to be a woman or a man. Both men and women declared their superiority in the kitchen, suggesting their superiority in other areas as well. Thus these cookbooks became a battle site in the war of the sexes.

Thomas D. Petitjean, Jr., focuses on the difficulties the daytime soap operas faced in depicting realistic female characters in an era when women's roles were changing dramatically. He argues that soap operas portrayed women no longer as entirely either saints or sinners, but more complex and nuanced characters.

The last three chapters focus on teen fandom, *Charlie's Angels*, and disco, all three of which have been disparaged by scholars as antifeminist.

These chapters offer a different perspective on how women might have been empowered by being fans, watching *Charlie's Angels*, or performing disco music. In Chapter 9, Ilana Nash argues that teen-idol fandom provided girls with a venue to exercise their own type of second-wave feminism. Teenyboppers were young girls who idolized popular singers such as Shaun Cassidy and Leif Garrett; they can be better understood, Nash suggests, by analyzing their roles as fans of Cassidy, Garrett, and other musicians. In particular, teenybopper magazines like *16* and *Tiger Beat* helped readers build an empowering fan culture. Turning from Shaun Cassidy to Farrah Fawcett, Whitney Womack in Chapter 10 studies the impact of *Charlie's Angels* in the 1970s. While most scholars have considered the program denigrating to women, Womack argues that it actually encouraged women to be independent by showing the Angels to be self-reliant, seldom depending on men to rescue them. She then turns to the more recent *Charlie's Angels* film, examining how it presents a more stereotypical view of women and femininity.

In Chapter 11, Judy Kutulas explores the changing music scene for women, as the singer-songwriters of the early part of the decade (Carole King, Carly Simon, Joni Mitchell, and Joan Baez) gave way to the disco divas of the late '70s (Gloria Gaynor and Donna Summer).[10] Kutulas argues that this shift was indicative of many social changes, especially in feminism. King and her cohorts thrived in a society in which the reverberations of early feminism were felt everywhere—including in the music studio. These musicians wanted some of the musical control that earlier women singers had not possessed, in the process showing that women could take charge of the entire songmaking process. But Gaynor and other disco divas represented an important shift away from the singer-songwriters. The divas lacked the freedom of the earlier singer-songwriters; they were produced and packaged by and for men. The divas sent a reassuring message to a mainstream audience that feminism could be controlled because, after all, weren't they sexualized in a fashion to appeal specifically to men? Kutulas concludes by suggesting that the disco divas represented a safer, more sexualized version of feminism, less threatening to men but also attractive to women.

It is easy to pass over our current fascination with the 1970s as simply the newest fad, something ephemeral and trivial, but, as this book shows, there is more to the decade than macramé hangings and magic eight balls. The 1970s have become, according to Shelton Waldrep, author of *The Seventies: The Age of Glitter in Popular Culture* (2000), "the place to look to for the answer to the question: Who have we become at the century's end? . . . The clue to our own present seems mysteriously locked somewhere in that slippery decade."[11] Somehow, understanding American society today means better understanding those "strange feverish years."

Perhaps because it was in this era that so much of today's American culture was starting to develop—everything from the personal computer to MTV—we need to turn back to it to interpret our experiences today.

It is, of course, impossible to untangle all the ways the 1970s have shaped U.S. society, so *Disco Divas* has a more modest goal: to discover some of the ways that women's roles were influenced by popular culture. The essays here present a wide-ranging exploration of 1970s popular culture and its influences. *Disco Divas* will leave its readers with a more complex understanding of an era that continues to influence us. Pull up a beanbag chair, switch on the lava lamp, and settle down to explore how the 1970s have shaped our lives.

Part I
Second-Wave Feminism and the Media

Chapter 1

Madison Avenue Versus *The Feminine Mystique*

The Advertising Industry's Response to the Women's Movement

Steve Craig

In 1963, Betty Friedan, a writer for women's magazines with a background in psychology, published what many consider to be the most influential work of feminism's second wave. *The Feminine Mystique* gave voice to the unhappiness and frustration many women found in male-dominated society and helped motivate the political and social action that brought about many of the changes that followed. In her book, Friedan described what she called "the problem that has no name"—the vague feelings of dissatisfaction in some women who, despite being financially secure and well educated, found themselves trapped in "the comfortable concentration camp" of suburbia. Friedan argued that American culture's "mystique of feminine fulfillment" was a sham.[1]

Friedan's book became a runaway bestseller, purchased and read by millions of women in the United States and around the world. Calling it "the book that changed lives," second-wave historian Flora Davis argues that *The Feminine Mystique* "laid the groundwork for the new mass movement and provided the first inkling that women's rights might attract broad support."[2]

The publication of *The Feminine Mystique* was especially consequential for the advertising industry because Friedan placed much of the blame for women's unhappiness on America's postwar consumer society and especially on advertisers' exploitation of women.

It is their millions which blanket the land with persuasive images, flattering the American housewife, diverting her guilt and disguising her growing emptiness. They have done this so successfully, employing the techniques and concepts of modern social science, and transposing them into those deceptively simple, clever, outrageous ads and commercials, that an observer of the American scene today accepts as fact that the great majority of American women have no ambition other than to be housewives. If they are not responsible for sending women home, they are surely responsible for keeping them there.[3]

As might be expected, early responses of the advertising industry to the charges made by Friedan were extremely defensive. During a session of the 1965 Advertising Federation of America's convention, female advertising executive Jo Foxworth called *The Feminine Mystique* "a mistaque" and challenged Friedan to a debate.[4] Foxworth said the book was "depressing," and she disputed the whole notion that the American woman—in her interpretation of Friedan—"is a pitiably frustrated creature . . . who is eaten up with agony over her lot in life." According to the *New York Times* account of the session, "the speaker appeared to delight her audience, which had a heavy sprinkling of other advertising women." Foxworth went on to offer "Nine Commandments for Women in Business," which included "Thou shalt know when to zip thy ruby lips and let the men do the talking," and "Thou shalt carry no stick, save lipstick."[5]

Despite such initial reactions, Friedan's complaints about advertising, along with those of others in the women's movement, were ultimately to have a major impact on the industry. Two main factors were decisive. First, the advertising industry had a significant number of women workers in positions of responsibility. Many of these women agreed with at least some feminist aims and felt that the charges against objectionable ads were legitimate. A significant number of women in advertising took up the call for change and worked from within the industry to bring it about, campaigning not only against exploitative portrayals of women in advertisements but also against the sexual discrimination in hiring and promotions they had personally experienced. As insiders, their actions helped legitimize women's complaints in a largely male-dominated industry. Second, *The Feminine Mystique* spoke to (and for) a new kind of oppressed group, not a poor, exploited minority, but rather the middle-class women who were the major purchasers of many of the products advertised so heavily in American media. As these women began to take the movement seriously, advertisers realized they had a crucial economic interest in responding to their concerns.

"How Can Anyone Object to That?" The Campaign Against Advertising

One of *The Feminine Mystique*'s major themes was that the American advertising industry consciously manipulated its portrayals of women to ensure they would continue serving as good consumers of the thousands of products and services sold by the food, drug, beauty, and fashion industries. As Friedan wrote, "the perpetuation of housewifery, the growth of the feminine mystique, makes sense (and dollars) when one realizes that women are the chief customers of American business. . . . [T]he really important role that women serve as housewives *is to buy more things for the house.*"[6]

Friedan pointed out that, although advertisers did not create the feminine mystique, "they are the most powerful of its perpetuators." By portraying housekeeping and other "feminine duties" as the ultimate goal of
the modern woman, "ads glorify her 'role' as an American housewife—
knowing that her very lack of identity in that role will make her fall for
whatever they are selling."[7]

By the late 1960s, women (and a few men) had begun organizing to
promote feminist objectives, and several of the newly formed groups
began actively campaigning against the advertising industry. The largest
and best known of these is the National Organization for Women (NOW),
founded in 1966 with Friedan as president. From its earliest days, NOW
had a heavy agenda of political and social action in several areas, including campaigning against advertising images.

Tactically, the targeting of media images made a great deal of sense.
Feminists saw advertisements as clear and tangible evidence of a sexist
society.[8] The advertisements were ubiquitous and so served as constant
public reminders of the issue. In addition, advertisement content was controlled by a relatively small number of organizations that could easily be
identified and targeted for political action. But perhaps most important,
the advertising industry was highly vulnerable to economic retaliation by
women. Few advertisers are interested in insulting their target audience,
so the specter of legions of housewives boycotting certain products
because of offensive advertising would certainly have a powerful effect.

Beginning in 1970, NOW and other women's groups began an organized all-out assault on the advertising industry. Disruptive acts, such as a
day-long sit-in staged in the New York editorial offices of the *Ladies' Home
Journal* and the shouting down of CBS Chairman William S. Paley at the
company's annual stockholders' meeting gained national attention.[9]
Other tactics included placing stickers stating "This Ad Insults Women"
and "This Exploits Women" on advertising posters in subway trains and
other public places.[10]

Advertisers began to take notice of this growing wave of feminist objections, and efforts were made to gauge just how influential their ideas were
becoming. The research department at one of the nation's largest advertising agencies, Batten, Barton, Durstine & Osborne (BBD&O), organized
two feminist focus groups to determine what products and ads these
women found most objectionable.[11] The *New York Times,* in a style all too
typical of the early 1970s, reported that nineteen women participated and
that all were "well educated and articulate, many were good looking."
BBD&O reported that the women expressed "resentment against advertising's constantly reinforcing the women's-place-is-in-the-home idea."[12]

Any industry doubts about feminism's growing influence were dispelled
in June 1970, when congressional hearings on discrimination against

women were held in Washington. NOW vice-president Lucy Komisar testified against discrimination in both advertising portrayals and media employment practices. Citing objectionable ads for products and companies as diverse as Barbie dolls, Parker pens, and Iberia airlines, Komisar told the Special House Subcommittee on Education that NOW's members would be boycotting products they felt were demeaning to women.[13] Subcommittee member Edith Green, Representative from Oregon, agreed with many of Komisar's comments. Green even announced her own personal boycott: "I have made a personal resolve not to buy certain products advertised by ridiculing women; and I would hope that [women's groups] would really carry on a systematic boycott of products that in their advertising depict the woman as a supercilious idiot."[14]

Two months later, NOW and a coalition of other women's groups did call for boycotts of four specific products: Silva Thins cigarettes, Ivory Liquid detergent, Pristeen feminine hygiene deodorant, and *Cosmopolitan* magazine. Advertiser response to the threat was mixed. A spokesman for Procter and Gamble (makers of Ivory Liquid and countless other household products) was quoted as saying the company "would be interested in hearing what the objections were," while Warner Lambert, the maker of Pristeen, responded that "Pristeen is for femininity, freshness and women's confidence. How can anyone be against that?"[15]

Although it is unclear whether NOW's call for boycotts was ever heeded by enough women to have a significant economic impact on advertisers, it doubtless caused a good deal of uneasiness in corporate boardrooms. However, it is clear that by the close of 1970, the women's movement had made significant progress in its goal of focusing attention on advertising.[16]

"The Lady of the House Is Dead": Advertising Women Speak Out

The movement's campaign against objectionable ads received a good deal of help from within the advertising industry itself. As noted earlier, a significant number of women held influential positions in advertising, and a number were outspoken in their support of feminism.[17] Others, however, were ambivalent, and a few even expressed contentment with the status quo. Many advertising women worked for agencies that produced the campaigns activists found objectionable and so remained publicly silent to avoid harming their careers.[18] As one woman executive explained, "It might scare off prospective male clients."[19]

As time went on, a significant number of advertising women did actively campaign for change from within the industry. During the 1970s, when the feminist critique of the industry was at its height, the trade publication *Advertising Age* carried numerous stories about seminars and workshops called to discuss industry practices in regard to women, almost all of which were conducted or hosted by advertising women. Trade publication articles calling for reform were also common during this period, and virtually all of these were written by advertising women.[20]

But the most persuasive argument for change in the industry was based not on feminist philosophy but on plain economics. Especially influential was the campaign waged by Franchellie Cadwell, president of Cadwell Davis, Inc., a New York advertising agency. Cadwell said she saw the need for change more as pragmatism than as politics—revising the image of women in advertisements simply made good business sense.[21] In a two-page ad in the April 1970 issue of *Advertising Age*, Cadwell's company announced in huge type, "The lady of the house is dead," and went on to point out that women constitute "53% of the population of the country with 85% of the spending power," and suggested that "at the very least women deserve recognition as being in full possession of their faculties."

As an advertising agency with a woman president and specializing in selling to women, we are deeply involved in what transpires in the feminine mind. . . . Women's "arms" are their spending power. Their attack will be not identifying with the advertising images that demean them, leading to a product boycott. . . . An upheaval in women's thinking is here. The advertiser who doesn't move to meet it is going to bear its full brunt. And he deserves it. No force has demeaned women more than advertising.[22]

As the movement gained more support and increasing numbers of women found ads objectionable, many advertisers came to agree with Cadwell's conclusion—offending women was just bad business. The National Advertising Review Board (NARB), an industry self-regulation group, appointed a "consultive panel" drawn from its own membership to study "advertising portraying or directed to women." In its report released in early 1975, the panel conceded that the industry had a problem and provided a "checklist" of questions that advertisers were supposed to ask themselves when creating advertisements. These included, "Do my ads portray women as more neurotic than men?" and "Do my ads portray women actually driving cars?"[23]

At the same time, advertisers found that the women's market was quickly changing. Increasingly, women were casting off the stereotypical role of stay-at-home housewife and going to work outside the home. Industry forecasts suggested that these "working women" would have less time to "putter around the kitchen" and would purchase more clothing, shoes, and cosmetics. It was also suggested that they would become prime targets for advertisers of traditionally male-oriented products such as life insurance, credit cards, and rental cars.[24]

"You've Come a Long Way, Baby": Advertisers Begin to Adapt

By the end of the 1960s, many advertisers had begun to respond to women's concerns. While some simply avoided portrayals women found objectionable, others mounted new campaigns aimed at currying favor with consumers who had become sensitized to feminist issues. Whole new brands were created specifically to exploit the excitement many women felt about the movement.

One of the earliest and most successful of these new brands (at least from the industry's point of view) was Virginia Slims, a cigarette created by Philip Morris. The new brand was introduced in the middle of 1968 with a huge advertising campaign featuring clever and appealing advertisements that linked the new product with three themes: (1) smoking helps women control their weight; (2) smoking is a way women can flaunt their independence; and (3) smoking is glamorous and sophisticated. The cigarette itself was slimmer than other brands, and the use of thin fashion models subtly recalled the belief held by many women that smoking curbs appetite and helps in weight control. Advertisements tied the cigarette to personal freedom—and specifically to the women's liberation movement—by basing the campaign on fictional events set during the suffrage period. Finally, each ad featured slim and glamorous models in chic clothing holding the product.

The first Virginia Slims television commercial proved especially appealing to viewers and set the theme for the remainder of the campaign. Taking a satirical jab at male chauvinism, it offered a series of quick fictional vignettes portraying men who had "caught" women smoking during the early part of the century. In the first scene, a woman is discovered by her husband "smoking in the gazebo." As viewers watch the sepia-toned footage, the announcer intones, "She got a severe scolding and no supper that night!" Another woman is "caught smoking in the cellar behind the preserves. Although she was 34, her husband sent her straight to her room! Then, in 1920, women won their rights."

The ad ends with a chic model holding a Virginia Slims cigarette walking toward the camera accompanied by the distinctive jingle, "You've come a long way, baby." Other television ads and print advertising followed this same basic format.[25] The Virginia Slims campaign evidently struck a chord with many women whose sympathies had been aroused by the women's movement. The humorous satirizing of male chauvinism was extremely popular, and the Slims slogan became a national catchphrase. Despite the campaign's popularity with many women, others argued that the ads commercialized feminism and trivialized the movement's message. They pointed out that, despite what the ads claimed, women had not really come very far at all (and they added their own new catch phrase, "and don't call me 'baby'!"). NOW condemned the Virginia Slims ad agency by issuing one of its "Old Hat" awards for ads that demean women.[26]

But such objections went largely unnoticed by most women. The introductory Virginia Slims advertising campaign has been called "wildly successful," and one industry observer claims that "millions of women were compelled to try this new brand, even women who did not smoke."[27] The remarkable success of Virginia Slims and its introductory campaign had a major impact on the advertising industry. As one marketing executive put it, the campaign "bounced most of us on our ears" and "set a new tone in women's products advertising."[28]

Not all companies were as sophisticated as Philip Morris in their advertising to the "new woman." One simple strategy was to reverse the gender roles in an advertisement. This had the effect of seeming to admit the injustice of past stereotypes while holding out the promise of a future where women's treatment would be more equal—all thanks to an advertiser with a "raised consciousness." This approach was encouraged by Lucy Komisar, vice-president of NOW, who praised counter-stereotype portrayals and urged advertising agencies to adopt them.[29]

A perusal of 1972 copies of *Ms.* magazine reveals the following fairly typical examples of counter-stereotype ads. A double-page spread for Leilani Hawaiian Rum asks, "Why shouldn't a woman make a good daiquiri? And why shouldn't she go on from there?"[30] An American Express ad features a male model addressing the camera: "It's time women got their own American Express Card and started taking *me* to dinner." Readers who wished to apply for the card were asked to fill out an attached "Women Only" application.[31] Dewar's Scotch Whiskey featured twenty-eight-year-old physicist Sheila Long in one of its "Dewar's Profiles." Long is pictured as a well-dressed, attractive young woman with flowing hair staring into the camera in a fashion model pose. She holds a long, slender piece of chalk in her hand; behind her is a blackboard filled with complex math equations.[32]

Many of these counter-stereotype ads explicitly suggested that the advertiser agreed with at least some of the social aims of the women's movement and was undergoing fundamental changes to accommodate them. For example, AT&T ran an ad in *Ms.* magazine picturing one of its "first women telephone installers" perched high atop a telephone pole, working on a line.[33] A similar ad a month later featured "one of several hundred male telephone operators."[34] The gender reversal strategy became so trite that it was even satirized in an ad by Dana fragrances. The company's Tabu ads had run for years illustrated by a Victorian painting of a male violinist passionately kissing a woman seated at a piano. The 1974 version had the roles reversed with the violinist a woman dressed in male evening-wear.[35]

Feminism and the Beauty Industry

Yet the women's movement's most serious challenge to advertisers was not in its objection to stereotypical portrayals. The most radical feminists were calling for nothing less than the abandonment of a whole class of products traditionally purchased by women—those produced by the beauty industry. For the radicals, all fashion and cosmetics were simply tools of sexual objectification and therefore instruments of male oppression to be discarded. For many women, this was a compelling argument and even more moderate feminists began to shun makeup.

As the movement evolved, the beauty industry became concerned about this trend, and its fears were somewhat justified. The decade of the 1970s did see cosmetics, fragrance, and hair-care products suffer flat or declining sales.[36] But notions of femininity and beauty and their interdependence with the fashion and cosmetics industries have been very deeply ingrained in American culture. While some women began to reject these products, many others did not. As feminist pioneer Susan Brownmiller points out, "An unadorned face became the honorable new look of feminism in the early 1970s, and no one was happier with the freedom not to wear makeup than I, yet it could hardly escape my attention that more women supported the Equal Rights Amendment and legal abortion than could walk out of the house without eye shadow."[37]

Many women, saturated since childhood with the importance of beauty products, were reluctant to give up the psychological security they bestowed.[38] Then, too, those entering the workplace for the first time believed that fashionable clothing and artful use of cosmetics were essential elements of corporate success. Still others feared that without makeup they would appear to be a part of the "radical feminist fringe," a not unreasonable fear since media coverage of the time often attempted to marginalize feminist ideas by questioning the femininity of the women involved.[39]

The beauty industry, feeling the threat of women's changing attitudes, sought new approaches to the women's market that would allow them to exploit the excitement generated by the movement. The seam between sexual objectification on the one hand and many women's fear of losing their femininity on the other offered an ideal location in which advertisers could reposition their products. Advertisements began to appear that said, in essence, "We know you are liberated and deserve equal rights, but you must still present yourself as feminine and desirable."[40]

By the early 1970s both the advertisements and the editorial copy of popular women's magazines had become fixed on redefining feminism as simply a new form of consumerism. For example, an editorial on the status of the American woman in the June 1972 issue of *Vogue* read: "She's looking great. She feels great. The American woman has a whole new view of herself pioneered out of self-reliance and a 'divine discontent' with just making do as wife/woman, mother, chauffeur, cook, lawnmower, keeper of family dogs, cats, hamsters . . . and, always, a knockout."[41] The remainder of *Vogue*'s issue was, of course, devoted to fashion layouts and cosmetics ads.

Ironically, even the fashion industry used the movement to promote new clothing styles. In 1970, readers of *Vogue* found ads for "the Liberated Wool Sweater," courtesy of the American Wool Council: "It's part of a whole new generation of liberated looks that give you freedom of movement, freedom from wrinkles, and freedom to wear any hem-length you like. Shown here, the embodiment of the new freedom. Stripes walk softly, but carry a big look-at-me message."[42]

Cosmetics companies followed suit. In 1973, Revlon introduced Charlie, a fragrance designed for and marketed to the "new woman." Charlie advertisements featured what purported to be a no-nonsense single and independent working "girl" with a fashion model face and figure, usually pictured in a pantsuit. Charlie swept the market and became the nation's best-selling fragrance in less than a year, and other fragrance companies rushed to introduce their own "liberated" scents.[43]

Selling makeup presented a seemingly more difficult problem for advertisers. How could the industry convince liberated women who purportedly rejected sexual objectification that they should continue to buy and wear makeup? One successful approach was to portray the cosmetics as "natural," or, in some cases, "invisible." For example, Revlon's Moon Drops was pitched as a "demi-makeup," and ads told women that it was "the makeup that *is* and *isn't*." An ad in a 1970 issue of *Vogue* read, "Moon Drops Demi-Makeup. . . . It looks so convincing you'd swear it isn't makeup. . . . People will think it's your own fresh, flawless skin. (Let them.)"[44] Other brands took similar approaches. Max Factor advertised its Geminesse false eyelashes as looking "for all the world as though they were born there."[45] Another *Vogue* ad showed a closeup of the face of a dramatically lit model with the words, "if she never stops being told how lucky she is not to need make-up. . . . She's got to be covered with Germaine Monteil's fabulous new Acti-Vita cream foundation."[46] New women could look like they'd given up cosmetics without ever really having to—the perfect solution to the dilemma over makeup that many women confronted. The beauty industry was more than happy to supply new "invisible" products, along with a steady steam of reassurance.

As consumer feminism grew, several new magazines were established to exploit the increased market for advertising. *New Woman* first appeared in 1972 with editorial content geared to flatter the newly liberated "working woman." For example, the January–February 1974 issue contained the following articles: "I'm 40, Still Single. And Love It," "Are You the Type for a

Business of Your Own?" and "Entertaining Your Clients Can Be Fun."[47] Although the articles, photos, and cartoons featured counter-stereotypical situations and stressed the joys of liberation, sandwiched between were the same ads for beauty products and fashions that were appearing in *Vogue* and *Mademoiselle.*

The incongruity of advertising and editorial content became an important issue when *Ms.* magazine (founded by Betty Friedan, Gloria Steinem, and other feminists) began publication in 1972. Although the *Ms.* editors said they wanted to run only advertising consistent with the aims of the women's movement, there were sometimes disagreements as to exactly what this meant. While the radical and socialist wings of the movement found most mainstream ads objectionable, more moderate "liberal" women controlled *Ms.* and sought to make the nonprofit magazine available to as many women as possible by attracting a large, mainstream advertising base.[48] The first regular issue ran a controversial ad for Coppertone suntan lotion inside its front cover that featured a slim blonde woman in a bikini and said the product "helps more people get a magnificently deep fast tan."[49] The magazine later ran an ad for Virginia Slims that also provoked a negative reaction in the readership. As time went on, *Ms.* editor Gloria Steinem even tried unsuccessfully to attract cosmetics ads from Revlon and other companies.[50]

Madison Avenue Versus *The Feminine Mystique*: So, Who Won?

In *The Feminine Mystique,* Betty Friedan placed much of the blame for the unfair treatment of women on American business, arguing that it was through advertising that companies established and reinforced the images of women as subservient household drudges. Many women responded to Friedan's arguments and began to seek political and social change through the formation of NOW and other activist groups. By the end of the 1960s, advertisers were beginning to feel pressures both from protesters and from women within the advertising industry itself. As it became clear that Friedan's criticisms had struck home with many women, companies concluded that the old offensive stereotypes were simply bad for business and that new advertising and marketing strategies were in order. Many firms had begun to replace traditional portrayals of women with counter-stereotype ads that suggested sympathy with women's complaints. Other companies introduced new products and brands designed to exploit the spirit and rhetoric of the women's movement.

Academic researchers investigating the images of women in advertising suggest that things did, indeed, change during the 1970s, but perhaps not exactly in the way feminists would have liked.[51] While the most offensive stereotypes disappeared from ads aimed at the "working women" who advertisers felt were most likely to be offended, they often remained in other ads targeted to housewives and men.[52]

In retrospect, it appears that while the campaign against objectionable stereotypes helped the women's movement define its struggle against sexism in a tangible way, it also let advertisers off the hook too easily. Rather than adopting new attitudes toward the role of women in society, advertisers tended to exploit the enthusiasm of the women's movement, coopt its rhetoric, and present audiences with the images they wished to see. The fashion and cosmetics industry—those most threatened by liberation—even exploited many women's fear of lost gender identity to recoup lost market share.

Although advertising images did change, the goal of these changes was to redirect the emerging "new woman" into the role of "new consumer." Today, advertisements still define women in terms of buying things, offering consumption of goods as a substitute for the fulfillment many women are yet to find.

As Diane Barthel has pointed out, "It is wrong to assert that corporate America has been unresponsive to feminism. On the contrary, it has responded in its own predictable fashion."[53] Although feminism's second wave did bring about change in the way women are portrayed in advertising, it was not in the way that organizers of the movement had envisioned.

Chapter 2

"It's a Rip-Off of the Women's Movement"
Second-Wave Feminism and The Stepford Wives

ELYCE RAE HELFORD

Soon after the 1975 film *The Stepford Wives* opened in movie theaters across the country, to economic success but mixed reviews, a special screening was organized for one hundred women "opinion makers" at New York's Magno Sound screening room. As reported by Judy Klemesrud in a *New York Times* piece provocatively titled "Feminists Recoil at Film Designed to Relate to Them," the screening was followed by an "awareness session" that encouraged women to discuss their feelings about the film's politics. The event was hosted by feminist screenwriter Eleanor Perry (*Diary of a Mad Housewife*) to promote the film among women. She embraced this opportunity. "Finally, a movie that is not about two guys and their adventures," she enthused before the screening.[1] By the time the film was over, however, groans, hisses, and laughter rang out from the audience. Typical were comments such as writer Linda Arking's: "It confirms every fear we ever had about the battle of the sexes, and it says there is no way for people to get together and lead human lives."[2]

After ten minutes of the "awareness session," Betty Friedan (founder and president of the National Organization for Women) suggested, "I think we should all leave here. I don't think we should help publicize this movie. It's a rip-off of the women's movement."[3] The session concluded, for those who chose to remain, with the opinion voiced that women must write and direct their own films. Nonetheless, at a subsequent smaller gathering at Eleanor Perry's home, Gael Greene opined, "I loved it— those men were like a lot of men I've known in my life. They really do want wives who are robots." And Perry agreed: "The film presses buttons that make you furious—the fact that all the Stepford men wanted were big breasts, big bottoms, a clean house, fresh-perked coffee and sex. I thought Betty Friedan would stand up and say, 'Yes, this is just the way that men treat women.'"

Such complex and contradictory responses typify reactions to *The Stepford Wives*. The popular press of the time lauded *The Stepford Wives* as the first U.S. film to address the subject of feminism and the women's movement directly;[4] a text that "women's lib can take for a manifesto";[5] or at least "the only viable, intelligently conceived movie about women and their future made in the past decade."[6] Simultaneously, the press forcefully condemned the film as insulting to women and equally demeaning to men.[7] Descriptions of the film range from "far more cerebral than visceral" and "disquieting" to "sleazy"; and from "glib," "gimmicky," "silly," driven by "facetiousness," and "wildly funny"—perhaps unintentionally in places—to "ridiculous."[8] By the time one has read the many critical pronouncements that emerged after the box office release, one might conclude that the "black humor and sophistication of the plot is handled extremely well"[9] or, just as easily, "maybe they just should have skipped the whole thing."[10]

Many films, of course, earn contradictory reviews. However, taken together, the specific conclusions these critics draw regarding the film's tone and message suggest more. The film and the critical response it provoked offer compelling insights into 1970s U.S. media culture's representations of and popular responses to feminism. As is the case with *The Stepford Wives*, most popular media representations of feminism have come from the minds and pens of white men of privileged class. The media have satirized feminism, rendered women's efforts to attain equality and justice as both comedy and horror, and identified the women's movement as far more cerebral than visceral (more talk than action), as disquieting, sleazy, glib, gimmicky, driven by facetiousness, unintentionally funny, and ridiculous. The women's movement, like *The Stepford Wives*, has been blamed for making "domestic bliss suddenly . . . as pernicious as anemia"[11] and for "hit[ting] men below the belt and tell[ing] them it's for their own good."[12]

In this context, the following pages take the film *The Stepford Wives* as a case study in the relationship between second-wave feminism and 1970s popular media. Like Bonnie Dow in *Prime-Time Feminism*, I proceed from the premise that media texts serve the function of "interpreting social change and managing cultural beliefs."[13] Specifically, I study *The Stepford Wives* as it negotiates the media's cooptation of some of the primary principles of second-wave U.S. feminism, including the binding claim "Sisterhood Is Powerful" and the consciousness-raising mantra "The Personal Is Political."[14]

These are not the only significant concepts of the 1970s women's movement in the United States, but they give a helpful indication of the direction of feminist thought and action during this era. The motto "Sisterhood Is Powerful" signified the need for women to work together and reject competition. Popular media of the 1970s trivialized the concept of sisterhood, ridiculing women's public demonstrations and demonizing feminists as abrasive, unattractive malcontents. Moreover, the press engaged in efforts to divide women, such as the arbitrary championing of the fashionable Gloria Steinem over the less media-assimilable Kate Millett as the "leader" of a movement that publicly denounced the concept of leadership as anti-feminist. However, the media simultaneously capitalized on calls to sisterhood by pitting men against women through the use of antagonistic and warlike rhetoric. Nowhere was this strategy better exemplified than in the televised tennis match between Billie Jean King and Bobby Riggs. ABC entitled this 1973 spectacle "The Tennis Battle of the Sexes."

The slogan "The Personal Is Political" emerged in the context of consciousness-raising groups in which predominantly white and middle-class women met to explore the details of their personal lives and, through this experience, to form political agendas. These groups helped such women to understand that their personal and family lives kept them isolated, dependent, and limited in their sphere of cultural/economic/political influence. Entertainment media of the era trivialized this insight, giving us women who could exit the domestic sphere and wield power but chose not to (*Bewitched* and *I Dream of Jeannie*) or struggling tokens who were unmarried but still caretakers of friends and coworkers (*The Mary Tyler Moore Show*).[15]

Before I apply these concepts from 1970s feminism to *The Stepford Wives*, those unfamiliar with the film may need an overview. The film tells the story of Joanna Eberly, a young, thin, white middle-class woman from New York City who reluctantly moves to the suburbs with her lawyer husband and two daughters (Figure 1). In the fictional suburb of Stepford, she wrestles with conflicts over her roles as wife-mother and amateur photographer (with somewhat vague goals of professionalism) as she encounters the vapid, idealized housewives who populate the town. Though the other women frighten and disgust her, Joanna soon meets the more rebellious Bobbie Markowe. Bobbie, similarly, is a young, white middle-class woman; she differs from Joanna primarily in that her husband masks his ethnic (Jewish) identity by having changed his last name from Markowitz to Markowe, she has fewer conflicts regarding housework and parenting (she simply does the bare minimum), and she has no career ambitions whatsoever.

Joanna and Bobbie watch in horror as the women of Stepford, one by one, become zombies. They learn that longtime resident Carol Van Sant used to be president of a local women's organization but now prizes only domesticity and pleasing her husband. And Charmaine Wimperis changes before their eyes from a glamorous, pampered amateur athlete to a sub-

Figure 1. Joanna (Katherine Ross) is not as certain as her husband Walter that she will like her new life in Stepford.

missive hausfrau, tearing up her backyard tennis court and firing her maid. Joanna and Bobbie fear there might literally be something in the water that causes this transformation but come up empty when they seek advice from Joanna's chemist ex-boyfriend. Before they can pursue other possibilities, Bobbie falls prey to what we soon learn is a plot of the local Men's Association. With the help of Dale "Diz" Coba, a former creator of animated figures for Disneyland, the men are murdering their wives and substituting indistinguishable robots for them (Figure 2). Though Joanna makes a noble effort to uncover the plot or at least rescue her children and flee, she is ultimately caught, killed, and replaced (Figure 3). The film ends with a scene of all the Stepford wives on display at the supermarket, slowly pushing their carts and droning their inane "hello's" and "how are you's" in sexualized stage whispers as they reach daintily for the best brand of floor wax, while the town's newest residents—the first black couple in Stepford—argue in the aisle. We move from this ominous scene to a shot of the robot Joanna walking blandly toward the camera with large, vacant eyes. A freeze frame on the eyes ends the film.

Perhaps the most famous aspect of *The Stepford Wives* is its title, which has become shorthand for white women of privileged class who seem entirely submissive and obedient to their husbands' wills. This rhetorical practice, like the film from which it comes, is ambiguous in message. Is calling someone a "Stepford wife" an attempt to address our culture's oppressiveness in encouraging women to surrender their independence and voices for social and interpersonal approval and the "security" of a traditional marriage? Is it a critique of the gendered dynamics of race and class privilege? Because both answers invite valid interpretations, the film and the label that has emerged from its title exemplify polysemy—the availability of texts for multiple readings. However, this does not mean that we can draw no meaningful conclusions about the cultural work of such polysemic texts. In fact, the very multiplicity of interpretations available for *The Stepford Wives* makes it a particularly productive text through which to examine U.S. media culture's diverse and sometimes contradictory responses to the 1970s women's movement.

When Sisterhood Becomes a Battle

The Stepford Wives identifies feminism as a quintessential 1970s sound bite, "the battle of the sexes." This phrase masks far more than it exposes. Seeing women's oppression as a battle means reworking significant imbalances in power into an aggressive conflict between equal but different opponents. And the "battle," conducted primarily on mass-mediated turf, was not so much between the "sexes" as between white, heterosexual individuals of privileged class. The goal of this war was to prove who was "better": smarter, more fully equipped to handle power, more worthy of respect. Though it did not originate in the 1970s, the rhetoric of a gendered battle increased in popularity at this time at least in part as a response to the concept of sisterhood central to second-wave feminism. Women who came to feminist consciousness in the 1960s and '70s could see that they were isolated from one another by structures of gender, race, and class. They also saw that the media culture of the era put them in competition with one another, especially for men's attention. The notion of sisterhood encouraged women to see similarities and solidarity instead of separation and rivalry. Working collectively was about a "utopian desire to submerge individual ego for the greater political good," argues Susan

Figure 2. (*overleaf, top*) Robot Bobbie (Paula Prentiss), who loves her coifed hair and uplift bra, offers a panicked Joanna a nice cup of coffee.

Figure 3. (*overleaf, bottom*) A terrified Joanna searches for her children, knowing she will be the next to become a Stepford wife.

Brownmiller,[16] author of the landmark 1975 text *Against Our Will: Men, Women, and Rape.*

However, the media made competition-driven spectacles of this utopian desire. On one hand, there was the catfight, epitomized in the media-driven "battle" between Gloria Steinem and Phyllis Schlafly over the ERA.[17] Putting women on camera as they vehemently disagreed over feminism or aspects of the movement could disprove sisterhood and champion the status quo of individualism, competition for feminine perfection, and the approval of men. On the other hand, there was also money to be made and ratings to be garnered by accepting the ideal of sisterhood and exploiting it through gendered sports competition. If "Sisterhood Is Powerful," then let it prove its power in a symbolic battle of the sexes.

In addition to reaffirming the centrality of individualism and competition in U.S. culture, battle of the sexes rhetoric also excludes the possibility that men can be pro-feminist or that anything but violence can be the result of gendered interactions. This well describes *The Stepford Wives* perspective. As sociologist Herbert J. Gans comments in his review for *Social Policy*, "the film sees the [women's] movement as setting women against men, thus ignoring the many feminists who have argued that women's liberation cannot be achieved without larger social change that also liberates men."[18]

Though the husbands clearly have more power than the wives (economic, political, and social), *The Stepford Wives* focuses primarily on the men's determination to keep their dirty little secret and Joanna and Bobbie's efforts to uncover it. The Stepford husbands' specific motives are left unclear. At times, they seem implausible, as with Ed, husband of Charmaine, a woman who "is already the perfect image of plastic beauty and stunted thoughts."[19] Even more often their motives are nonexistent, as with Joanna's husband, Walter, and the architect of the plan himself, the unmarried Dale Coba. *Village Voice* reviewer Molly Haskell thus creates her own cinematic metaphor in explanation: "We are meant to be witnessing a tribal ritual: the male community closes ranks to purge the evil in its midst, namely the wife who wants to *be* somebody."[20]

Most critics generally agree that the men in the film are threatened by the women's movement and the liberation it promises, but they cannot say exactly why. Gans argues, "Neither the initial [Stepford women's group] organizers nor Bobbie and Joanna were particularly militant, nor did they contest the male domination of the town or demand equality within the family."[21] Thus, in typical 1970s fashion, the film focuses on a question it can answer: Who will "win"? The battle of the sexes is the vague but appropriate driving force of the film.

Joanna must battle against the men of Stepford for her life. They toss jibes in her way to throw her off course, just as Bobby Riggs hurled chauvinistic quips at Billie Jean King to try to make her miss her shots. Early in the film, for example, the members of the Men's Association come to Joanna's house with little notice for a cocktail party at which she is to prepare refreshments. While she is in the kitchen making coffee, Diz stands in the doorway ogling her. When discovered, he remarks, "I love to watch women doing little domestic chores." Joanna must parry, and she does. When Diz tells her he got his nickname from working at Disneyland, Joanna states that she disbelieves him because, frankly, he does not look like the kind of man who would enjoy making children happy.

Joanna engages in the sport of verbal parrying with men several other times in the film, showing her admirable competitive sports(wo)manship. After Joanna complains to her husband that she has been excluded from the decision to move to Stepford, from his decision to buy the particular house they would live in, and from his decision to join the separatist Men's Association, Walter tries to lure her away from such concerns by encouraging her to have sex. "Have you ever made it in front of a fireplace?" he asks.

"Not with you," she retorts, exemplifying her sexual liberation and unwillingness to lie to fulfill her husband's expectations.

In contrast to this verbal display, literal sports play by women is forbidden in Stepford. This fact is made plain by the robot Charmaine's destruction of her tennis court so her husband can put in a pool by which she can lounge. In obviously trivialized form, this scene echoes then contemporary battles over women's involvement in athletics, especially team sports. Only with the passing of Title IX in 1972 could women obtain financial and moral support for team athletics at the high school and college levels. Sports for women of the 1970s were certainly political. As Billie Jean King says of her match with Riggs, "It wasn't about tennis; it was about social change."[22] When we read *The Stepford Wives* through the metaphor of sports competition, the film's men are deplorable because they recognize the "sport" (the battle of the sexes) but prevent women from playing it.

In what is perhaps the film's most famous scene, in which Joanna finally confronts Diz about why the men of Stepford are murdering their wives, he smugly replies, "Because we can." Joanna can find no parry for this, and she and feminism are silenced. Thus, she also loosens her grip on the fireplace poker she has been carrying as a weapon to defend herself in a battle that has become literal, and Diz easily takes it from her. When read through battle of the sexes rhetoric, we find that what ultimately silences Joanna and leads to her demise is her inability to counter his taunt that if women could, they too would make robot men to serve their needs as they grew older and less desirable. The film's self-fashioned game is over; the men have proved "feminism" a fraud by winning the battle.

Mocking Consciousness Raising

Moving away from this suggestive metaphor, the film also addresses another key example of 1970s feminist rhetoric, the phrase "The Personal Is Political" and the related concept of consciousness-raising. *The Stepford Wives* offers the ideal setting for the subject in its white upper-middle-class suburb of Stepford, full of patriarchal nuclear families in which the men work outside the home while the women live mired in isolated domesticity. In the postwar culture of 1950s America, mass-produced suburbs became the norm for white middle-class Americans. A combination of the GI Bill, FHA housing loans, and racist zoning practices made the white middle-class patriarchal nuclear family living in a suburban tract home a "government sanctioned ideal."[23] A key facet of this new way of living was its contribution to the decline of traditional community life in urban areas. The home functioned as "a kind of fallout shelter from the anxieties and uncertainties of public life" of the era, leading to a "nostalgic return to the Victorian cult of domesticity that was predicated on the clear division between public and private spheres."[24]

Given this dramatic cultural shift, it is easy to see why the women of these early suburbs came to exemplify perfectly Betty Friedan's description of the feminine mystique. For the privileged class of 1950s women Friedan wrote about in a book that for many historians jump-started the second wave of feminism, life was about fulfilling beauty norms, pleasing husbands, and taking all responsibility for housework and children without pursuit of any public or professional life. Women who fell prey to this worldview often suffered from what Friedan termed "the problem with no name," including symptoms of depression and anxiety. The resulting figure, writes Friedan, is childlike, empty, "an anonymous biological robot in a docile mass. She becomes less than human," and "the longer she conforms, the less she feels as if she really exists."[25] It is difficult to imagine a description that better fits the fate of the Stepford wives (see Figure 4).[26]

Friedan's *The Feminine Mystique* offered one textual starting point for feminism, as did her establishment of NOW in 1966. Many women began to understand that what the culture insisted was one's "private" life was actually deeply political and shared by so many women that Friedan could discuss the problem with no name as a syndrome of epidemic proportions. Arriving at such conclusions was vital to women's creation of individual and collective change. A primary second-wave feminist method of moving from understanding to action was the formation of consciousness-raising groups.

More than televised sports events, consciousness-raising groups were important to many of the white middle-class women who constituted the majority of feminist organizations such as NOW in the 1970s. Small discussion groups where women could articulate their own problems and

Figure 4. The Stepford wives, exemplifying Friedan's "feminine mystique," enjoy their shopping.

goals and hear those of others (however similar to their own based on demographics and prejudices) enabled the participants to build plans and programs for change together. As Kathie Sarachild describes in a 1973 talk to the First National Conference of Stewardesses for Women's Rights in New York City, "Consciousness-raising—studying the whole gamut of women's lives, starting with the full reality of one's own—[is] a way of keeping the movement radical by preventing it from getting side-tracked into single issue reforms and single issue organizing." Such groups were organized on the premise that "all women would have to see the fight of other women as their own, not as something just to help 'other women,' that they would have to see this truth about their own lives before they would fight in a radical way for anyone."27

The Stepford Wives capitalizes on the popularity of these groups while trivializing their goals in its representation of a consciousness-raising session in Stepford. Urban women at heart, Joanna and Bobbie experience increasing feelings of isolation in their single-family suburban homes, deep alienation from the other women of Stepford and their glorification of the feminine mystique, and distance from their own Men's Association–obsessed husbands. They experience suburban life as "blocks composed of total strangers [who represent] friendships only at the abstract level of demographic similarities in age, income, family size, and occupation," as well as race, and they quickly learn that "the neighborhood ideal [brings] with it an enormous amount of pressure to conform to the group."[28]

Rather than being absorbed into the homogeneous Stepford mass of mystique, Joanna and Bobbie attempt to initiate a consciousness-raising group for the neighborhood's women. At first, a pre-robot Charmaine is the only other woman in town willing, remarking, "I'm no fanatic, but I'm really interested." She goes on gleefully to label the gathering a "bitching" session, though Joanna is quick to offer, "Maybe, if we're lucky, we can get into something more constructive."

After much effort and a little blackmail, Joanna and Bobbie gather the women of Stepford to discuss issues of importance in their lives. Tentatively, Joanna begins, stating, superficially and without much conviction, that sometimes she thinks her husband loves the law more than he loves her. Charmaine follows with greater intensity, asserting that she knows her husband has never loved her at all, having chosen her for her appearance alone. Then the robot women get their say. Kit Sundersen laments that she cannot get enough baking done in a day because of all the other housework she must do. Joanna tells her she does not have to bake at all. The automated women find this suggestion incomprehensible. Suddenly, another housewife comes to Kit's rescue when she mentions how much time Easy-On Spray Starch will save her. She effuses over the product, eyes glossy, ecstatically declaring that she would not only do a commercial for the product if asked but would do it for free. Bobbie's disbelieving "Wow" ends the scene.

There are many conclusions we can draw about second-wave feminism from this scene. Simply depicting a consciousness-raising group is outside the scope of most Hollywood films of any genre or era. Moreover, the protagonist's motive for doing so is certainly feminist in *The Stepford Wives*. She wants these subservient women to gain (or, in some cases, regain) their self-respect, set some goals apart from housework, and achieve some level of awareness of their oppression. However, the film also offers feminist commentary through its overstated and oversimplified representation of consumerist beauty queens. In particular, the scene provides an unexpected critique of Friedan's theory of the feminine mystique.

Friedan relies on images in women's magazines as proof of the existence of the mystique. Then she implies women's entirely passive reception of these images in order to assert their inescapable power.[29] Positioning audiences as uncritical dupes was common for feminists and others well into the 1970s, as illustrated by Alice Embree's claim, published in Robin Morgan's 1970 anthology *Sisterhood Is Powerful*, that the mass media "shaped people into one-dimensional receivers of communication—people who were more easily channeled into the roles of unprotesting consumers." This positioning renders women passive "emotional nonintellectuals." [30] The consciousness-raising scene in *The Stepford Wives* takes this theory and uses humor to illustrate its implications. Media audiences are not simply passive cultural dupes, the scene seems to argue, or perfectly coifed women who can do nothing other than wax poetic about spray starch would be the inevitable result.

A less critical facet of the consciousness-raising scene is the way it ignores that "the personal is political" for diverse women, including working-class women and women of color. In 1974, a group of black feminists founded the Combahee River Collective in order to condemn the implicit and explicit racism within the second-wave women's movement. Of greatest emphasis was the concept of simultaneity of oppressions: black women face a multilayered oppression based on their gender, race, and class, and these three aspects of identity are inseparable. In their 1978 treatise, "A Black Feminist Statement," the collective asserts,

A political contribution which we feel we have already made is the expansion of the feminist principle that the personal is political. In our consciousness-raising sessions, for example, we have in many ways gone beyond white women's revelations because we are dealing with the implications of race and class as well as sex. . . . We have spent a great deal of energy delving into the cultural and experiential nature of our oppression out of necessity because none of these matters has ever been looked at before. No one before has ever examined the multilayered texture of Black women's lives.[31]

The Stepford Wives is entirely uninterested in the texture of black women's lives. Nonetheless, the film does feature some commentary on race and class issues in its reference to and inclusion of a token black couple in the film's final scene.

Joanna and Bobbie find inspiration for their consciousness-raising group when they stumble onto knowledge that there used to be a women's organization in Stepford during a discussion with the Welcome Wagon Lady. This unnamed crone, a busybody who chronicles the changes in Stepford in her column for the town newspaper, shares the news that a black family is moving into Stepford. She remarks that this change is "good" and notes that Stepford has always been a "progressive" community. When Joanna and Bobbie react to this statement with bemused disbelief, she announces that Stepford was the first town in the county to have a Chinese restaurant and then mentions the now-defunct women's organization.

This scene is easy to overlook as a commentary on racial difference. Casting is particularly careful in the film, even in small roles such as Nettie, Charmaine's maid, who is white and referred to as German. Thus, when Charmaine notes that members of some cultures are born to serve, she insults Germans and the film skirts issues of racism. The slight is offensive, to be sure, but Charmaine emerges as classist not racist.

The black couple who move to Stepford appear only in the final scene. Their dialogue is purposefully obscured, for their function in the film is to make plain that Joanna is not the last woman to resist life in Stepford, nor will she be the last to die there. From the little we can gather from body language and tone, the husband seems to be exasperated and attempting to quell his wife's concerns. She, by contrast, is vigorous in her display of frustration with Stepford, more vigorous, in fact, than was Joanna. Perhaps this woman may even be able to stop the Men's Association once and for all.[32] Nonetheless, issues of racial difference remain unexplored. The couple is allowed into Stepford apparently because the husband sees eye-to-eye with the white men of the town. He shares their misogyny and class perspective, and this is enough to permit the couple's presence in white-dominated east-coast suburbia.

Another issue related to second-wave feminism is slighted by the film as well. The consciousness-raising scene also comments on what it deems to be excesses in radical feminists. Seemingly afraid to appear too radical even to Bobbie, Joanna hedges her enthusiasm for feminist activism in Stepford by saying, "I'm not contemplating any Maidenform bonfires, but they could certainly use something around here."[33] The image of bra-burning originated in the popular press response to feminists' 1968 demonstration at the Miss America pageant. To signify women's desire to free themselves from media-inspired fantasy images of feminine bodily perfection, items identified as "woman-garbage" were tossed into "a huge Freedom Trash Can," including "bras, girdles, curlers, false eyelashes, wigs and representative issues of *Cosmopolitan, Ladies' Home Journal, Family Circle*, etc."[34] However, the bras were not burned, as was popularly reported.

Bra-burning, as opposed to throwing away one's bra as a small but significant part of a mass gathering to protest media objectification of women, offered an irresistible spectacle, a "metaphor that trivialized feminists and titillated the audience at the same time." Susan Douglas argues:

For the press, burning bras was a natural segue from burning draft cards. It fit into the dominant media frame about women's liberation and equated the women's movement with exhibitionism and narcissism as if women who unstrapped their breasts were unleashing their sexuality in a way that was unseemly, laughable, and politically inconsequential, yet dangerous. Women who threw their bras away may have said they were challenging sexism, but the media, with a wink, hinted that these women's motives were not all political but rather personal: to be trendy, and to attract men.[35]

If Douglas is correct in her conclusions, *The Stepford Wives* exemplifies them. The film scripts Joanna as needing to qualify her feminism as clearly *not* radical, not threatening. It does so by having Joanna use the plural,

"Maidenform bonfires," suggesting that such mythical events took place not only at the 1968 Miss America protest but repeatedly. (Similarly, as quoted above, Charmaine qualifies her interest by noting she is "no fanatic.") In the conservative words of *Los Angeles Times* reviewer Kevin Smith, "The radiantly beautiful Miss [Katharine] Ross [who portrays Joanna] expresses perfectly the sentiments and predicament of many well-educated young wives who don't necessarily want to march or burn bras, yet want a sense of identity and accomplishment of their own."[36]

Through such references, *The Stepford Wives* teaches that there are justified and unjustified forms of feminism. The men in the film are oppressive and distasteful, and we are meant to sympathize with the protagonist and the other women of Stepford who have been murdered by them. We must also keep in mind, however, that only by remaining extremely limited in how she practices her feminism will Joanne remain sympathetic. Though Richard Schickel laments that the film is "too glibly on the side of the fashionable angels" in his *Time* review,[37] it is vital that these women are as perfect as angels, and fashionable ones at that.

Bralessness, in the mid-1970s, could signify feminist liberation, but, as Douglas notes above, it also offered excellent titillation for those opposed to feminism. And bralessness abounds in *The Stepford Wives*. Even as Joanna and Bobbie self-righteously attack the housewives of Stepford for their obsession with dressing up and looking attractive for their husbands, it is our heroines who sport the most fashion-conscious garb in town. With the long, thin bodies so in style during this era and sporting the hippest clothes—from halter tops to hot pants—Joanna and Bobbie argue for women's lib without ever risking identification with the stereotype of feminists as fat, hairy-legged frumps with unstyled hair. In a moment of politically problematic foreshadowing, Joanna even quips, "What I wouldn't give for a chest like that," on first glimpsing Charmaine. Despite their critique of the excessive make-up Stepford wives wear just to do the dishes, neither Joanna nor Bobbie ever appears without lipstick and eyeliner.[38] Of course, this is as much about Hollywood film standards as about the ambiguities of *The Stepford Wives* and 1970s culture; however, such evidence does make plain why Friedan called the film "a rip-off of the women's movement" as she left the screening.

The Stepford Legacy

Ultimately, the gendered images of *The Stepford Wives* do not encourage a unified statement on the women's movement or the role of feminism in the lives of 1970s women. We see sisterhood reduced to a battle of the sexes on white middle-class men's terms. We see feminist goals limited to the vague and elitist goals of a classist, racist, and heterosexist suburban club of young, thin, "beautiful" women. And we see a consciousness-raising group that renders grassroots activism absurd excess. Yet we also see depictions of articulate, sincere women attempting to resist the white middle-class feminine mystique and a critique of the reduction of intelligent women to media dupes.

Despite the film's polysemy, however, the narrative ends on an entirely pessimistic note. The women have lost not only the battle of the sexes but also their lives. The men of Stepford have defeated any attempts at genuine sisterhood, producing instead obedient consumerist automatons who think alike only in that they do not think at all. No amount of consciousness raising can empower a murder victim. The men have acknowledged their patriarchal control but have taken no moral responsibility for their privilege.

So, is *The Stepford Wives* a feminist commentary on white middle-class women's disempowerment at the hands of their husbands? A triumphant backlash against the women's movement? Or simply a Hollywood "rip-off," written to make money by invoking the language of gender conflict during the 1970s? Regardless of our answer, the film is politically compelling and historically significant as a commentary on media negotiation and exploitation of popular elements of 1970s feminism.

In addition, *The Stepford Wives* has not ceased to affect audiences, available as it now is in VHS, Laserdisk, and DVD formats and on cable television. Internet reviews have recently flourished, praising and attacking the film with relish equal to that of original era critics and with even greater emotional and linguistic excess. Also, as they did at its initial release, promoters of the film enlist feminists in their cause. The American Movie Classics website, which has dubbed the film a "classic" by virtue of showing it, actually got Susan Brownmiller to write a review, provocatively entitled, "Domestic Engineering: A Feminist Deconstructs *The Stepford Wives*." Brownmiller, like Kael before her, notes Joanna's appearance as "altogether too Stepfordian from the very first scene," which makes it "hard to imagine she bears a plausible inner life that is in mortal danger of being snuffed out." Yet, she concludes, "Whatever its flaws, 'Stepford' deals with the serious themes of suburban conformity, women's aspirations, and men's fears and desires in a highly entertaining, thriller-chiller fashion."[39]

As Brownmiller exemplifies, critics and fans still respond to *The Stepford Wives* with a mixture of appreciation and loathing. All we can be certain of is that the film continues to enjoy popularity, even in college classrooms,[40] and that Gans was wrong when he predicted in 1975 that, "years from now, if *The Stepford Wives* is remembered at all, it will be only for its misogynous way of bringing women's liberation to the screen."[41] *The Stepford Wives*, as this discussion has endeavored to illustrate, offers compelling historical commentary on the tensions and contradictions of popular representations of the U.S. women's movement of the 1970s.

Chapter 3

"He Said, She Said"
Popular Representations of Sexual Harassment and
Second-Wave Feminism

CARRIE N. BAKER

Law professor Anita Hill, Navy lieutenant Paula Coughlin, Stanford doctor Frances Conley, *Boston Herald* sportswriter Linda Olsen, and Arkansas government employee Paula Jones were just a few of the women at the center of sexual harassment scandals that rocked the nation in the 1990s. The media frenzy surrounding these scandals brought the issue of sexual harassment into the mainstream of American consciousness. While press coverage raised awareness of sexual harassment, it also reflected many of the old stereotypes about women—the same ones directed toward rape victims—that they asked for it by their dress or manner, that they were lying, that they were oversensitive.[1] This tendency was perhaps most forcefully reflected in the media's enthusiastic reporting of the later infamous slander of Anita Hill that she was "a little nutty and a little slutty."[2] For feminists, media coverage of sexual harassment was a double-edged sword— raising awareness of the issue but also reinforcing biased attitudes against women.

These tendencies have roots going back into the 1970s, when sexual harassment first emerged as an issue in popular culture. Early media coverage of sexual harassment on the editorial pages and in news reporting had a Dr. Jekyll/Mr. Hyde quality. The largely male editorialists found endless amusement mocking and scorning those who took the issue seriously. These writers trivialized the issue, portraying sexual harassment as simply a matter of bad manners, immodesty, or immorality. As courts began to rule in favor of sexual harassment victims, editorialists around the country had a field day condemning efforts to combat sexual harassment as the latest leftist plot to involve bureaucrats in the lives of citizens and to take all the fun out of the workplace. On the other hand, news coverage, which often appeared in the "style" section of newspapers and was written by female reporters, offered a serious and concerned treatment of the issue.

Feminist activists had a powerful influence on the early portrayal of sexual harassment in popular culture through this news reporting. In the spring of 1975 in Ithaca, New York, feminists coined the phrase "sexual harassment" for a media blitz to promote the first speakout on the issue. In the mid-1970s, reporters turned mostly to feminists for information and perspectives on sexual harassment because they were the only ones working on the issue. As a result, coverage often reflected feminist understandings of the causes and meaning of sexual harassment and feminist strategies for combating it. Newspaper and magazine articles described the activities of feminists organized against sexual harassment, discussed strategies to combat harassment, and provided information about resources for harassed women. The voices and stories of harassed women were prominent. Much of this coverage had an activist slant, delving into the underlying power issues and focusing on solutions to the problem—what to do and where to go for help.

Discussions of sexual harassment in the media played a critical role in feminists' efforts to raise public awareness and in turn fueled early anti-harassment organizations by bringing new clients to them and giving the issue an air of legitimacy. Women's stories and feminist perspectives on sexual harassment permeated popular culture, helping to transform public consciousness. Rather than seeing sexual harassment as a personal sexual or moral problem, people began to understand that it was a widespread social problem with debilitating consequences for women's workplace participation. This cultural backdrop led to the creation of legal remedies for sexual harassment by enabling feminists to convince judges that sexual harassment in the workplace was serious enough to amount to sex discrimination. In this way, despite the reactionary editorials, popular culture played a tremendously important role in raising public awareness of sexual harassment, legitimating the issue, and facilitating the development of solutions to the problem.

Forming a Movement: Resistance to Sexual Harassment in the 1970s

Sexual coercion in the workplace was not a new problem when feminists began to organize around the issue in the 1970s. American industrialization brought great numbers of women into mills and factories, and these women often faced sexual coercion from bosses and foremen. Nineteenth-century social reformers first conceptualized sexual coercion in the workplace as a social problem, but framed it as a moral issue. Reformers were concerned with the moral degeneration of women in the workplace, so they advocated protective labor laws that limited women's participation in the workplace to shield them from these influences.[3] The issue again came to the attention of activists as women flooded the labor market in the 1970s. Feminists reconceptualized the problem of sexual harassment as a civil rights issue. Concerned with women's equal employment opportunities, feminists argued that sexual harassment was sex discrimination.

In the early 1970s, several individual women stepped forward to challenge sexual coercion in the workplace. They sued under Title VII of the Civil Rights Act, which prohibits sex discrimination in employment, arguing that sexual harassment was sex discrimination. Often represented by civil rights attorneys, these early pioneers of sexual harassment law risked their livelihoods and subjected themselves to invasive, costly, and extended litigation for an unlikely victory. Federal courts were initially reluctant to hold that sexual harassment was sex discrimination, however, because they believed that sexual harassment was merely a "personal matter." Judges dismissed many of these early cases.

By the mid-1970s, several feminist anti-sexual harassment organizations had formed. The 1975 speakout in Ithaca resulted in the creation of the first organization to address sexual harassment—Working Women United, which later became the Working Women's Institute and relocated to New York City. In Boston in 1976, another group formed to combat sexual harassment—the Alliance Against Sexual Coercion. This group, which grew out of the rape crisis movement, produced much of the early theory about sexual harassment, drawing in large part upon feminist theory on rape. Feminists argued that sexual harassment was an abuse of power arising not out of sexual desire but out of men's desire to retain power as women entered the workplace in greater numbers. They also argued that harassment affected women as a group, not just individual women, because sexual harassment lowered the status of female workers and reinforced sex segregation in the workplace. The Working Women's Institute, the Alliance Against Sexual Coercion, and other groups conducted research on the incidence and impact of sexual harassment, provided information and support to victims of sexual harassment, and worked to raise public awareness of the problem.

As noted earlier, these feminist groups used the media to raise awareness of sexual harassment. At the first speakout on sexual harassment on May 4, 1975, Working Women United excluded the press but held a press conference the next day. This was the beginning of a long and fruitful, but sometimes troubled relationship between the founders of the movement against sexual harassment and the media. Feminist activists used the media to spread their message, find other women who had similar experiences, and promote their analysis of this only recently named but widespread phenomenon. As the 1970s progressed, magazine and newspaper coverage of sexual harassment that mentioned the Working Women's Institute and the Alliance Against Sexual Coercion generated an enormous number of clients for these organizations. By the end of the 1970s, many feminist organizations were working on sexual harassment, including those dealing with the concerns of women just beginning to break into nontraditional occupations such as coal mining and construction.

Breaking the Ice: The First Media Coverage of Sexual Harassment

In the early 1970s, before feminists began to speak out on the issue, media coverage of sexual behavior in the workplace was rare and completely lacked a critical perspective, often focusing on how to seduce one's boss, à la *Cosmopolitan* founder Helen Gurley Brown's *Sex and the Single Girl*.[4] The underlying power dynamics were ignored. Toward the end of the decade, as a result of feminist activism, press coverage of the issue increased. While the topic of sexual harassment only rarely appeared in the popular press before 1976, by the end of the decade most major women's magazines and many other mainstream magazines and newspapers had covered it. Newspapers and magazines often included stories of women who had experienced sexual harassment, and they incorporated feminist critiques of sexual harassment as an abuse of power. They quoted feminist activists and provided contact information for feminist organizations working on the issue. These stories raised awareness about the issue, causing more women to speak up about harassment, to name the experience as a violation, and to fight it. Women began to question coercive sexual behavior in the workplace that they would before have accepted as the status quo. In this way, media coverage helped generate a movement that resulted in new laws against misconduct and transformed understanding of appropriate behavior in the workplace.

The first mainstream newspaper to address the issue of sexual harassment was the *New York Times*, which published an article on August 19, 1975 by Enid Nemy, "Women Begin to Speak Out Against Sexual Harassment at Work."[5] Appearing in the family and style section, the article "was syndicated nationally, to a tidal wave of response from women across the country."[6] The author discussed the Ithaca speakout and the founding of Working Women United, described as launching a "campaign to expose the problems of sexual exploitation of women on the job." She quoted feminist activists and sexually harassed women. Lin Farley, a founder of Working Women United, said that workplace sexual harassment was "extremely widespread," but often "treated as a joke." NOW president Karen DeCrow said sexual harassment was "one of the few sexist issues

which has been totally in the closet." Nemy discussed potential legal remedies at the local, state, and federal levels. She quoted Eleanor Holmes Norton, who at that time was Commissioner of Human Rights for the City of
New York and later became a key player in the development of federal sexual harassment law as chair of the Equal Employment Opportunity Commission. The second half of the article discussed the experiences of five
sexually harassed women, three of whom were from Ithaca, one from New
York City, and one from Washington, D.C. They experienced harassment
in varied occupations—waitressing, nursing, and real estate. One woman,
Jan Crawford, reported that her supervisor demanded sex "after making
it clear he didn't approve of women working outside the home." Another
woman, Susan Madar, complained of the economic disadvantages of "not
being attractive enough," which she described as "more subtle" but still
sexual harassment.[7] This article appeared in over a dozen newspapers
around the country, including the *Philadelphia Bulletin* and the *Chicago Tri-
bune.*

Several months later, in January 1976, the *Wall Street Journal* published
its first article about sexual harassment, "A Cold Shoulder: Career Women
Decry Sexual Harassment by Bosses and Clients," by Mary Bralove.[8] This
article was longer and more business-oriented than the *New York Times* article. Quotes from activists were fewer and briefer, while several business
professionals were quoted, including Eli Ginzberg, a professor of economics at Columbia University's Graduate School of Business, and Margaret Henning, codirector of the Simmons College Graduate
Management Program. As in the *Times,* the article recounted several stories of sexually harassed women, but the women tended to be business
professionals. However, Bralove described, "small pockets of working
women . . . boldly speaking out and seeking protection against unwanted
sexual advances by bosses or clients." She mentioned United Nations
employees publicly airing harassment charges, the recently established
Los Angeles Screen Actors Guild morals complaint bureau, student pressure to include a curriculum on harassment at the Simmons College
Graduate Program in Management, the work of the City of New York
Commission on Human Rights, and the Working Women United speakout and survey in Ithaca.

In the same month that the *Wall Street Journal* article appeared, *Redbook*
published a questionnaire on sexual harassment in the workplace, the
purpose of which was "to have a reliable and factual basis on which to
judge the problem" and "to amass a significant body of information about
sexual harassment."[9] These three articles were the first mainstream
reporting on the issue of sexual harassment, which by the end of the
decade would be commonplace.

Grow Up or Get Out: The Editorial Trivialization of Sexual
Harassment

The first critical voice to emerge in the popular press was that of Rhoda
Koenig in the February 1976 issue of *Harper's*.[10] This scathing opinion
piece came in response to Enid Nemy's article in the *New York Times*.
Describing sexual harassment as "flirtation," Koenig trivialized the issue by
commenting that "a lot of women would feel deprived without a reason-
able quota of sexual harassment per week." Similar to critiques of feminism that emerged in the 1990s from women such as Camille Paglia and
Katie Roiphe,[11] Koenig condemned feminists for characterizing women as
"miserable," "weak," oppressed, and helpless victims. Suggesting that feminists were charlatans and women were masochistic dupes, she argued,
"With Jesuitical ingenuity, they go about convincing white, middle-class
college-educated women that society has done them wrong, like the snake
oil salesman whose suggestible listeners began to feel all the symptoms of
sciatica, dropsy, and the botts." She condemned feminism for encouraging women to hold society responsible for their own failures and for discouraging independent thought and action. As opposed to the feminist
characterization of men as aggressive, Koenig argued that men were
"more like shy woodland creatures, fawns peeping through the thicket of
masculine self-protection." Ironically, she predicted that "sexual harassment probably won't make its way onto the picket lines or the evening
news" and "antiharassment forces will [never] work up enough steam to
roll over the rest of us." Koenig was the first of many editorialists to suggest that feminists were exaggerating the problem of sexual harassment
and that women were to blame because they were hypersensitive or had
asked for it.

Two months later, a torrent of critical editorials surfaced in newspapers
around the country in response to the first federal court declaration that
sexual harassment was sex discrimination in violation of federal anti-dis-
crimination law. In April 1976, Judge Charles Richey in Washington, D.C.
ruled in favor of a young black woman who lost her job because she
refused to submit to sexual demands from her boss. The press coverage of
this case was tremendous. The Associated Press and United Press International broke the story on April 20, the same day the case was decided.
On April 21, over fifty newspapers from over twenty states around the
country picked up the story. Major newspapers covering the case included
the *New York Times, Wall Street Journal, Washington Post, Atlanta Constitution,
Los Angeles Times,* and *Houston Chronicle*.[12] Coverage continued in the days
that followed, and numerous editorials appeared, largely critical of the
decision and often mocking the judge. That the case had touched a nerve
was clear in the vitriolic outrage of editorials that appeared around the
country.

Editorials criticizing Judge Richey focused in particular on one footnote in the decision. He had ruled that sexual harassment was not isolated personal conduct but a serious violation of equal employment guarantees because it created an "artificial barrier to employment which was placed before one gender and not the other, despite the fact that both genders were similarly situated."[13] Defendants had argued that such a ruling would lead to the absurd conclusion that the "sexual preference" of the supervisor would determine whether conduct was discriminatory. In the critics' favorite footnote Judge Richey briefly commented that a finding of discrimination could not be made if the supervisor was bisexual and made sexual advances toward both genders.

Editorialists jumped on that brief footnote with scornful glee. The most widely reprinted editorial was by Art Buchwald of the *Los Angeles Times*. His column appeared in over forty newspapers around the country between April 27 and May 3, 1976.[14] He began by sarcastically describing Judge Richey's decision as one of the most important legal decisions of the last fifty years because the ruling "sets new guidelines for how bosses can behave during and after office hours all over the country." Focusing on the footnote mentioning bisexuality, Buchwald recounted a fictional conversation between a boss, Mr. Novak, a female employee, Miss Roseberry, with whom Mr. Novak seeks a sexual relationship, and Mr. Callihan, Novak's legal foil. Novak invites Roseberry on a date, but also brings Callihan in order to avoid a lawsuit. When Novak compliments Roseberry on her sweater, he also compliments Callihan on his shirt. Novak asks both employees to stay late, takes them both out to dinner at a small French restaurant, and then takes them both to Roseberry's apartment afterward. When Callihan objects and says he's tired, Novak replies,

"Who isn't tired? You think it's fun having to worry about being sued every time I take someone from the office out to dinner? You can take Miss Roseberry anywhere you want to. But if I take her I have to take you, too. I don't make that kind of money, Callihan."
"I guess it does take the fun out of being a boss, Mr. Novak."
"Oh, forget it. Why don't you get into something more comfortable, Miss Roseberry? . . . You too, Callihan."
"Why me, Mr. Novak?"
"Because, dammit, it's the law!"

Despite mounting evidence that sexual harassment harmed many women, Buchwald assumed male sexual prerogative in the workplace and trivialized women's concerns.[15]

Often editorialists characterized sexual harassment as a matter of manners or morals. An editorial in the *Los Angeles Times* entitled "Sex Rears Its Mixed-Up Head" portrayed sexual harassment as simply a matter of bad manners, having no deeper sociological causes or implications. Describing Judge Richey's decision as "lively," the editorial focused on the footnote mentioning bisexuality. Suggesting that the lawyers "drop their law books momentarily to consider the dispute in a wider context," the writer asked, "Why must the clanking machinery of the law have to be set in motion to resolve problems in human relations that could be settled by the simplest code of ethical conduct?"[16] The editorial characterized sexual harassment as a question of etiquette and ethics, scoffing at the idea of legal relief for the problem. An editorial in the *Wall Street Journal* also portrayed sexual harassment as a moral question that the law should not address. "The Law and Threats to Virtue" chided, "Judge Richey's opinion would suggest that there are some situations where a little discrimination might still be a good thing."[17] These editorials completely ignored the feminist argument that sexual harassment had a serious negative impact on working women, but instead repeatedly turned back to how Judge Richey's decision infringed on men's freedom to pursue women sexually in the workplace.

The repeated focus on the bisexuality footnote reflected the editorial writers' viewpoint that sexual harassment was a matter of sex, not harassment, a question of male sexual freedom, not equal opportunity for women. Condemning Judge Richey's decision as "grotesque," Dick Hitt of the *Dallas Times Herald* focused almost entirely on Richey's footnote about bisexuality. Describing the decision as "the Richey Ruling on how bisexual bosses may be insulated from sex discrimination suits," Hitt argued that Richey had "carved [bisexuality] in stone" and suggested that progressive companies "may even now be appointing a vice president in charge of Promiscual Equality."[18] Jim Wright of the *Dallas Morning News* described Judge Richey as "the creative jurist who recently laid down the first federal guidelines for office hanky-panky." According to Wright, the "chief significance" of the decision was that "the so-called Sexual Revolution is over." He declared: "Judge Richey has done more than any man since Cotton Mather to detour society off the primrose path." As Hitt did, Wright trivialized the decision by focusing on Richey's footnote on bisexuality, ruminating about how a particularly resourceful boss might engage in nondiscriminatory lechery. He then concluded, "Judge Richey, in brief, did for the conduct of office hanky-panky what other judges and federal guideline writers have previously done for the conduct of business: he didn't actually make it a crime; he just wrapped it in so many miles of ridiculous red tape that it no longer seems worth the trouble."[19] These editorials erased the distinction between unwelcome coercive sexual advances and voluntary sexual relations and willfully ignored the power dynamics underlying sexual demands in the workplace.

Editorialists condemned other successful legal cases as well. In response to the first federal appellate court ruling in favor of a sexual harassment plaintiff, an editorial appearing in the *Washington Star* and reprinted in William F. Buckley's *National Review* asked, "how are we going to breed more little bureaucrats if the court rules that a he-bureaucrat cannot make time with a she-bureaucrat?"[20] A similarly caustic, trivializing attitude appeared in editorials responding to the first sexual harassment case filed against an educational institution.[21] These writers focused on condemning the women bringing the case. The *New York Times* published an editorial on July 26, 1977, lambasting the students filing suit. Under the title "The Courts of First Resort," Russell Baker described sexual harassment as a "nuisance" and simply a matter of bad manners. Rather than resorting to the "ponderous and expensive machinery of the courthouse," Russell suggested "quicker and cheaper ways of making professors mind their manners," like calling on the services of a "robust father . . . carrying a shotgun," "a large brother or boyfriend," or simply by using a "hat pin" or "a few simple words thrust neatly into his vulnerable asininity."[22] In this appalling display of sexist stereotypes, Baker revealed his complete ignorance of the power dynamics and serious repercussions of sexual harassment for women. But he was by no means alone in his male-biased ignorance. A similar sentiment was expressed by a Yale University official quoted in a *New York Times* article reporting on the case: "if women students aren't smart enough to know how to outwit some obnoxious professor, they shouldn't be here in the first place."[23] This disrespectful attitude toward the female students appeared again in a *Time* article entitled, "Bod and Man at Yale," which quoted Yale's attorney José Cabranes denouncing the students' lawsuit as "reckless and obviously designed to attract maximum publicity for groundless charges."[24] These men repeatedly attacked the credibility and character of the victims alleging harassment.

Outside the editorial pages, some news articles trivialized sexual harassment by focusing on the sexual aspects of the behavior rather than the inherent abuse of power. A *Time* article called "Executive Sweet: Many Office Romeos Are Really Juliets" described a study by Barbara Gutek and Charles Nakamura finding that many men reported being victims of sexual harassment. From the cartoon showing a man being chased around a desk by a woman with hearts floating around her head to the concluding sentence that, "as more women rise to supervisory positions, it will become harder to tell who is chasing whom around the desk," the article trivialized the issue by ignoring power differentials based on sex and the differential impact of workplace harassment on men and women.[25]

Similarly, several magazines published articles on "office romance," with little or no discussion of the potentially coercive nature of relationships between male bosses and female subordinates. An article in a 1976 issue of *Harper's Bazaar* described sexual harassers as "office Romeos" and harassment as "office sex" or a "pass." Several articles suggested solutions focusing on female behavior: women were encouraged to dress modestly and be more assertive, including making eye contact, using authoritative body language, speaking with conviction, and not diluting the message by smiling.[26] As late as July 1979, *Working Woman* published an article that similarly assumed that assertiveness was an adequate solution to the problem of sexual harassment and even discouraged legal solutions.[27] Several articles discussed sexual relations in the workplace or educational setting without addressing the underlying power dynamics. Even some explicitly feminist magazines were slow to understand the issue. In the August 1976 issue of *Ms.*, an article on allegations of sexual advances toward students made by the women's track coach at UCLA did not discuss the situation as sexual harassment, nor did it mention feminist activism on the issue.[28]

In the 1970s, editorials on sexual harassment consistently focused on how prohibitions of sexual harassment infringed on male sexual prerogative in the workplace. They characterized the issue as a question of misunderstandings about sex rather than abuse of power, and they ignored the mounting evidence of the negative impact of sexual harassment on women's workplace participation. Finally, they condemned women who resisted harassment, characterizing them as oversensitive or silly.

Taking Sexual Harassment Seriously: News Coverage Spreads the Word

Despite the early condemnation and trivialization of sexual harassment by editorialists and some news reporters, media coverage of the issue generally reflected feminist understandings of the issue. Enid Nemy's August 1975 article in the *New York Times* and Mary Bralove's January 1976 article in the *Wall Street Journal* broke the ice in mainstream news reporting of sexual harassment. By the end of the 1970s, the issue had appeared in a broad array of national and local newspapers and magazines. Law professor Elvia Arriola has criticized early media coverage of sexual harassment, arguing that women's magazine editors "struggled to define the law's reorganization of social attitudes in terms that did not challenge many of the embedded cultural attitudes that surrounded male-female sexual relations." Furthermore, Arriola has argued that the media portrayed sexual harassment as a problem affecting only white-collar women, excluding the experiences of blue-collar women.[29] Certainly some articles appearing in women's magazines lacked a critical perspective on the issue, portraying it as simply a question of romantic involvement, not male abuse of power. But generally women's magazines incorporated feminist ideas that challenged traditional sexual roles, often quoting feminist activists and including contact information of organizations providing counseling and referrals. Women's magazines also often incorporated discussion of the experiences of blue-collar women. In this way, the media spread the feminist message and fueled the movement against sexual harassment in the 1970s.

Most of the coverage in women's magazines in the late 1970s characterized sexual harassment as a serious issue that affected women in a broad range of occupations. An article by Claire Safran in the November 1976 issue of *Redbook* reported on *Redbook*'s January 1976 survey on sexual harassment. Quoting extensively from a broad cross-section of women who answered the survey, including a legal secretary, a factory worker, and a college professor, Safran described the problem as "pandemic," occurring "in the executive suite, in the steno pool [and] on the assembly line." She reported that changing one's behavior or dress rarely worked and that women resented the implication that they were to blame. She argued, "Both sexes arrive at work lugging the emotional baggage of a lifetime, all the childhood teachings about what's masculine and what's feminine, the cultural myths and social reflexes that make men and women behave as they do toward each other. We've just begun to unpack that baggage, to look at it and try to replace the worn-out, obsolete bits and pieces."[30] Safran then suggested ways to handle sexual harassment, including legal avenues of relief. In April 1978, *Redbook* published a follow-up report on judicial and legislative developments on sexual harassment and described the Working Women's Institute, providing contact information.[31]

Contrary to Arriola's claim many women's magazines challenged "the embedded cultural attitudes that surrounded male-female sexual relations." For example, in an April 1978 article in *Redbook*, Margaret Mead argued that society needed a taboo on sex at work.[32] She explicitly recognized the power dynamics underlying sexual harassment and advocated changing the culturally embedded attitudes about how men and women interact. She noted, "so many men use sex in so many ways as a weapon to keep down the women with whom they work" because "at home and at school we still bring up boys to respond to the presence of women in outmoded ways." Mead argued that the law is not enough to change behavior, but that society needed to create a taboo against sex at work, similar to incest taboos, in order to root out sexual harassment in the workplace.

Other women's magazines also published articles that condemned the gendered power dynamics underlying sexual harassment. In the June 1977 issue of *Ladies' Home Journal*, feminist and *Ms.* editor Letty Cottin Pogrebin wrote an article analogizing rape and sexual harassment, which she described as "a virulent form of economic coercion practiced by men who have the power to hire or fire, promote or demote, give raises or deny them." She noted that often "personal solutions count for nothing."[33] Similarly, *Ms.* published a cover story on sexual harassment in November

1977, which focused on the economic vulnerability of sexually harassed women. The article recounted stories of sexual harassment by women in a broad range of jobs—an executive secretary, an advertising agent, an assembly line worker, a medical administrator, a waitress, a congressional aide, and a student—but the author argued that those hardest hit by harassment were waitresses, clerical workers, and factory workers because they were economically vulnerable.[34] This and other articles in the issue explained the work of the Alliance Against Sexual Coercion and the Working Women's Institute, discussed surveys of sexual harassment, reviewed legal developments, described the effects of harassment, and provided suggestions for how to deal with harassment. As a whole, this issue of *Ms.* questioned the suggestion that women could control sexual harassment through their behavior, pointing instead to the larger structural causes of the problem. Women's magazines challenged many of the embedded cultural attitudes that blamed women for sexual harassment. Even women's magazines that did not specifically address the abuse of power underlying sexual harassment still treated the issue seriously, often drawing on the expertise of the Alliance Against Sexual Coercion and Working Women's Institute.[35]

In addition to women's magazines, many mainstream newspapers and magazines published articles on sexual harassment. These articles often reported on the activities of the Working Women's Institute, such as a 1977 speakout on sexual harassment in New York City. Often the press coverage focused on public policy developments, including legal cases and government hearings.[36] Many articles discussed resources for dealing with harassment, often providing contact information. Sometimes these more mainstream sources had radical critiques, such as in an article in the April 1977 issue of *Across the Board*, a business periodical. The author argued that the real issue behind sexual harassment was not sex itself, but power—sexual abuse and coercion were means by which men socially and economically exploited women in the work force.[37]

Sexual harassment of blue-collar women received attention not only in women's magazines but also in mainstream newspapers and magazines, especially toward the end of the decade, when women were first breaking into nontraditional blue-collar occupations in significant numbers. In August 1977, the *New York Times* reported on new Labor Department regulations designed to facilitate women's entrance into the construction industry, including a requirement that contractors "ensure and maintain a working environment free of harassment, intimidation and coercion." In 1978, the *Los Angeles Times* reported on the sexual harassment of women in the construction industry. An August 1979 article appearing in the magazine *Coal Age* provided the first in-depth article addressing the sexual harassment of blue-collar workers—female coal miners. Soon many other newspapers were covering sexual harassment of female coal miners, including the *New York Times, Washington Post, Baltimore Sun,* and *Village Voice.* The *Richmond Times* reported about sexual harassment of women in several nontraditional jobs, including mining, manufacturing, carpentry, and construction. Sexual harassment in the military also received much media attention.[38]

Media coverage fueled the movement against sexual harassment. This can be seen most clearly from coverage of the 1977 speakout on sexual harassment in New York City sponsored by *Ms.* magazine and Working Women's Institute. About two hundred women attended the four-hour speakout held on Saturday, October 22 at the Community Church of New York on the Lower East Side. Gloria Steinem spoke at the event. Ten women, including Lin Farley, presented prepared testimony. Then many more women spoke during an open mike period. Unlike the 1975 speakout, the organizers allowed journalists, but they excluded male journalists during the "open mike" period. Journalists were prohibited from photographing or recording the speakers, and they were required to maintain the anonymity of the speakers in their news stories.[39] Despite these limitations, the speakout received extensive television and newspaper coverage, including a *New York Times* article quoting the Institute's leaders, Susan Meyer and Karen Sauvigné. In addition to the November cover story in *Ms.,* many other magazines ran stories on sexual harassment around this time and mentioned the Working Women's Institute. Meyer and Sauvigné began to appear regularly on television and radio shows, including *Good Morning America, The Phil Donahue Show,* and *The Mike Douglas Show.* Due to this exposure, the Working Women's Institute began receiving hundreds of letters and phone calls a week from sexually harassed women seeking advice.[40]

The *Ms.* cover story had an effect on the Alliance Against Sexual Coercion similar to the one it had on Working Women's Institute. The magazine included an article on the work of the Alliance, providing contact information. This coverage led to an explosion of calls to the Alliance Against Sexual Coercion from sexually harassed women and from the press, as it had for the Working Women's Institute. Many other magazines and newspapers then discussed its work. A 1979 *Business Week* article on sexual harassment quoting member Freada Klein led to the Alliance's first corporate client, the State Street Bank in Boston. By 1979, the Alliance was self-supporting from fees collected from literature, speaking engagements, consulting, and training workshops.[41] These examples show how popular culture played a tremendous role in raising public awareness of sexual harassment.

The Honeymoon Ends

Feminist activism had a powerful influence on news coverage of sexual harassment in the 1970s, which in turn had a powerful influence on the development of the movement against sexual harassment. Many articles discussed the work of the Alliance Against Sexual Coercion and Working Women's Institute and quoted the leaders of these organizations. This press coverage often incorporated feminist perspectives, contributing to a growing awareness of the abusive nature of sexual advances in the workplace because of the underlying power dynamics between male supervisors and female subordinates. While some early news articles viewed sexual harassment as a personal problem warranting individualized solutions, most encouraged women to talk to other women in the workplace, to get help from women's organizations, and to act collectively. Often news coverage told riveting stories of sexually harassed women, and the women whose stories they told were both white-collar and blue-collar workers. This discussion of sexual harassment in popular culture was critical to the creation of the movement against sexual harassment that led to a transformation of workplace norms about sex.

Ironically, news coverage of sexual harassment in the 1970s offered a much deeper analysis of sexual harassment as a social problem than did later news coverage, which became much more focused on the legal maneuverings of lawyers than on the voices of victims or feminist analyses of the problem. In the late 1970s and early 1980s, as feminists succeeded in raising awareness of sexual harassment, courts and policymakers took center stage as they developed remedies. Government officials and lawyers came to dominate discussions of sexual harassment. Feminists succeeded in gaining legal remedies for sexual harassment, but they lost control of the public discussion of the issue.

As feminist influence on the public discussion of sexual harassment has waned, feminist perspectives on the problem have receded from prominence in popular culture, replaced by powerful stereotypes of women claiming sexual harassment. In the 1980s and 1990s, as legal cases came to drive the media coverage of sexual harassment, stereotypes of and biases against women came to permeate the public discussion of the issue. As women sought relief in courts, harassment defendants attacked the credibility and character of their accusers, just as rape defendants have been doing for centuries. According to University of California at Santa Cruz political science professor Gwendolyn Mink, women complaining of sexual harassment face a "regime of disbelief."[42] Anita Hill was a vivid example—Clarence Thomas's supporters called Hill psychotic, a lesbian, a pathological liar, a slut, and a nymphomaniac. In addition to attacking the reputation and motivation of women alleging harassment, many trivialized sexual harassment by characterizing the behavior as a matter of private sexual conduct rather than an abuse of power.[43]

The news coverage of sexual harassment in the 1990s often distorted the issue. Women alleging harassment were characterized as oversensitive and investigations into sexual harassment were portrayed as witch hunts.[44] The media reveled in focusing on examples of bad policy decisions involving sexual harassment. In the fall of 1996, the media extensively covered two separate instances in which boys aged six and seven were disciplined for "sexual harassment" after kissing female classmates against their will, leading to a public outcry against "political correctness."[45] Hollywood put a twist on the issue with the 1994 movie *Disclosure*, in which Demi Moore played a corporate executive who sexually harassed a male subordinate, played by Michael Douglas.[46] Even a board game called Harassment was released in 1992 to favorable reviews.[47] In the 1990s, much of popular culture addressed sexual harassment in a reactionary or trivializing manner, in many ways similar to that of the early editorial writings on sexual harassment.

Feminists continue to work actively against sexual harassment, fighting to shape public discussions of the issue and improve public policy. However, feminist perspectives often get lost in a sea of voices, many unsympathetic to the plight of sexually harassed women. The debate today occurs within a legal/bureaucratic framework that fundamentally shapes public discussions of the issue, often upholding the status quo. In the 1970s, on the other hand, when the women's movement had a strong influence on popular culture, sexual harassment activists were able to use the media effectively to shape public consciousness about sexual harassment and create legal relief for its victims.

Chapter 4

"Airheads, Amazons, and Bitches"

Cheerleaders and Second-Wave Feminists in the Popular Press

MOLLY ENGELHARDT

One of my college professors reminisced in class once about being in high school during a time when Wittgenstein was the rage among young intellectuals. As he put it, "everyone" was reading him, and then with a chuckle he added, "unless, of course, you were a cheerleader or something." What made the joke work was the professor's collapsing of two mutually exclusive terms—cheerleading and philosophy—into the same syntactical frame. The image of a bouncy, ever-eager, intellectually challenged cheerleader trying to read and make sense of such a male-oriented, rigorous discipline as philosophy was so absurd that we had to break out laughing. What I remember thinking at the time was how odd it felt to be laughing alongside my academic colleagues at an image that was in fact me, since in high school I had had no idea who Wittgenstein was and was way too busy cheerleading to care. Not only was the joke on me, but by responding in the conventionally appropriate way I was disavowing my own past while simultaneously using it as the "other" against whom to construct a new identity, one I presumed to be more enabling in my quest toward "becoming" a doctor of philosophy.

Catching myself in the act of disavowing my girlhood past has helped me realize the significance of these classroom antics in terms of feminism and gender politics. For one thing, cheerleading in the 1960s, as I remember it, was a fairly respectable activity—one of the few calisthenic activities available to girls outside P.E.—and those doing it were not only school leaders but very likely to grow into ablebodied intellectuals. My professor, however, was projecting another kind of cheerleader, one residing outside lived experience and constructed for the most part through various forms of popular culture. While "the cheerleader" is not a fixed sign—everyone's understanding of the activity and the performer doing it is context-driven—"the cheerleader" as a cultural icon circulates for the most part as white, middle-class, female, and dumb. We know this figure because we see her on television, in advertising, and in movies. She is the frivolous, vacuous, "Oh my god!" cheerleader in *Buffy the Vampire Slayer*, the "usual airhead bitch" cheerleader in the 1988 teen movie *Heathers*; she's routinely the butt of jokes, the naive sex victim in B-rated movies, the tease who lures people to porn web sites. The class laughed because it knows how to "read" popular culture, which in part requires arresting the memory of lived experience to participate instead in the pleasures of the reconstructed, fictionalized "real."

While my purposes are neither to redeem cheerleading nor to condemn it, I do find it symptomatic and unfortunately typical that an activity participated in by so many women—second-wave feminists certainly among them—is so uncritically accepted as a sign of naiveté, stupidity, bitchiness, and hypersexuality. That these negative associations are ambiguous—a stupid bitch? A naive nympho?—is rarely questioned. Despite the fact that the demonic high-school girls in the movie *Carrie* are indeed *not* cheerleaders, viewers often *remember* that they are, giving evidence to how welded the images of cheerleaders and demons are in the cultural imagination.

A colleague of mine tried to resolve my perplexity over cheerleader-bashing by dismissing the question altogether and asserting with absolute knowingness that "cheerleaders are bashed because they are bitches." Another took issue with this claim: "No, it's because people are jealous of cheerleaders; they either *desire* them or desire to *be* them." Former athlete Mariah Burton Nelson disparages cheerleading in her *Embracing Victory: Life Lessons in Competition and Compassion* (1998) because girls doing it "celebrate other people's victories, not their own."[1] While Nelson's claim corresponds with themes that grew out of 1970s feminism, the competitive nature of the activity in recent years makes her statement anachronistic. Cheerleading in many parts of the country is fiercely competitive, and it is not unusual for girls' squads to choose their own competition over the football game when schedules conflict. My point is that the cultural assumptions and meanings attached to cheerleading do not necessarily align with the material reality of the activity. As a cultural icon, she/it exists extraneous to lived experience.

My aim is to revisit the 1970s via pop culture to locate historically the resignification of cheerleading during the decade from a leadership position (1950s and '60s) to something low, ridiculous, and for feminists best left forgotten. The cultural devaluation of cheerleading, I argue, was connected with the backlash against second-wave feminism manufactured, in part, by the media's dissemination of negative stereotypes through which to deflect the cultural disquiet provoked by public exhibitions of radicalism. Using representations of the cheerleader figure from widely circulated texts during the 1970s (*Esquire, Playboy,* Jack Heifner's *Vanities,*

Animal House), I show how the constructed dichotomy of the feminist/ intellectual, cheerleader/dumb blonde that might have succeeded in opening up the meanings attached to the signified "woman" simultaneously left both signs vulnerable to popular vilification.

Cheerleading during the 1950s was an institution that conformed to and reified conservative American ideology: it perpetuated patriarchy and competition, and it created a forum for the unified expression of loyalty and love of community. It likewise endorsed the male, heterosexual, American dream already available—work hard and you, too, can be a winner (and win a cheerleader). The project of radical feminism, on the other hand, was to erase social hierarchies and reorganize the institution of marriage and family to realize a global sisterhood free of patriarchal oppression. The best way to succeed in this mission was to vacate positions that were subordinate to male activities (like cheerleading) and become political—the two could not coexist in the same cultural frame without compromising the cause. The continued circulation of these counternarratives not only weakened the momentum of both but allowed patriarchy to do its insidious work of pitting women against women to further undermine feminist goals. Popular culture facilitated this work by ridiculing women from both sides of the divide.

Gendering the Sidelines

Going back to my professor's joke about philosophy and cheerleaders in the classroom, it is ironic that the person credited with first organizing cheerleading as a school activity was a professor of mental and moral philosophy. Thomas Peebles was an undergraduate at Princeton in 1880, and it was Princeton where the first recorded cheer was performed: "Ray, Ray, Ray! Tiger, Tiger, Tiger! Sis! Sis! Sis! Boom! Boom! Boom! Aaaaaah! Princeton, Princeton, Princeton!" Peebles was appointed to a faculty position at the University of Minnesota in 1884 and, as legend has it, he took the cheer with him. It was here that organized cheerleading originated.[2] Often spectators would spontaneously lead the crowd in a cheer, and at the University of Southern California the first cheerleader was in fact a "frock-coated professor."[3] Universities needed recruitment devices and some sort of extracurricular spectacle to build school loyalty and generate an alumni base that would support the school financially; football and its supportive component, cheerleading, served this function. Interestingly, in spite of the advent of girls' sports in colleges and high schools during the 1890s, cheerleading remained entrenched as a boys' activity until the latter part of the 1920s. While the athletic girl was extolled in the 1903 University of Minnesota newspaper as the "truest type of all American Co-eds," with her basketball performance so popular at all-female Smith College that the entire student body participated in a virtual pregame frenzy, boys continued to dominate the sidelines as cheerleaders.[4] Gertrude Morrison's 1914 young adult novel *The Girls of Central High at Basketball*, in fact, describes boys leading cheers at a girls' basketball game.[5] The subordinate rank of the sidelines in this case is more male-gendered than the playing field.

Before the women's suffrage movement had reconstituted sports into a viable pastime for women, cheerleading had been linked to the masculine ideal—bulk, power, aggression—because of its association, albeit in a subordinate form, with football. But women engaging in contact sports challenged the perception that physicality was a predominantly male endowment, and by the advent of World War II the rhetoric of cheerleading shifted into gender neutrality. The demands of war usually take precedence over social order—gender hierarchy being one such ordering—and World War II was no exception. Thus we see cheerleading manuals published during the 1940s paying tribute to nationalism without regard to gender. One of the most widely distributed manuals of the decade was the 1945 *Cheerleading and Marching Band*, which opens with a dedication to "the gallant men and women whose courage and determination . . . whose bravery and sacrifice . . . have secured for future generations of our people the right and privilege of assembling."[6] The propaganda campaign engineered and funded by the U.S. government to return Rosie the Riveter to her kitchen had not yet begun, as evidenced by the inclusion of "gallant women" in the dedication. The qualifications for a good cheerleader were likewise gender neutral and were more oriented to function than to performance: pleasing personality, appearance (with neatness rather than beauty emphasized), imagination, organizing ability and leadership, acrobatic ability, and a commanding voice.

Such gender neutrality ended along with the war, however, and, in keeping with the conservative, postwar mood of the country, cheerleading manuals began to impart messages to girls that they could participate in such a physical, public activity if "they act[ed] as girls should." Thus an activity that during its inception helped conceptualize the masculine ideal now became a site for constructing femininity. The tone and message in physical education instructor Stella Gilb's 1955 manual *Cheerleading, Pep Clubs, and Baton Twirling* suggested a concern in public sentiment about girls in sports and femininity in general. Cheerleading had obviously suffered a setback in terms of status because Gilb's opening remarks alluded to a shortage of funds and inadequate training materials.

Gilb claimed that she wrote the book after being "besieged with requests for help concerning the *problems* of cheerleading" (emphasis added).[7] While cheerleading in the past had been about controlling the crowds, it now seemed to be the cheerleaders themselves who needed controlling. Gilb introduced her book with the claim that cheerleading and baton twirling had been elevated overnight as extracurricular activities for girls to compensate for "many states rul[ing] out competitive sports for girls." She stated that the "elimination of girls basketball from the school curriculum is probably one of the reasons we find some schools with all girl cheerleaders" (1). As if banning what had been one of the most popular athletic outlets for girls wasn't enough to set America straight, old rhetoric about "true womanhood" and preserving femininity reemerged, but ambiguity over the gender of this activity persisted. Gilb wrote, "There can still be found in every school and community some faculty member or parent who questions the value and desirability of permitting girls to be members of a twirling corps or cheerleading group. To some, it is merely a means of attracting attention in undesirable ways." The key to the problem, Gilb argued, was the sponsor, who should be "appointed to show [cheerleaders] the way" (viii). A new age-determined binary of power—adult sponsor, student cheerleader—became instituted in the schools to better discipline an ambiguously gendered activity by imposing upon its female participants new codes of femininity.

The conflict was obviously won by advocates for girls' cheerleading after compromises were struck to alleviate fears of school administrators and parents while still giving high-school girls something extracurricular to do. What such compromises involved was a restructuring of the activity to comply with a social hierarchy that understood boys' activities as being more institutionally significant than girls'. Jane Flax argues that such unequal dichotomies mirror Western philosophy's project to "create an illusory appearance of unity and stability by reducing flux and heterogeneity of the human and physical worlds into binary and supposedly natural oppositions."[8] When the veil hiding the social construction of categories of difference is lifted, as often happens during crises such as war, the hegemonic center of society creates binaries to impose order, which Flax argues reveals a desire for control and dominance. Feminists have long pointed out that the systematic subordination of women in patriarchal societies is based not on the actual nature of the social activity, but on the position within the hierarchy of the gendered subject assigned to do it. Accordingly, when boys were cheerleaders, it was a valued occupation and those doing it were recognized for their leadership abilities and commanding presence. But girls leading crowds called into question the gender of leadership, and the signification of the activity shifted to that of spectacle. Rather than lead or control the crowds, cheerleaders were expected to organize and excite them.

Bubble Heads and Amazons

Narrative myth and the restabilizing efforts of the country after the war played an important role in this popular reconception of cheerleading.

To watch boys cheer for boys was too close to the homosocial dynamic many men experienced during the war.[9] Men were now being directed toward business, competition, and building a family, with the fruits of mass consumerism serving as the prize for hard work and conformity. The cheerleader was one such fruit, her value embodied by her beauty and athleticism; she represented on a symbolic level the makings of what the 1980s referred to as the trophy wife for those men possessing "the right stuff." Just as the football player represented the masculine ideal, the cheerleader represented the cult of feminine virtue, and together these two reenacted the American Dream, which was by necessity heterosexually bound. The cheerleader was the heroine, the football captain the hero, and both were the best the school had to offer in terms of beauty, respect, intelligence, and potential. In spite of the war's end, eugenics remained embedded in nationalist mythmaking.

The American Dream that promised to reward patriotism was ruptured by the radical movements that occupied most of the 1960s and the early part of the 1970s. The radical feminist movement and its lesbian component conflicted with the postwar nationalist spirit that understood masculinity as the force that made possible the American Dream. The enlightenment "truth" that knowledge in the hands of the legitimate people would assure both freedom and progress was reworked by radical feminists, who used the same set of laws but assigned the collective group rather than the individual or hero as the legitimate people. Rather than reforming society, the radical feminist agenda was to develop new structures that would prefigure the utopian community of the future. One point on which liberal, radical, socialist and Marxist feminists agreed, at least in the beginning, was that "the male-dominated, child-centered nuclear family was the single most important site of female oppression."[10] As Betty Friedan put it in *The Feminine Mystique*, "the problem that has no name" was the oppressive nature of the ideology of domesticity, which had flung women out of the work force and into suburban homes to suffer their "housewife's blight" alone.[11] The family was the primary site of gender socialization, the site where boys learned to wield power and girls learned to gain fulfillment from taking care of others. In other words, the American Dream that celebrated marriage as the pinnacle of romance began to crumble when married women opened up in female-centered consciousness-raising groups to tell stories of the emptiness and despair that awaited them after the honeymoon.

An alternative dream available to women through feminism was global sisterhood, with compulsory heterosexuality giving way to women identifying with women. While it is true that many socialist feminists believed that men should be included in the women's collective—Shulamith Firestone reportedly responded when asked her opinion of the matter, "What's a party without men?"[12]—a larger component of second wavers identified men as the enemy and agent of patriarchy. The inviolability of marriage and family as social institutions became most salient when outsiders to the movement shifted the critique to the protesters themselves, deriding the feminist platform as a site where shrill, overly aggressive, man-hating, humorless, deliberately unattractive women were charging the entire world with sexism. These stereotypes were manufactured in large part by the mainstream media, which exaggerated the political moves of feminists to create a rhetoric of sexual derision best exemplified by the commonly used phrases "braless bubbleheads," Amazons, "the angries," and "bands of wild lesbians."[13]

The intensity and pervasiveness of the backlash against feminism demonstrates how threatening the politicized woman was in the public's mind. Despite its ideological diversity and consequent strife, the purpose of women's liberation as a political movement was radical and called for nothing less than an entire restructuring of American society. Robin Morgan states in the introduction to the 1969 feminist anthology *Sisterhood Is Powerful* that the first step toward eliminating the oppression of women by patriarchy is to recognize one's participation in the regime: "To deny that you are oppressed is to collaborate in your oppression. To collaborate in your oppression is a way of denying that you are oppressed—particularly when the price of refusing to collaborate is execution."[14] A group of New York feminists calling themselves The Feminists produced a leaflet brandishing subtitles like "Do You Know That You Are Your Husband's Prisoner?" and "Do You Know Rape Is Legal in Marriage?" and circulated it at a demonstration held at the New York Marriage License Bureau. The text ends with the words, "We must free ourselves. And marriage is the place to begin."[15] Many feminists assumed that any woman with an intellect would be transformed by the literature circulating about the oppressive structures of white middle-class femininity, so that when certain groups of women such as beauty queens, brides-to-be, and cheerleaders failed to see their situation as entrapment, they were categorized as either slaves to the patriarchal network or too naive, stupid, or socially irresponsible to notice. Despite the fact that cheerleading had been made available to girls as a result of a small-scale but nonetheless viable struggle during the 1950s, it was no longer perceived as a symbol of leadership but as a politically incorrect activity that retarded rather than enabled the grander purpose of social transformation.

An opinion piece by Mary-Ellen Banashek in *Mademoiselle*, entitled "Memoirs of an Ex-Cheerleader" (1976), not only invoked feminism with its adaptation of Alix Kates Shulman's classic memoir but also gave voice to the progress toward gender equality that required burying, or better yet forgetting any ties to a cheerleading past.[16] Representing an imaginary antifeminist voice she writes, "You were all joiners. . . . In high school the in-thing was to be a cheerleader, so you joined. In college radicalism was chic, so you jumped aboard with the same rah-rah spirit. Why, you're probably into women's liberation now." Banashek illuminates the damage a cheerleading past might inflict on a feminist's reputation—being a joiner and a former cheerleader looked suspiciously insincere. Those who didn't join the women's movement and continued to cheer and support men's activities might have had the sincerity, but it was sorely misplaced; rather than fighting the system, they were offering themselves up as the embodiment of the damaging marks of patriarchal exploitation.

Feminism, too, received its share of parody in popular culture, one example being an episode of *The Partridge Family* (1970)—"Keith Becomes a Feminist"—that ridiculed the polemical stance undertaken by many young, newly politicized women. Keith's (David Cassidy) new feminist girlfriend Tina wants him to help her promote the upcoming POW (Power of Women) rally by enlisting the family's talent for the event, which he does without first getting their consent. The humor is directed at the "moral watchdogs," who are afraid that feminism will make their daughters dig ditches, but it is directed even more at the politically awakened Tina, who calls every social convention Keith uses to show his affection for her condescending to women and meaningless. Canned laughter follows her every statement. Right before the family begin to perform at the rally, Tina tells Keith he must change the lyrics to make them compatible with feminist philosophy, a demand he refuses because he loves music more than anything, including Tina; censorship, he makes clear, is a worse evil than sexism. The show positions Keith at its moral center by showing the softening effects of the music and lyrics on the irrational and naive Tina, who by story's end has exchanged her radicalism for the more relational-friendly stance of moderation.

This *Partridge Family* episode appeared on the heels of one of the biggest media sensations (barring the Bobby Riggs, Billy Jean King tennis tournament) in feminist history. During the Miss America contest on September 7, 1968 (the middle of football season), more than one hundred women's liberationists went to Atlantic City to protest the pageant's exploitation of women, which meant that millions of home viewers watched as an enormous banner emblazoned with the words "Women's Liberation" was unfurled just as Miss America read her outgoing speech. In addition to chaining themselves to a Miss America puppet and throwing "instruments of torture to women" such as high heels and girdles into a "Freedom Trash Can," some of the signs they carried had messages directed at "other" women that were downright mean: "Miss America is a big falsie" and "Up Against the Wall, Miss America."[17] As Alice Echols remembers in her political history of radical feminism, *Daring to Be Bad*, the protest got out of hand and women "distorted the original message, transforming it from an attack on the pageant to an attack on the contestants themselves."[18] It is true that cheerleaders were a different subculture than beauty contestants, but because both occupied the same conservative, heterosexual frame, attacking Miss America was similar to attacking all the proponents of the American heterosexual dream, including cheerleaders.

Not only were men the enemy, so were women who refused to listen to reason or abide by newly constructed ideologies that were arguably as dogmatic as those upholding hegemonic values. The irony here goes without saying: if women were the enemy too, who would want to share a vision of global sisterhood? The media pushed the irony even further by representing the 1973 speakout between liberal and radical feminists as a name-calling catfight. The *New York Times* referred to the event as a classic "kill the mother" fantasy-drama, with Betty Friedan poised as the enemy mother.[19] Friedan had mentioned in an earlier memoir that outside "disrupters" of the movement in 1970 had tried "to push lesbianism or hatred of men" onto others, a comment that outraged lesbians and other members of the radical wing. The headline, "Mrs. Friedan's Essay Irks Feminists," deemphasizes the diversity among the women at the event by subtly creating a binary of sexual difference—"Mrs." Friedan, the married heterosexual, and "feminists," the champions of lesbianism. But while most of the speakout's participants were respectful to Friedan, the reporter begins the article with a listing of insults cast from both factions, implying that paranoia rather than reason motivated the debate. Friedan was concerned about "a possible take-over of the women's liberation movement by man-haters, lesbians, 'pseudo-radical infantilists' and infiltrators trained by the F.B.I. and the C.I.A." Critics countered by calling Friedan "severely myopic, a lesbian-phobe, a dyke-baiter, . . . a disgrace to any movement . . . a conjurer of phantoms and a narcissistic and self-congratulatory polemicist who had reached new heights of paranoia and egotism." A few of Friedan's comments were directly quoted, but none of the insults hurled back at her were, suggesting a degree of fabrication on the part of the reporter to heighten the sensation of the story. Not only are stereotypes constructed in this article, their origins are located within the women's movement itself.

Just as the heterosexual romance of love, home, and family was fissured by the feminist decree that marriage was slavery and heterosexuality equal to sleeping with the enemy, so was the romance of sisterhood when it became apparent that women could be as oppressive as men and sisterhood as divided as marriage. By the mid-1970s, the dissolution of these counter-narratives embraced by women from opposite political positions began to manifest itself even more blatantly through negative stereotypes of both feminists and cheerleaders in consumer magazines, newspapers, and film. Out of the same political context emerged a dichotomy that contained signifiers on both sides of the divide equating "woman" with the ridiculous. Two seemingly opposite stereotypes—the man-hating, hairy-legged feminist and the blonde bomb, no-lights-are-on cheerleader—were in fact interconnected and mutually constituted.

An article in a 1974 issue of *Esquire* suggests that the backlash against feminism beginning in the mid-1970s had a trickle-down effect on girls' cheerleading and the myth it embodied. A cross-section of athletes were interviewed, and alongside individual in-action photographs appeared a blurb that detailed the intellectual pursuits of each. Linebacker Andy Russell said, "I've really gotten into Dostoevski," and Oakland pitcher Ken Holtzman read Proust, preferring to read French authors in the original language. Kareem Abdul-Jabbar read *Siddhartha* and *The Prophet* and "they started [him] thinking about different ways to observe the universe."[20] Adjoining this feature that was obviously intended to contest the dumb-jock stereotype by uncloseting intellectual athletes was a satiric review of girls' cheerleading called "The Girls of Autumn."[21] The age-determined word "autumn" is accented by the subtitle, "For Ex-Cheerleaders, the Pompoms Sag But Life Goes On," the humor being directed at the physical degeneration of the cheerleader, whose spirit lives on despite the sagging body. The writer, Nancy Collins, ridicules the cheerleader, but does so surreptitiously by covering her own critical voice with that of a feminist interviewee who, once a cheerleading hopeful, "insists all that stood between her and the squad was her tush. The hair you can always fake, the other is up to God." By putting the two in opposition, Collins can ridicule cheerleaders *and* feminists who ridicule cheerleaders, while assuming a loyal front to both.

Collins disparages "sisters in the movement" who "insist that women are brainwashed into believing that if you can't handle the ball, you may as well handle the ballcarrier" as if she's sympathetic to cheerleaders, but then she uses the word "power" to satirize the small-mindedness of cheerleaders, who think of power in terms of getting to wear their uniforms to school on Friday and being the first to kiss the winning football player. The photograph accompanying this section on cheerleading was carefully propped and studio lit and is clearly a lampoon, since the model wears bright red lipstick accentuated by a mouth grotesquely stretched into a scream. Under her name and profession (she is a designer) are the words, "A cheerleader is a show girl, you know, close to the men, kicking and twirling and all that." The intent of *Esquire* is clearly to change a negative stereotype of male athletes, while creating a new one altogether for the cheerleader—rather than a heroine, this cheerleader is a joke. But because Collins uses political rhetoric to be ironic about serious cheerleaders and includes an interview with a feminist embittered over not having been a cheerleader, the two are operating in opposition, resulting in a lampoon of both.

What this suggests is that the cheerleader was suspect not only to feminists attempting to script a new social order but also to members of mainstream society who no longer believed in her as a representative of the feminine ideal. The cheerleader was marginalized, explaining in part her sexualization during the 1970s for the purpose of marketing professional football. Tex Schramm, owner of the Dallas Cowboys, took advantage of the moment when he decided in 1972 to upgrade his cheerleading component in order, as he put it, to excite the audience. Exchanging high-school sweetheart types for women whose provocative costumes demanded the gazes of spectators, Schramm was partially responsible for reconstituting the popular conception of the cheerleader from the girl-next-door to the erotic dancer, who performs in public without taking it all off. Schramm was quoted in *Playboy* as saying that when the Cowboys moved to their new stadium in 1971 he decided "to make our cheerleaders more or less atmosphere producers."[22] *Playboy* capitalized on the new sexualized cheerleader persona during the 1980s by showcasing college girls from different football conferences, whose nakedness was decorated with cheerleader iconography. The early 1970s also saw a proliferation of B-rated movies (*The Cheerleaders*, 1972; *The Swinging Cheerleaders*, 1974; *Cheerleaders Wild Weekend*, 1975; *The Pom Pom Girls*, 1976; *Satan's Cheerleader*, 1977) representing the cheerleader in various plot formulations but always within a hypersexual register.

Cher and Flip Wilson capitalize on the sexy cheerleader theme in a skit on *The Cher Show* when Laverne (the trampy, gum-chewing Cher) and Geraldine (Flip Wilson in drag) reminisce during a high-school reunion about the good ole days when the football team was their constant companion. Laverne's behavior with these football players was so bad that she had to spend the last year of high school in a girls' school. The two ogle men, brag about their curvy bodies, and perform a suggestively naughty old cheer. When Geraldine promises to call the next day, Laverne warns her that if a man answers she is to hang up—not because her husband does not like phone calls but because he's not at home. The skit ends with both happy that they are still up to their old tricks.

Gary Alan Fine analyzed twenty-nine versions of the "Promiscuous Cheerleader" legend—occupying the same playing field as Cher and Wilson's parody—collected from college students at the University of Minnesota, who had first heard the story during high school in the early 1970s.[23] The legend tells of a cheerleader who, after having sex with every player on the football team, has to be rushed to the hospital, where an inordinate amount of semen is pumped from her stomach. Ironically, an activity that began at a university with a philosophy professor at the helm had become after seventy-five years a subject for smutty jokes.

The first time I remember laughing at cheerleaders was in 1976, when Jack Heifner's three-act play *Vanities* appeared on stages across the country.[24] While the sexual connotation of cheerleading is less direct than that found in *Playboy* or in legends about promiscuous cheerleaders, it is still operating actively in the play. The first scene opens in a gymnasium, the year 1963, with a cheer, "Two bits, Four bits, . . ." Three girls argue over whether something as sacred as "Two bits" can be changed, and they worry about the mistake at the last pep rally when instead of spelling out "Yea, Team" they spelled out "Yea, Meat." They also argue over what theme they should pick for the upcoming football dance, but their biggest concern is how far they should go sexually with their boyfriends and what to do with "that trashy Sarah." The most conservative of the group, Joanne (Kathy Bates played this part in the original cast), doesn't understand why the chant "Go all the way, all the way" might imply sexuality to expectant spectators. *Silas Marner* has intellectually stumped the three, and Joanne gets "all confused when [she] finds out that George Eliot was a woman." When an announcement comes over the loud speaker that the president has been assassinated, the girls think it's the president of the student council and are relieved when they hear that the football game will go on that night as scheduled.

The meaning of the play resides in its title, *Vanities*, signifying that these girls are vain and vacuous because they privilege boyfriends, beauty, and reputations over social concerns occurring in the public sphere. While I don't mean to suggest that pep rallies are more important than national events, I do think that the theme of *Vanities* and the humor constituted by it worked in 1976 because at that time audiences still perceived real culture as being located within the business, economic, and political fields and certainly not on the sidelines of football. These cheerleaders were not simply a symbol of teenage silliness but represented something much more potent and interconnected with the fissure of American ideology that the play is recalling in a context twisted with cynicism.

Such fears over the "times they are a changing" open Scene 2 of the play, with the three now Kappa Kappa Gammas living together in the sorority house and worrying about the contaminating effects of jeans, smoking, and guitar players, which all three agree should be outlawed. Joanne says, "I don't care what the girls do in private, but they shouldn't smoke in public. It's unlady-like." Their current challenge is to come up with a theme for Spring Carnival that is not controversial. After ruling out *Fiddler on the Roof* (the Jewish sorority always does that), *West Side Story* (Puerto Rican so that's out), and *Flower Drum Song* (oriental), they decide unanimously on *Hair* because it is "about peace and love and sunshine," and anything having to do with hair must be important without being scary. The mention of antiwar activity draws an "Ugh, politics" from Joanne, followed by, "I told Ted I didn't understand why he had to get involved. The Viet Cong aren't bombing the campus."

The heterosexual myth of living happily ever after conflicts with the feminist myth of shared sisterhood in Scene 3, set in 1974 in the garden of Kathy's apartment. Having traded feminism for Society, Mary dismisses as insignificant the moment when she burned her bra during a demonstration: "I staged the whole thing." Kathy asks, "And that liberated you?" Mary responds, "Christ, it was a joke. Remember jokes?" As Joanne steadily gets drunk while talking about her kids and husband Ted, we discover that this same Ted is having an affair with Kathy and in fact pays for her apartment. Heifner's parting shot is Mary's comment, "Shall we toast our by-gone days?" to which Kathy replies, "Let's drink to forget them." In one sweep, Heifner deflates the experience of many white middle-class women, who, whether they are former radical feminists or conservative cheerleaders, are represented as dupes, not only of the system but also of their own sisters. And the cause of such betrayal was their own naiveté.

Vanities was a big hit for over a decade, in part because it capitalized on the wave of nostalgia that hit America during the post-Viet Nam/Watergate era. The cheerleader and her pom poms, bubble hairdo, and giggle functioned in the nostalgia films of the mid-1970s as a potent symbol for taking viewers back to their more innocent, nonpolitical past. Paradoxically, however, while the cheerleader might have helped people return to their past, she was also a reason they would want to come back. She was represented no longer as a desirable object but rather as a target of ridicule and in some cases the roadblock to, or a diversion from, male intellectualism.

Two of the most memorable films of the 1970s were *American Graffiti* (1972) and *Animal House* (1978), both set in 1962, that era when in theory, anyway, the American Dream still reigned. In *Animal House* the cheerleaders Mandy and Bev look the part—they are giggly, have blonde bubble hair, and are adequately bitchy—but their virtue depends on physical rather than moral cleanliness; Mandy makes sure to slip on her rubber gloves before going parking with her football player boyfriend Greg. While the cheerleaders in the film are represented as ridiculous, the intellectual link is equally so, as characterized by the English professor (Donald Sutherland) telling his class Milton was a joke and turning his students on to pot rather than literature. The film does not allow us the pleasure of recuperating our lost innocence because we are too busy laughing at it. And not only is cheerleading our means to this end, but so is intellectualism, that field of perceived heresy out of which dangerous ideas like feminism are generated.

American Graffiti was released six years before *Animal House*, and George Lucas is obviously more interested in revisiting the cultural past than satirizing it. The plot centers primarily on four relationships, three of them variations of the heterosexual romance, with one conforming completely to the head cheerleader/football captain trajectory mentioned before. Of the four romances, the cheerleader/football player story is the most uninteresting, perhaps because we already know it so well, but the novelty in Lucas's film is the subtle demonization of the cheerleader character. The film's tension derives from Richard Dreyfus's character's indecision over whether to leave his hometown and accept a scholarship to college. Added to this are the head cheerleader's (Cindy Williams) attempts to keep her boyfriend, captain of the football team (Ron Howard), home with her rather than going off to college with his friend. The last scene takes place at the airport, where we see these two high-school sweethearts waving goodbye to Dreyfus's character as he goes off to college, Howard's arm protectively around Williams's waist. The implied message is that the cheerleader has successfully sabotaged the intellectual pursuits of the hero.

Feminist Revisioning: Something to Cheer About?

In these three representations of an era "before the fall," cheerleaders are targeted as the ones responsible for disrupting progress by manipulating others or "daring to be bad." This association of deviant power with an activity that in the 1950s was understood as conservative and was participated in by clean-cut, preppy girls suggests a shift in its popular reception connected on several levels with radical feminism. The meanings associated with cheerleading could no longer be perceived as innocent because women yelling and raising their fists to crowds had become resignified by radical feminism. Raised fists and shouts are by tradition associated with revolution, and regardless of their purpose—in this case, female support of a male activity—would have connoted to some degree the unruliness of the times. And considering the association of feminism with lesbianism, a group of hand-holding girls, arms linked, bodies swaying, must have ruptured some aspect of the ritualized space of the football game, especially that of the heterosexual romance. The best way to assuage the discomfort produced by women attempting to restructure a social order was to lampoon all women, with cheerleaders the readiest and most vulnerable target. Having been disinherited from feminism as an activity too contaminating to embrace as one's own, cheerleading was left politically defenseless and open to the demands of popular culture.

Ironically, while the radical edge of feminism has waned considerably since the 1970s, cheerleading has become in some parts of the country as competitive as football. Its popularity did suffer somewhat during the 1970s, but the activity never died and today remains at the center of girl culture, along with athletics. The debates over whether cheerleading should be given sports designation suggest that politics have indeed shifted to the sidelines. To compete, cheerleaders need funds for uniforms, entrance fees, and travel, but to be designated as a sport, cheerleading no longer needs football; it is this that football aficionados abhor. Nevertheless, private for-profit companies are cashing in on the current craze for competitive cheerleading by sponsoring state and national competitions with prize money.[25] Cheerleaders now include briskly paced dances, tumbling and stunts, and human pyramids in routines that are becoming increasingly sophisticated, innovative, and dangerous. While the ambulance at the game used to serve as a reminder of how dangerous football was, today it is just as likely that a cheerleader will be injured as a football player. In 1990, a Consumer Product Safety Commission sampling of hospital emergency-room reports showed that 12,405 injuries were the result of high-school and college cheerleading.[26] In other words, by disavowing cheerleading as something embarrassing, something "low" and degrading for girls, feminists are working against efforts to fund an activity that many girls want to do, not as subordinates but as competitors.

Cheerleaders and radical feminists share similar histories of derision, not only because they were victims of negative stereotyping during the 1970s, but also because the memories associated with the history of both are riddled with ambivalence. One way some (though not all, certainly) second-wave feminists resolve the discomfort of the past is to conveniently forget it, a tactic Adrienne Rich calls "historical amnesia." Ellen Willis writes in her foreword to Echols's *Daring to Be Bad* that "mistakes and failures [of the radical feminist movement] are typically used not to learn from its flaws but to dismiss its whole project."[27] What prompted Echols to re-visit the events of the late 1960s and early '70s, in spite of the discomfort in doing so, was to search for mistakes so as to better understand them. One of the most glaring mistakes she found was the failure of white middle-class feminists to take into account the differences among women, which from the onset caused enough infighting and backstabbing to turn the image of a shared sisterhood into tragic burlesque. By examining the interconnection of two seemingly divergent cultural groups—radical feminists and cheerleaders—I hope to have made a space for cheerleaders in the current revisioning work being undertaken by feminists as they attempt to make viable and productive a politics of "intersectionality." By including cheerleading in women's cultural history, feminists can further textualize the unsettled complexity of women's political and social past and celebrate the expansiveness of women's experience rather than trying to pare and prioritize it.

Part II
Women's Changing Images

Chapter 5

Foxy Brown on My Mind
The Racialized Gendered Politics of Representation

STEPHANE DUNN

I was about ten years old when I first saw *Foxy Brown* (1974). For years, my strongest memory of the movie was the visual image of Pam Grier as Foxy Brown: "She's super badd, Ms. Foxy Brown." Watching her dance in the movie's opening dance sequence, I marveled at Grier, a beautiful black woman who was the star of a Hollywood movie. I admired her sexy, 1970s style super diva outfits and her super cool, bold persona. She was not just another pretty black woman in tight clothes, filling in the background of a movie. And Grier's character had attitude. She wore that sassy, take no mess from anybody style the way she wore her clothes—confidently and without apology.

Later, when I watched the movie again as an adolescent in the 1980s and a young adult in the 1990s, I became more captivated by Foxy Brown's fearlessness and the fact that she outsmarted and outfought both the bad guys and the evil white female character, Katherine. Watching the movie yet again more recently, I am struck by the contradictions in the film. On one hand, the movie offers an image of a tough woman as action hero who wins out over the bad guys, a significant change in the tradition of Hollywood films where men are usually cast as action heroes rather than women. The film is further unique because its heroine is a black woman, depicted as beautiful, feminine, and desirable. This dynamic marks it as very special, since Hollywood still rarely invests in this particular image of black women. On the other hand, the film's potential for being truly radical is limited because it does not ultimately upset the sexist and racist white patriarchal iconography of the black female. Foxy Brown stands somewhere uncomfortably between the stereotype of the dangerous sexual black woman, the strong black superwoman, and a potentially new kind of heroine—a black woman who cannot be defined by traditional notions of black femininity in popular culture.[1]

Foxy Brown's tough nature suggests a feminist revision of the traditional film representation of toughness as a quality associated solely with men. In addition, the characterization of Foxy Brown illustrates the shifting historical tropes of black female imagery in popular culture. She is far removed from the asexualized black mammy representations of black femininity that dominated Hollywood films up through the 1950s. Yet *Foxy Brown* perpetuates the historical erotic sexualization of the black female body and continues the performance of dangerous eroticism associated with the persona of many black female performers in the twentieth century.[2] Concurrently, traces of the stereotypical inscription of black women with a sort of subhuman toughness remain in the treatment and characterization of Foxy Brown.

One of the few 1970s blaxploitation films starring a black woman as the lead,[3] *Foxy Brown* was written and directed by legendary exploitation director Jack Hill,[4] who was a pioneer in making films focusing on tough women. Like its male counterparts *Superfly* and *Shaft*, *Foxy Brown* has endured as a 1970s cult classic.[5] Almost thirty years after she was introduced to primarily black movie audiences, Foxy Brown continues to appeal to adult audiences and has emerged as a popular icon in post-1970s black culture movements. Over the years, I have been struck by how *Foxy Brown* continues to elicit enthusiastic responses from black women across generations. The enduring iconic status of Foxy Brown is further evident in the obvious cultlike adoration shown by *Pulp Fiction* director Quentin Tarantino. He resurrected Grier's Hollywood career by casting her as Jackie Brown in the movie of the same title, which obviously capitalized on stylistic elements of 1970s blaxploitation movies as well as Grier's continued popular association with the Foxy Brown character.

In general, though, *Foxy Brown* has been critically dismissed as one of the cheap, moneymaking, technically flawed blaxploitation movies with too much sex and violence.[6] Or it has been regarded as merely the most famous blaxploitation action movie with a female hero and as the movie that confirmed Pam Grier as the reigning black woman star of the genre. To my mind, this film has not adequately been studied. Despite its obvious technical flaws and aesthetic limitations, it opens up some interesting spaces for critical consideration of popular culture. *Foxy Brown* illuminates both progressive and problematic racial and gender politics in U.S. feminist and black nationalist movements of the time.

A distinctly 1970s depiction of a black superwoman, *Foxy Brown* capitalizes on the romanticized black militancy of the era. The movie was created in part because of the "Black Is Beautiful" and "Black Power" themes that permeated the civil rights struggle and swept over African American communities. Thus the film represented the changing demands of the industry on black moviegoing audiences.[7] Popular culture representations of both black masculinity and black femininity indicated the changing tide of racial politics in America. Significantly, though, the black nationalist ideology of black social and political liberation that infused the public framing of Black Power became as informed by the politics of race as by the politics of gender.

Foxy Brown also emerged during a period of sweeping change in views of women's sexuality. Reflecting on the sexual and racial atmosphere of the period in a 1997 interview, Grier remembers it as "a time of sexual revolution." She asserts, "We redefined sexuality for America. Suddenly it was acceptable to desire a black lady."[8] Black women were the primary female viewers of *Foxy Brown* and *Coffy*, but Grier garnered some attention from the mainstream women's movement. She appeared on the August 1975 cover of *Ms.* magazine.

These intriguing interlocking racial and gender dynamics of *Foxy Brown* provoke the questions that I wish to explore. What are the progressive feminist implications of the tough woman characterization of Foxy Brown? How is she a radical representation of women, particularly black women? How is the feminist potential of the character undermined or contradicted in the movie? What accounts for her appeal to post-1970s generations of black female music performers?

Foxy Brown signaled a welcome change from the usual image of the black female in the black urban ghetto dramas of the 1970s. In the three most popular blaxploitation films, *Shaft* (1971), *Superfly* (1972), and *The Mack* (1973), women are peripheral yet primary sexual objects who validate the sexual prowess and masculine power, hence super-"baddness," of the black male lead. In these "buckmania" films[9] women are graphically portrayed as "bitches" and "ho's." Historically, sexual black women in Hollywood movies have always, as bell hooks states in *Outlaw Culture*, been portrayed as "whores or prostitutes."[10] In the male-dominated 1970s blaxploitation films, women are deemed "bitches" because, according to the films' male perspective, they are irrational and jealous, given to catfighting and vindictive behavior, and completely occupied with existing for the sole purpose of men's sexual pleasure as well as abuse. In addition, in the glorified pimp culture of the Mack or Priest (*Superfly*), women are more often than not literally prostitutes.

Introducing the "Superbadd" Mama

Cleopatra Jones (1973), starring Tamara Dobson as the "Superbadd Supermama,"[11] and Pam Grier's two roles as "Supermama" in *Coffy* and the even more "Superbadd" *Foxy Brown*, flipped this script. In these movies, the black heroine does not play the role of a "bitch" in the sense of the traditional blaxploitation screen portrayal. Instead, the heroine is a "Superbadd Mama," "Badd Bitch," or, in the words of Foxy's brother Linc

(Antonio Fargas) "a whole lotta' woman" who didn't "take no mess." In other words, she is a tough woman, outwitting and outfighting the evil forces. In Grier's first major starring film, *Coffy*, she plays a nurse on a mission to avenge the drug addiction and death of her baby sister. Coffy survives finding out that her boyfriend is involved in the drug game and numerous fights with other men and a white woman before shooting her traitorous lover and toppling the drug lord.

The financial success of *Coffy* led to what was supposed to be its sequel but was instead transformed into *Foxy Brown*. In this film, Grier plays a woman involved with a noble black undercover agent, Dalton Ford, who is killed by a drug and prostitution operation led by a white woman, Katherine, and her lover Steve. Foxy Brown's brother Linc, a petty player in the operation, ends up being murdered by Steve after setting in motion the murder of Foxy Brown's lover. Brown goes on a mission to avenge their deaths, which provides the showcase for her amazing toughness.

Her toughness and untraditional role as a black female action hero who fights back and wins rather than accepting white supremacist patriarchal power and male abuse, perhaps appealed strongly to African American women. Importantly, for many young African American women Pam Grier was the first big black female movie star they had seen in Hollywood whose beauty and sexy screen persona were heralded by both white and black media. *Foxy Brown*'s generous servings of action, violence, sex, and other popular staples of the early 1970s action movie genre probably accounted for the relatively small yet significant attention it garnered from white moviegoers. No doubt, American International Pictures (AIP) and director Jack Hill's emphasis on Grier's physical beauty and heterosexual feminine appeal helped make a movie starring a black woman alluring to African American male viewers and exploitation film fans.

Hollywood had cemented the tough guy icon as a staple of the male action hero long before the 1970s. In the blaxploitation films, the black male lead's toughness most often manifests itself in his rebellion against "whitey," mirroring the black power ethos of the more militant African American civil rights activists of the 1960s and early 1970s.[12] The tough "buck" also possesses a signature style, including his "cool" dress, talk, and street-smart attitude. The black male hero's signature trait rests in his sexual and physical power over women. Foxy Brown represents a particular feminized toughness; her "baddness" in some ways marks a departure from the traditional characterization of the tough hero and her black "buck" counterparts.

Foxy Brown exhibits a physical and mental resilience that could risk being merely a model of traditional masculine features or the superwoman black female stereotype. Yet, while her image certainly embodies traces of the latter, the movie projects throughout an image of her as sexy and feminine yet uncompromisingly tough. She does not merely *survive*— while looking great doing it—she wages a fight and, in the end, she is literally the last woman standing. She possesses many of the "tough woman" traits that Sherrie A. Inness outlines in her book *Tough Girls: Women Warriors and Wonder Women in Popular Culture* (1999), though, as a black female character fighting both the *gender* and *racial* status quo, Brown does not fit neatly into this model in all ways.

Inness provides a useful explanation of the four elements that make up the tough woman figure: body, attitude, action, and authority.[13] Foxy Brown/Grier does not have a physical body that signifies a traditional masculine physical toughness, often a trademark of the tough woman in contemporary popular culture; she possesses soft curves rather than bulging, hard muscles. The absence of more traditional masculine indicators of physical strength in Brown is actually one of the radical aspects of Foxy Brown as an action character in the male tradition. Her curvaceous yet fit body represents a woman whose physical toughness is not largely a product of brute strength. Instead, her toughness rests in her mental stamina, instincts, and intelligence as well as her physical fighting ability. Here, too, though, Brown does not show much evidence of martial arts expertise— the precise sharp kicks to the head or karate chops that were and continue to be staples of action heroes in movies. She relies on her quick intelligence, resourcefulness, preparation, and, at times, a gun.

Foxy Brown illustrates another major element that Inness identifies as essential to the movie representation of the "tough woman." When Foxy Brown goes on her mission of revenge, her style of dress is crafted to signify her toughness. After her lover's murder, an angry, Afro-wearing Brown bursts into her brother's apartment in a snug-fitting black leather outfit, then uses a gun to force her brother to give her information about Steve and Katherine's operation. Inness points out that masculine clothing, such as a black leather biker's jacket, signifies toughness and "serves as a visual reminder that a woman has distanced herself from femininity." When Grier steps out of her softer, more feminine, brighter colored dress style into the black leather pants outfit, it parallels her move toward action. The outfit serves to emphasize further Foxy Brown's "superbadd" nature and her fitness for the task of taking down Steve and Katherine's operation.

Furthermore, Brown's toughness could not be effectively conveyed without the daring, determination, and fearlessness that define her attitude. Inness calls the absence of fear or taking action in spite of some fear a necessary component of the tough woman. Even though she's outnumbered most of the time, with few of the powerful resources of Steve and his men, Brown doesn't exhibit any fear of her enemies. Instead, her unwavering determination and fighting spirit assure us that Foxy Brown will eventually triumph. More than any emotion, she shows her anger toward those responsible for her lover's death. Yet, even in anger, Foxy Brown demonstrates her quick wit and intelligence as well as strength and resourcefulness in every dangerous situation. Last, her take-control representation of her self and her actions exude an authoritative attitude—also, Inness describes, a key trait of the tough woman.

Foxy Brown embodies more than some progressive qualities in the representation of female film characters. Her specifically African American female identification is an important element in her character. Grier has said that she "exemplified women's independence."[14] She comments further that she projected shades of her African American women relatives' tough attitude and no-nonsense business persona into her portrayal of Foxy Brown. "I based my screen characters," Grier reveals, "on my mother, aunts, and grandmothers. They were the kind of women who would fight to their last breath before they'd give their purse to some punk robber." Grier herself came up with some of the most creative and resourceful survival maneuvers in both *Coffy* and *Foxy Brown*. For example, in the former, Coffy escapes a violent encounter with some other women by pulling out a switchblade that she's hidden in her Afro. In the latter, Foxy Brown uses her car to rescue her brother, and in another scene, the infamous lesbian brawl, Foxy artfully uses a chair to fend off some hostile Amazon-sized women.

The black feminist potential of Foxy Brown is perhaps most indicated by her liberating efforts on behalf of an oppressed black woman. After Brown goes into disguise as a prostitute in Katherine's operation, she takes responsibility for protecting and freeing Claudia, a young mother and wife, who is trapped into staying in Katherine's "stable." Foxy Brown fiercely protects Claudia from a lesbian's aggressive unwanted advances. Furthermore, she risks her own freedom when she stays behind to fight Steve and his men so that Claudia can finally escape Katherine and Steve's grasp. Foxy Brown's treatment of Claudia highlights the racist, classist, and sexist oppression of black women and suggests black women's collective responsibility toward each other and action as a means of achieving liberation.

It is true that Brown uses Steve and his rich clients' lust and sexual objectification of women for money, her sexual attractiveness, and, by extension, their construction of her as an exotic sexual black female in order to infiltrate Katherine and Steve's operation. The fact that she must disguise herself as a high-priced prostitute speaks to the sexist positioning of women within the blaxploitation movie genre as sexual objects; however, Foxy Brown subverts this role. She does not have sex with Judge Fenton—her first and last "client." Instead, she gets Claudia to rebel along with her and humiliate the corrupt Fenton, simultaneously making sure he will punish two of Steve and Katherine's men in court. Hence Brown merely pretends to accept the sexual role Katherine gives her—she defies being a passive sexual object in this instance. Foxy Brown's care for her brother and Claudia and her general anger toward those whose greed motivates them to prey on the weak are progressive elements in her characterization.

Toning Down Foxy Brown

One of the important indicators of the racialized gender politics functioning in the treatment of Foxy Brown is the representation of the anti-slavery neighborhood committee. This vigilante group of black men advocates the idea of collective communal responsibility and care in the war against drugs, nihilism, and violence in poor black urban environments. The film portrays the group's members sympathetically, especially their efforts to protect and advance their community by discouraging and punishing black involvement in the drug trade. Early in the movie, when Dalton Ford and Foxy Brown witness the work of the vigilante group, she calls their style of justice "as American as apple pie." But, problematically, the group endorses a black self-sufficiency and responsibility ethic embedded in a very macho action orientation.

The representation of the group highlights the troubling gender dynamics in the movie and emulates the sexist nature of late 1960s and early 1970s black nationalism. Generally, despite some of their progressive social ideas, in real-life black nationalist groups, such as the Black Panthers and the Black Muslims, and in the civil rights movement in general, sexism was a central feature. In *Black Macho and the Myth of the Superwoman*, Michelle Wallace describes the "Black Movement" as a struggle revolving around the black man's quest for manhood.[15] As the civil rights movement continued, Wallace asserts, "little attention was devoted to an examination of the historical black male/female relationship, except for those aspects of it that reinforced the notion of the black man as the sexual victim of 'matriarchal' tyranny."[16]

Furthermore, the gender politics implicit in the film's representative Black Power group follow the romanticized popular film representation of such organizations even in more serious, thought-provoking 1970s revolutionary black films like *The Spook That Sat by the Door*. Here, as in *Shaft*, *Superfly*, and even *Foxy Brown*, women operate merely as sexual entities in subordinate roles to the male characters. If they enter into the revolutionary social or political action, they do so via their sexual roles, as in the case of Foxy Brown's disguise as a prostitute.

Rather than upsetting this orientation because a woman teams up with the vigilante group, the movie maintains the masculine engendering of black revolutionary groups. Foxy Brown is not a member of the group, and there is little indication that she will become so after her mission is complete. While she is familiar with the men in the group before her quest begins, she is clearly uninvolved with their struggle. After her escape from the ranch, Foxy Brown must seek their aid to accomplish her crusade against the powerful forces of Katherine and Steve. She aligns herself with the group temporarily because her personal mission complements their social mission. Black male action heroes, and certainly, white male Hollywood action heroes then and now, are most often cast as successful one-man revolutionaries who rarely seek such help. It would be difficult to imagine a male hero, Shaft, for instance, coming to a group of black women for such aid.

The gender politics implicit in the representation of the vigilante group are interlocked with the social critique illuminated by the group's mission. This critique is in large part directed toward the failure of the official, mainstream criminal justice system to prevent the exploitation of black communities in terms of drugs and violence. The failure of Brown's lover, a black man working within the criminal justice system, to destroy Katherine and Steve's illegal operations, and his subsequent murder point to this same critique. Both indicate the difficulty of destroying such operations because to do so, the higher racist and classist echelons of power behind those operations must be shattered. Foxy Brown's justice speech to the group, perhaps her most eloquent, self-revealing words in the whole movie, highlights the limitations of the group's scope in their struggle for justice and progress for the economically and socially troubled black community: "I want justice for all of them. And I want justice for all the other people whose lives are bought and sold so a few big shots can climb up on their backs and laugh at the law and laugh at human decency."

Up to this point, the group has only impacted individuals—black individuals who are mere lowly players in the white-controlled capitalistic drug enterprise. Despite its war on drug activity, the group's impact has been small because it has not reached out to effectively attack the larger forces responsible. When the men team up with Foxy Brown, they extend their collective struggle by fighting the external white supremacist capitalist forces that exert such power over the condition of their community.

Yet, while Brown's speech expands the idea of the group's fight as one that must be lodged against those in power outside the community as well, it also points again to the disturbing gendered implications of her mission. Foxy Brown's central motivation is the man she loved. She concludes her passionate speech: "And most of all, I want justice for a good man. This man had love in his heart. And he died because he went out in his neighborhood to try to do what he thought was right." Hence her mission is primarily about avenging her lover rather than any progressive sociopolitical desire to have a positive impact on her community or other black women. When one of the brothers replies that Brown is after revenge rather than justice, she replies, "You just take care of the justice, and I'll handle the revenge." When she says revenge, it reinforces her as a woman with a familiar type of female motivation rather than one who shatters our notions of woman's nature. Foxy Brown is fighting for her man. From the beginning of the movie until the end, she has no job or life—not revealed to us anyway—outside being a caretaker to her brother, devoted woman to her lover, the noble Dalton Ford, and avenging angel. It is disturbing that the movie conveys her ability to be tough enough to accomplish her mission as largely a product of her love for her man.

This is not the only problem with the film's radical potential. The excessive sexualization of Pam Grier's body and the fact that except for Katherine and Foxy Brown, the other women in the film appear as one of two popular culture stereotypes, masculine lesbian or brainless prostitute seriously undercut this potential. The visual emphasis placed on Grier's body hardly offers a new alternative for presenting women in Hollywood movies. The excessive attention given to her sexy, feminine body helps to mediate Foxy Brown's tough, potentially masculine, and feminist edge. Shots like the one in the beginning of the movie are common. Here, the camera moves in close to Brown as she gets out of bed clad only in bikini panties and gets dressed, providing a top to bottom shot that is obviously there only to provide a seductive, sexual visual of Grier. This serves as yet another example of how differently male and female bodies are treated in films. It continues to be more common for females, as in the case of Grier, to be captured on screen through close-up partially nude or nude shots. The display of Foxy Brown's sexual appeal becomes treated as a defining essential part of her character.

Hill and AIP ultimately do not create a black female film character that can be taken as a reinvention of the traditional notions and treatment of the black female body in popular culture. Instead, they create in Foxy Brown a still typically sexualized, albeit more idealized black heroine whose ethnic beauty makes her an exotically different cinema heroine in the tradition of white and black tough male heroes, while maintaining the traditional imagery of sexual females in film. The film is as much characterized by the focus on Grier's "Brown sugar"[17] sexualized "exotic" beauty as by its lack of scenes where Foxy Brown appears in nonsexual, yet tender and emotionally revealing contact with anyone.

Even the name and title "Foxy Brown," coined by AIP,[18] draw attention to the exotic racial sexualization the creators inscribe in her. "Foxy" has roots in the African American popular urban vernacular words of the period. "Foxy" was an adjective black men might apply to a black woman they considered sexy and very attractive. She might also be referred to in the noun form of the word, as a "fox." "Foxy" plays on the social concept of a fox's nature as sly, cunning, and slick, though it metaphorically signifies Brown's ability to outwit and outmaneuver her enemies. The name "Foxy," teamed with "Brown" as the title of the movie and with the name and concept of the character invoke the racial and sexual identity of Foxy/Pam. AIP capitalized on the sexual-racial connotation of the name in advertisements for the movie. For example, one trailer read: "She's brown sugar and spice, and if you don't watch it, she'll put you on ice."

Pam Grier had little control over the image of Foxy Brown, though certainly she imbued the character with her charisma and intelligence. In the *Ms.* 1975 interview with Jamaica Kincaid, Grier commented on her lack of control over her on-screen image, noting the "black sex goddess" image of her in films that AIP favored. Grier critiqued the ongoing excessive emphasis on violence as well as on "tits and ass" that marked *Coffy* and her other films despite her protests to AIP.[19]

While audiences are supposed to view Foxy Brown as a woman whose power is as much attributed to her toughness as to her sexual attractiveness to men, Foxy Brown is not always in the position of having control over her body or avoiding merely using her sexual attractiveness to further her mission. She suffers sexual humiliation in a scene that seems a ritual of black female submission to white male phallic power. Nowhere does the film reinvest more definitely in the historical sexualization and devaluation of the black female than in the scene in which Brown's enemies punish her by sending her to "the ranch," obviously "plantation" in disguise. At the ranch, tellingly, a breaking place for troublesome girls in Katherine's stable and where drugs are stored and processed, Hill goes disturbingly far to achieve his "over the top" action goal.

The film reenacts the historical rape of black slave women and the breaking of spirited slaves through physical abuse by white masters with the complicity of the white mistress. Foxy Brown is roped to the bedpost and then repeatedly beaten, drugged, and raped by two white males who are obviously supposed to be the embodiment of the stereotypical redneck Southern character. The dialogue reinforces the historical racialized implications of the rape. The men call her a "black wench." So complete is the devaluation of her black female body and personhood, they tell her she is lucky to be getting "it" from them.

When I watched this scene recently, I found myself turning away from the camera, disturbed as it moved in on Grier's breasts and bruised face while the sinister white male character simultaneously moved in toward her, beating her and preparing to sexually violate her again. It is this scene that now lingers in my mind as I reflect on *Foxy Brown*. The scene represents a glaring reminder that as a woman, a *black woman*, Foxy Brown can be put in her place if she tries to shake the status quo of power too much.

Despite her toughness, she is subject to sexual abuse by white men and women in power in a way she cannot emulate. The scene reminds us that Foxy Brown is vulnerable.

On the surface, the scene might appear to end up shattering the historical master-black female slave narrative. Brown shows a mental strength that keeps her defiant despite her subordinate position and that sustains her throughout this extreme abuse. In spite of being physically weakened by drugs and physical abuse, she manages to blow up both the drugs and her violators. Yet, rather than shattering the white supremacist ideology that it represents, the ranch scene turns the historical rape and bondage of the black female body into an eroticized dangerous sexual fantasy. The overt play on the racial implications inherent in the scene functions more to increase the sexual and general shock level of the movie. Indeed, when the camera zooms in on Grier's battered body, it is appropriate to remember that off-screen, behind the camera, a problematic white male gaze—Hill's and AIP's—directs this black female imagery.

Though Foxy Brown's escape and revenge might have been intended to be an indictment of the brutal enslavement and rape she endured, it actually illuminates the sexist and racist politics at the core of the scene and Hollywood films in general. In such films, tough male action heroes may be beaten up, shot at, and knifed, but they aren't raped—sexually violated—by either men or women. Brown endures both, but her seemingly quick recovery and the sheer lack of any serious focus on her emotional response throughout or afterward do not speak to her toughness. In fact, they help dull the horror of the repeated brutal sexual violation she endures and its racist and sexist implications. The film reinforces the historic white supremacist notion that as a black woman she cannot really be horrifically brutalized or raped.[20] It places her not merely outside the realm of traditional womanhood because she is a tough woman but also outside the "cult of true womanhood" because she is the black superwoman.[21]

The end of the movie further lessens the feminist potential of the movie and the Foxy Brown character. The other tough, though disturbing female character, Katherine, completely breaks down into a passive, wimpy, heartbroken female. Throughout the movie, she offers an ugly portrait of the distorted tough woman and the traditional feminine ideal as she clings possessively to Steve. Her power as the key figure in the operation comes second to her obsessive adoration. Katherine also delights in oppressing and abusing other women, especially if Steve appears to desire them. When Katherine learns of Steve's castration, it is clear that her reign as the tough bitch running the operation, as well as her life, is over.

Foxy Brown's hard core castration of Steve might be interpreted as a gesture of female liberation. While I think the act is meant to function symbolically as her triumph over white patriarchal power, it ultimately fails to registers as such. Instead it ends up reinforcing the mythology of male phallic glory. Brown cuts off Steve's penis as an act of revenging the fact that she has been cut off from sexual contact with her man, Dalton. Thus the castration is not even represented as a way of avenging her rape. Brown wants Katherine to suffer as she is suffering, and that is why she chooses to castrate Steve rather than just killing them both. Hence, the movie's ending message tells us that the worst lot Katherine can suffer is not the demise of her successful illegal capitalistic enterprise or her life, but rather to be permanently cut off from Steve's sexual power.

Though *Foxy Brown* is still standing, tough and beautiful as ever, her last lines reinforce the motivation behind her "superbadd mama" actions and why she is still a safe female type in spite of it. Though she projects a gutsy spirit from the beginning of the movie, she is also, again, a woman without a known profession, whose life we only know in terms of her actions on behalf of the two men in her life—her brother and Ford. Before Ford's death, Brown was prepared to leave her life, whatever that comprised, and go away with her boyfriend, who had been given a new identity in the witness protection program. The last scene and her final speech to Katherine leave the image of two women left with incomplete, suffering lives. Thus, Foxy Brown's win over the bad guys does not register neatly as a fulfilling or radical triumph for her or for women.

Despite her limited control on screen, and to a significant degree off screen in the world of male-dominated Hollywood film companies, Grier exhibited a defiant attitude that would be worthy of a more complete Foxy Brown character. By 1974 she had formed a production company, Brown Sun Productions, after a pet name given to her by her grandmother. Her motive, she revealed in an interview, was to take control of, to change, the image of Pam Grier in films.[22] Grier was critical of the repeated Coffy-Foxy Brown movie formulas that AIP wanted to keep doing. She started Brown Sun Productions in order to create new roles for herself other than those stereotypical "black" roles AIP kept sending her way. Her opportunities for starring roles dwindled when Hollywood's love affair with the *Foxy Brown-Shaft* movie models died. Grier did go on to other movies quite different from *Foxy Brown*—though she has never broken the mold of her popular film image as Foxy Brown. Ironically, her late major career breakthrough film, *Jackie Brown*, borrows from the blaxploitation style and her *Foxy Brown* fame.

Foxy Brown's "Daughter"

Interestingly, the racist and sexist politics Grier encountered over her entertainment image in 1970s Hollywood finds a striking parallel in the situation of her very different contemporary namesake, rapper Foxy

Brown (Inga Marchand). When she made her debut at the tender age of fifteen, Inga Marchand decided to pay tribute to her movie idol Pam Grier by using "Foxy Brown" as her rap entertainment name. She says she chose the name because she loves Pam Grier, who "played the no-nonsense Foxy Brown."[23] In her study of hip hop culture, *Black Noise*, Tricia Rose describes the significance of self-naming by rappers as "a form of reinvention and self-definition."[24]

Some of the appeal of Grier and her on-screen character Foxy Brown for the rapper derives from both the tough attitude and actions of the character and the public media visibility of Grier as an African American beauty. Rapper Foxy Brown's experience speaks to the continuing problematic racist ideology informing images of skin color and female beauty in American society. Speaking of her daughter's skin color inferiority complex, Judith Marchand says that while she was growing up Inga didn't see "anyone in the media who looked like her."[25] Foxy Brown adds that her "number-one insecurity is being a dark female" because it wasn't viewed as cool.

It is unfortunate that Foxy Brown's reformulation of Pam Grier's "Foxy Brown" does not offer an image of black femininity that transforms stereotypes of black femininity or the performance of sexuality by black women performers in popular entertainment. As one of the few best-selling female rap artists today, Foxy Brown is best known for her successful participation in gangsta rap[26] or hardcore rap resulting from her adoption of the troubling sexist and nihilist values that permeate it. Foxy Brown has become famous through her profane, sexually explicit lyrics, her wild, sexual "tough bitch" visual image and her boldly proclaimed material girl motivations.

The blaxploitation movie genre spawned a black popular culture phenomenon that emphasized a style encompassing everything from fashion to funky urban-infused rhythm-and-blues music mythologizing the black urban ghetto. It has maintained its appeal as popular culture inspiration, as is evident from the new and continuing blaxploitation style elements and music that permeate hip-hop culture,[27] particularly in rap music. Many African American moviegoers of the 1970s felt that movies like *Shaft* and *Superfly* presented some realistic facets of black identity and black urban life in economically depressed communities. Furthermore, the heroes who bucked "whitey" and "the system" and signaled their rebelliousness and black macho pride with their dress and attitude represented a radical counterculture to mainstream society.

Significantly, neither male-dominated rap music culture nor the blaxploitation cultural phenomenon marks a departure from the sexist tendencies of the larger American society. The glorification of the stereotypical black male phallic reputation, of black male sexuality, along with the extreme sexual objectification of black women that pervaded blaxploitation movie culture, has found a kinship in rap music, especially the hardcore/gangsta rap category. As rap music has gained a global commercial following and success, both recognition of its sociopolitical radicalism and criticism of the misogyny, violence, sexism, and nihilism that infuses too much of it have increased.[28] In rap music, the linked sexual and gender politics are glaringly demonstrated in the prolific use of the terms "bitches" and "ho's" as synonyms for black women in particular and in rap music videos where the half-naked, sexually gesticulating bodies of black women have become an accepted signature trademark.

In spite of hardcore rap's sexist nature and violent overtones, women have begun to participate successfully in it, proving that they can be "iller [naughtier]" or at least just as "ill" as their male counterparts. Two of the most commercially successful of these rappers, Lil' Kim and Brown, have come under critical scrutiny, especially from black American feminists. Since Josephine Baker wowed Parisian audiences with her wild on-stage and off-stage antics as well as her performance of black female exotic primitivism, the question of to what extent a controversial sexual black female performer is being exploited or subverting that exploitation has been raised.[29] It is crucial that we continue to interrogate representations of black female sexuality in popular culture, including global hip-hop culture and rap music. In "Selling Hot Pussy," bell hooks asserts the importance of examining black women's absorption of negative stereotypes of black femininity:

Popular culture provides countless examples of black female appropriation and exploitation of "negative stereotypes" to either assert control over the representation or at least reap the benefits of it. Since black female sexuality has been represented in racist/sexist iconography as more free and liberated, many black women singers, irrespective of the quality of their voices, cultivated an image that suggests they are sexually available and licentious.[30]

Rapper Foxy Brown often appears on stage clad in lingerie and bikini-like costumes, perpetuating the performance of the wild, sexual black female image. Similar to Tina Turner's image, which hooks eloquently describes in "Selling Hot Pussy," rapper Foxy Brown appropriates the "wild woman pornographic myth of black female sexuality created by men in a white supremacist patriarchy," exploiting it in order to "achieve economic self-sufficiency."[31]

The current Foxy Brown bears little resemblance to the on-screen Foxy Brown of the 1970s. While both fictional movie character and rapper are women in a male-dominated arena who use sexual allure as a means to an end, their motivations and actions are strikingly different. While Grier's Foxy Brown was represented as a sister who was trying to change the game and dismantle it, rapper Foxy Brown's infiltration of the hardcore rap genre centers on her ability to play the game as it is, but just as successfully

as the male rappers. Brown seems to view her status as a commercially successful female participator in rap music as a progressive move. However,
she actually exemplifies the problematic concept that her participation in
marketing her public sexualization adopting the sexist "bitch" label to
denote her sexual prowess and allure, commercial success, macho toughness, and ghetto hardcore attitude mean that she represents a progressive
image of liberated black femaleness.

In the movie, Foxy Brown's motivation is love—though largely romantic—and a sense of justice. While the character has limitations, she is the
antithesis of the extreme capitalistic ethos that privileges money over
humanity. Indeed, as Foxy Brown's justice speech conveys, she is disgusted
with capitalistic motivations that take precedence over people's lives and
dignity. In contrast, rapper Foxy Brown's lyrics and public persona
demonstrate a distortion of the original Foxy Brown's going-after-what-
she-wants tough girl determination. Her music and public presentation of
her life in terms of being all about the "da Benjamins" (money) reveal the
extreme individualistic materialism driving her wild sexpot "Foxy Brown"
image. Though Grier's Foxy Brown functions in a world with nihilistic tendencies, there is also both hope and action directed toward combating
that nihilism. Rapper Foxy Brown perpetuates the nihilistic tendencies in
some rap music, displaying little evidence of the progressive social consciousness that exists elsewhere in rap music.

The movie's Foxy Brown uses her sexual appeal as a way to gain access
to the drug operation in order to bring it down, and the camera certainly
focuses on Grier's sexual body. However, neither Foxy Brown nor Pam
Grier seems to define herself primarily in terms of her sexual body. Rapper Foxy Brown invests in a devaluing sense of woman's power primarily
in terms of money and sex as well as the excessive sexualization of herself
through her on-stage and off-stage dress, erotic public poses, and ongoing
macho bravado about her sexual value and prowess. The sexually explicit
bravado in lines such as "My sex drive all night like a trucker"[32] and "Like
to be on top or, get it from behind. Either way I throw pussy like the free
throw line"[33] echoes throughout most of her rap songs.

Brown has taken on the sexual and sinister aspects of the label "bitch"
promoted in a lot of rap music by men. She projects herself, however, as a
"bitch" on top of the rap game due to her ability to "flow" (rhyme and
rap), and be as dirty and profane as the bad boys of rap. As she proclaims
in "Saddest Day": "Now I'm the type of bitch that's one of a kind / Y'all
know, the kind of bitch that like to sip fine wine." Foxy Brown's investment
in the equation of her female power with her ability to make money from
selling sex and profanity fails to signify a progressive politic.

Unlike Grier, who despite being continuously associated with the movie
character Foxy Brown has never appeared to define herself by her per-

formance, Inga Marchand's future connection with her Foxy Brown character is unclear. Brown has expressed an ambivalent interest in changing the direction of her image. Yet, at the same time, she clings to the fictionalized creation of herself as the Foxy Brown who is supposedly "keeping it real" by continuing the narrow trademarks of black ghetto identity that many of her male counterparts have glamorized.

Brown's current career and rap music success, as in the case of Grier, are inevitably tied to the politics of gender and sex. Brown is signed with the male-led and -controlled Def Jam record label that has cemented itself as a rap label with some of the most commercially successful hardcore male rap musicians today. In spite of her financial success, Chris Lighty of Def Jam Records acknowledges, decisions regarding Foxy's image and music are not under Foxy's total control.[34] This is dramatically illustrated by the lack of control Brown's own mother says she had over her then fifteen-year-old daughter's music image and musical direction. Burford and Farley's 1999 *Essence* cover story on Brown discusses contradictions in the matter of who controls Foxy's image. According to Foxy, she sought to change or rather tone down her wild, sexual image but was discouraged by Def Jam executives. In perhaps her most controversial public picture to date, Foxy appears on a 1998 December/January cover of the hip-hop magazine *Vibe*, wearing a bikini, clutching her crotch. Brown has said that she asked the magazine and Lighty not to use the shot, but the picture ended up on the cover (135–36).

In 1998, young Foxy Brown started her own label, ironically named "Ill Na Na" Entertainment, in order to assert more control over her own career (137). She has released a new album that continues her explicit lyrics, yet reveals the contradictions and problems of popular success achieved through her controversial "bad girl" image. Foxy Brown's predominantly regressive lyrics sometimes hint at her potential to offer important feminist and social critique within the rap music world:

No more Waitin to Exhale, we takin deep breaths.
   I be Foxy so peep this
Love thyself with no one above thee
Cause ain't nobody gon' love me like me.[35]

And she appears to recognize the nihilistic quality of her "high price" life in "My Life":

Wanted it all, now it's all mine
Loneliness, sorrow, confusion and pain
Nightmares, headlines, "Rapper found slain"
If it wasn't for my moms I'd drown in this pain.[36]

It remains to be seen how Inga Marchand will continue to play her version of "Foxy Brown."

Chapter 6
"Who's That Lady?"
Ebony *Magazine and Black Professional Women*

TONI C. KING

In the 1970s there was a plethora of resources for women in the popular culture genre of self-help and personal growth. They included books, magazines, videos, seminars, workshops, and encounter groups. Many of these resources were specifically geared to the concerns of professional women in terms of issues such as negotiation skills, corporate strategy, networking, mentoring, and a host of topics intended to ensure women's success in a gendered marketplace.

Paralleling the self-help literature on women and work was an explosion of self-help material in the area of adult development. Much of this literature, which appeared in the aftermath of the widely known *I'm Ok— You're Ok*, was directed toward women. During the 1970s, Manuel Smith wrote the best-seller *When I Say No, I Feel Guilty*. Subsequently, Nancy Friday wrote *My Mother, My Self*, and Gail Sheehy wrote *Passages 4*—also best-sellers—but these latter two were written by women for women.[1] These popular works ushered in an era of self-help literature marketed to women that continues today. All these books were geared at helping women understand and work through issues of adult development. By and large, however, neither category of self-help literature—women and work and women's development—included race in a significant way.

During this same decade, African American women, who already had a history of working in the paid labor force, were finding their way in greater numbers into a broader range of occupations than they had traditionally held.[2] Black women were moving from the traditional areas of health care, education, social services, and childcare into nontraditional areas such as law, engineering, business, and the sciences.[3] Popular culture resources were in vogue with white women in mind, but virtually nonexistent with women of color in mind. This omission of race in the self-help literature for professional women further exaggerated black women's invisibility and created a deficiency in this body of literature that would be difficult to correct. As Gloria T. Hull, Patricia Bell Scott, and Barbara Smith point out in *All the Women Are White, All the Blacks Are Men, But Some of Us Are Brave* (1982), when examining gender, white female identity is privileged to the exclusion of black female identity. Similarly, the social construction of race privileges black men over black women. This means that writing about white women has been assumed to speak for women generally, and writing about black men has been assumed to speak for blacks generally. This raced and gendered social construction essentially excluded black women from the popular media or scholarly literature of the 1970s.[4]

For black women who sought self-help via the genres of adult development and women and work, there was little recourse. This was a grave setback for black women in the new workplace contexts now open to them. It was unlikely that mothers and fathers, who had aptly prepared sons and daughters for traditional employment, could prepare them for this new workplace. Clearly, African Americans familiar with a segregated workplace would encounter new situations in the desegregated professional sphere. African American women—many of whom knew what it meant to work outside the home—could not have known what the dual stigma of race and gender would generate in coworkers, supervisors, and subordinates in new occupational arenas. In the 1970s these new performances of social roles had yet to be played out. As scholars would later demonstrate, black women's racial encounters in the workplace were distinct from those of black men and from those of white women.[5] Ultimately, the omission of race in the self-help literature for women added to black women's experience of isolation in the professional workplace and stymied their efforts to grapple with race-related episodes at work.

In contrast to this marked exclusion of black women's professional experiences and concerns in mainstream self-help literature, *Ebony* was filled with stories about black women's work experience.[6] For this reason I chose to look at *Ebony* as a potential text of black female "recovery." I use the term "recovery" to refer to the genre of self-help literature that gained in popularity throughout the 1970s to the current time. More specifically, I use the term as synonymous with bell hooks's term "self recovery" to talk about personal growth that includes recovering from race, class, and gender oppression.[7]

Ebony is the focus of my inquiry because of its longevity and wide circulation. The magazine began in 1945 and has historically been one of the most widely read African American magazines,[8] maintaining its popularity up to the present. During the 1970s it was rivaled in readership only by its sister publication *JET*. This smaller, concentrated magazine carried brief and hard-hitting pieces from the hallowed to the horrific. *JET* was known for keeping the public abreast of fashion trends, celebrity breakthroughs, breakups, hookups, and hoedowns. *JET* was also a virtual who's who in entertainment, business, politics, education, health, religion, and high society. In short, it was a magazine of the people. Call it gossip if you will, but *JET* let us know who in the community had been battered beyond recognition as well as who, after years of battering, betrayal, or emotional bashing, retaliated with a knife, gun, lye, or hot grits.

As long as *JET* existed for the people at large, *Ebony* could take the high ground and serve the needs of those in pursuit of the American dream Afrocentric style. Those who wanted to succeed in American society but also wanted to make sure they "gave back" to the black community could find in *Ebony* a longer version of the brief article from *JET* that named our heroes and she-roes, then gave an abbreviated accounting of their deeds of racial uplift. *Ebony*, in contrast, served up a full interview, complete with biographical highlights, some of the individual's own words, and examples of obstacles he or she overcame. *Ebony* offered a steady stream of "achievement against the odds" articles spanning the arts and entertainment, business and industry, religion, and community service. No area of professional expertise was overlooked in this magazine geared to motivate, encourage, and instill cultural pride in African Americans.

I also chose *Ebony* because I cut my teeth on it. During the late 1950s and throughout the 1960s, both *Ebony* and *JET* were part of the visual and literary fabric of my life. As early as four years old, I can remember sitting with my mother and turning the glossy pages of one of these magazines. Looking at *Ebony* and *JET* with my mother during my early years was a bonding ritual for us. As we studied the pages, I would ooh and ahh over pretty women and straight-haired little girls or group shots of families in their living rooms or kitchens where they read, sang, or played or danced with one another. Together, these magazines created a discursive rhythm of what I will call small talk and big talk. One—*JET*—was a stream of human engagement, both soap opera and opera. The other—*Ebony*—was the culminating mythology of a people in the process of overcoming racial oppression. While the voices of *JET* and *Ebony* overlapped in a communal chorus, it was *Ebony* that primarily celebrated victories against racism, discrimination, and poverty by revealing the lifestyles of successful African Americans.

Conscientization and Communality: "Can I Get a Witness?"

As an African American woman scholar, I wish to explore whether *Ebony* contributed to black women's well-being as they negotiated their personal and professional lives.[9] Research beginning in the late 1970s identified the inordinately high levels of stress black women experienced in responding simultaneously to three salient contextual demands: (1) significant others; (2) the black community; and (3) dominant cultural settings.[10] Entering new employment arenas affected them in all three areas. Often roles and expectations in one area conflicted with roles and expectations in another, producing dissonance and distress. If the work of recovery required at a minimum the awareness that black women were gaining ground in the professional sphere, *Ebony* made a definitive contribution in this regard. There was an abundance of articles each month dedicated to women and work, culminating in 1977 with a special issue devoted to the issues, concerns, and achievements of black women. Recovery from race, class, and gender constraints and the institutionalization of black female subordination requires understanding one's place within a larger matrix of intra- and intercultural experience. *Ebony* contributed to this for black women. Through *Ebony*, black women were able to witness each other in the role of professional pioneers.

A sampling of the titles that appeared throughout the 1970s conveys the variety of topics as well as the tone of the messages for their black readership.

The Lady Takes Charge: New Hospital Director Brings Sensitive Medical Care to Harlem's Needy.

The Drill Sergeant Is a Lady: Lady Marine Molds Lives of Young Recruits.

Med School Mom: Colorado Woman Blends Tough Medical Studies with Child-Rearing and Housewife's Chores.

A Together Prof at the University of Minnesota Law School.

She Manages the Mail: Woman Runs L.A. Postal Facility.[11]

These articles heralding black women's achievements consistently articulated whether the woman in question was the first black or the first woman or both to hold a particular position. Some of these "firsts" included the first black woman to serve as a member of a president's cabinet, the first black female Episcopal priest, the first black woman mayor of a Mississippi town, and the first black woman to head a major mental institution.[12] The magazine took particular pride in pointing out victories of integration taking place in the South. These articles bear witness to the reality of desegregation legislation; they also evidence the deeper level of cultural change that goes beyond legislation. Black Southern women were often depicted. For example, the magazine profiled Clara Ziegler in the article "Patrolling Alabama's Highways: State's First Woman Trooper: She Tackles Klan, Speeders, and Drunks."

The range of professions included in *Ebony* articles was broad. In addition to the state trooper, readers learned about a director of a state department of motor vehicles, a fashion designer, a military cleric, a realtor, a junior high school boys' football coach, a university chancellor, a gas company meter reader, a writer, and an Air Force aircraft navigator. *Ebony* affirmed and made visible the expanding scope of black female presence in both traditional and nontraditional occupations. The copious portrayal of black women as pioneering in so many arenas created for black Americans a powerful metanarrative in which black women embodied the societal changes promised by civil rights activism and institutionalized in civil rights legislation and affirmative action policies. Thus these articles were a visual and textual celebration of black women's ability to achieve despite race, class, and gender constraints.

Another element of recovery embedded in *Ebony*'s coverage of black professional women was the inclusiveness of the magazine across some categories of difference. *Ebony* included articles about women in working-class jobs, women in military careers, women in the fine arts, entrepreneurs, and career activists. This level of inclusion is not surprising, given that black communities commonly view professional status in broader terms than does the dominant culture. Perhaps because of the restricted opportunity structure blacks have historically encountered in the United States stemming from institutionalized racism, individuals with jobs within black communities were held in high esteem by community members.[13] This was particularly true for those who had a long-term identity in a particular occupation (teacher, firefighter, janitor). Here recovery occurred through *Ebony*'s recognition of black women across this broad array of work experiences, which ultimately fostered a sense of shared identity.

In addition to occupational diversity across blue-collar and white-collar jobs, *Ebony* also attended to diversity with respect to featuring disabled working women in a few of its articles, including "The Busy, Bright World of a Blind Woman: Sightless Psychologist Copes by Helping the Sighted Cope" and "A World Without Sight or Sound: Cleveland Woman Leads National Organization of the Deaf-Blind."[14] Appropriate to *Ebony*'s purpose of foregrounding professional achievements, these two articles focused on the contributions of the women to the organizations they served. By including women who differed in physical ability, *Ebony* effectively contributed to black women's recovery from race, class, and gender oppression by resisting normative standards that equated professional efficacy with ablebodiedness. While there were not numerous articles about disabled women, the ones that did exist added to a narrative of black women's ability to survive the challenges of multilayered oppressions.

The steady stream of articles in *Ebony* provided a communal resource for the African American community, who could witness black women's mass movement through doors previously closed. Recovery requires such witnessing. This witnessing and recognition is liberatory and makes black women more aware of their capabilities despite social constraints. If previous generations could not envision some of the opportunities that would become accessible to black women, it was important for black women to witness what was now possible in a world wider than what they could see in their immediate geographic location. Black communities have a long tradition of developing black women leaders by instilling in them the message that they must have "a belief in self greater than anyone's disbelief." Through this deluge of articles about black women achieving against the odds, *Ebony* was a vehicle for the transmission of this liberatory message.

Contested Accommodations: "Who's That Lady?"

At the same time that *Ebony* articles created a counter-narrative of achievement and professional gains that resisted stigmatizing societal messages about black women, these articles also accommodated dominant ideologies of womanhood. On the one hand, *Ebony* affirmed black women's transgression of race and gender norms by proudly proclaiming them as the first black or first woman to achieve a particular position. On the other hand, *Ebony* used language in ways that moderated the oppositional potency of this message.

For example, the language of *Ebony* articles about black women in the labor force liberally emphasized signifiers of femininity as if to ensure black women some measure of the privileges of the "lady" status historically reserved for white women. This tactic was most evident in the titles of the articles about black working women. The articles used such signifiers of femininity as "mom," "Mrs.," "feminine," "attractive," "charming," "demure," and "velvet gloved" in ways that positioned black women as culturally acceptable vis-à-vis their gender. This prevailing subtext of *Ebony*'s articles about black women served to normalize the transgressive nature of black women's successes. The subtext of "ladyhood" positioned the "together prof" as attractive, the university administrator as a "bachelorette," and the med school mom as a good housewife and nurturer.

This concession to white standards of feminine identity complicated black women's recovery. black women were constrained to the extent that they felt they had to uphold traditional standards of femininity as the price of their newly earned social status. In this post-civil rights era, with women moving even further away from traditional roles as keepers of home and hearth, it was incumbent on those role models who gained visibility to uphold standards of propriety for black women.[15] Being defined in the dominant culture as a "lady" was for black women an untenable and historically unattainable standard, to be sure. It was a standard that patriarchal hegemony had already stabilized through allegations that we were quintessentially incapable of achieving the ideals of proper womanhood.

We were, after all, Mammy, Matriarch, and Jezebel—all deficient in qualities essential to the "cult of true womanhood."[16] For some black women, tremendous role conflict could have emerged if they felt pressured to live up to or to uphold hegemonic ideals of femininity.

Curiously, *Ebony* articles appeared to assume this accommodationist posture of attaching feminine signifiers to professional women who held or aspired to the most high-status professional positions, including doctors, lawyers, private sector executives, entrepreneurs, and military officers. One example is the article "Black Women in Corporate America: Female Entrepreneurs Find Femininity Mixes Well with Business." Articles that discussed community service jobs or working-class occupations were less likely to put femininity at the center of the reader's attention with the same force: "A Very Special Volunteer: Six Years of Service Prepares Carolyn Payton for Top Peace Corps Post," "Casey Jones Would Be Proud: Silvia Duckens, 23, Carries On in Tradition of Legendary Engineer," and "Women in the Ring: Despite Opposition, Sport Is Growing Nationwide" are examples of articles without such signifiers.[17] The omission of signifiers for this group conveys the message that working-class women who work outside the home are not perceived to be transgressing norms of middle-class femininity. Thus, no special effort is made to reposition this group within the normative expectations for white middle-class women.

Although *Ebony* engaged in accommodating dominant ideologies of femininity in some respects, the magazine was also a contested space wherein black women were defining themselves in complex ways that subverted traditional notions of femininity. For example, in the article "A Together Prof at the University of Minnesota Law School," Joyce Hughes is described as a "pretty associate professor."[18] The article continued that, although "she holds her own, one never loses sight of her womanliness . . . Her youthful and feminine looks make it difficult to imagine that she is a cum laude graduate" (41). Here the article inadvertently presents the association between "good" looks and high intellectual achievements as both noteworthy and surprising. This accommodation to traditional gender norms reinscribes the dichotomy that one can be either intelligent or beautiful but not both.

Beyond the kind of accommodation to gender norms displayed in the article about Hughes is a contested space that has the potential to transform normative ideologies of femininity. This becomes most evident when *Ebony* uses the women's own voices or when the articles describe the women's behavior, actions, and interactions. When this occurs, the reader gets a much better sense that their gender role performance is a complex negotiation of agency and authority within these new professional contexts. In the Hughes article the author describes two incidents in which

Hughes demonstrates agency and authority during the journalist's interview with her:

> "Nope, wouldn't ever consent to that," she says firmly. She smiles, the colleague melts. "Since it's my first year teaching I want to remain as flexible as possible." Again the smile and the colleague swipes a cookie, shrugs his shoulders happily and suggests they pool their questions for the upcoming finals. She agrees enthusiastically. Shortly after he leaves the office, a senior law student comes in. He asks to miss one of her exams and make it up later. His wife just had a baby.
>
> "Can't do that," Joyce says. "It wouldn't be good for you." She smiles. "What if you had a day in court? You think the judge would excuse you from trial?" (41)

The complexity of Hughes's performance lies in her ability to situate her decision that she cannot let her law student miss a required exam in the context of gender role behavior for women. The firmness of Hughes's decision is cleverly contextualized within appropriate gender role expectations by her explanation that this decision is in the student's best interest. Positioning her response this way recontextualizes Hughes's authority and assertiveness as a developmental, nurturing response that is not only acceptable but expected for women across races.

Glossy Commodifications: Is the Rainbow Enough?

Ebony offered black women of the 1970s an opportunity to witness themselves negotiating new occupational terrain, while at the same time accommodating current mainstream ideologies of womanhood. Moreover, while black women's voices illustrated greater complexity of identity, overall their voices were constrained by a glossy journalistic format that permitted only a limited glimpse of their lives and implied a commodification of their achievements. At one level, this format helped black women find a sense of solidarity in their collective image of themselves as capable of achieving professional goals. At another level, however, *Ebony* in the 1970s was a vehicle for black aspirations of middle-class status, which often implies some level of assimilation. *Ebony*'s chronicling of black women's achievements through the journalistic conventions of the English language, particularly when that language is packaged within the popular magazine genre, invokes a dilemma articulated by Adrienne Rich: "This is the oppressor's language, yet I need to talk to you."[19] The outcome for black women is that their stories are reduced to easily digestible formats that minimize their day-to-day struggles.

A major pattern exemplifying this trend is the presentation of black professional women's experiences in terms of external enemies and internal solidarities. This journalistic pattern was designed for ease of consumption, particularly by the black community as a whole, because it promoted black solidarity and black nationalism. Black women's achievements were claimed as successes for the race. While this is not necessarily a problem in and of itself, it becomes a limitation for *Ebony*'s contribution to black women's recovery in that the main thrust of the articles identified an external enemy against which black women's successes and achievements were then defined. Yet the complexity of black women's experiences and the subsequent insights culminating in personal growth are marginalized or erased.

In many of the stories about black working women, the primary antagonist that dominates episodic conflicts is racism rather than sexism. For example, in the article, "Three Strikes Is Not Always Out: A Young Black Woman Fights Triple Prejudice,"a black woman physician moves to Alabama to practice at a rural clinic.[20] Once there, Dr. Cropper recounts difficulties in being accepted by patients in her role as their physician. Yet these difficulties are surmounted as she ultimately wins over even her most resistant patients. The article also refers to her staff as mostly white, yet harmonious and cooperative. There is no mention of tensions in their adjusting to work with a black woman physician as head of the clinic.

The most haunting stories in this article involve encounters with the Ku Klux Klan. On more than one occasion, KKK members pressured Dr. Cropper to leave the area. They visited her home and directly advised her to move away. On other occasions, fires were mysteriously started on her land. The most ominous story involves a late night call to the doctor to meet a patient who needed treatment at the clinic. Feeling uneasy about the call, she delays leaving for the clinic, and when she does arrive no one is there. Residents reported that just prior to her arrival, several cars with strangers in them had gathered in the parking lot. Dr. Cropper relayed that she was convinced that they meant to harm her.

Clearly her greatest threat was racial hatred. Yet beyond the hostility and the imminent threat to her physical safety, the article makes no mention of dynamics internal to her mostly white staff, the black community's expectations of this newcomer, or even Dr. Cropper's adjustment to this rural southern area. For black women less exposed to the urgent threat of blatant racial violence, the story does not offer an inside perspective on the subtle violations of modern racism. Neither Dr. Cropper's story nor the stories of other black women reveal much cross-race relational dynamics in which a black female held the role of authority.

A similar pattern of foregrounding an external enemy while glossing over internal dynamics occurs in the story, "Med School Mom: Colorado Woman Blends Tough Medical Studies with Child-Rearing and Housewife's Chores."[21] This time the adversaries are long and demanding work hours, a rigorous course of study, and minority status as both an African American and a woman. LaRae Washington is the second black to be admitted to the University of Colorado Medical School and one of only eighteen women in a class of 127 first-year students. She is also a thirty-year-old mother of four children ranging in age from three to twelve. In contrast to the external threat of the competitive school environment and the need to balance work and family, Washington's husband is depicted as supportive of her goals. To fulfill family responsibilities, she has the assistance of a live-in college student in addition to her husband's help. Washington is quoted as saying, "the full support of my husband is the main reason I'm making it." I do not question whether his role is supportive or whether his support is pivotal to her successful academic pursuits amid a thriving family life. Indeed, it would be difficult if not impossible for a mother of four to pursue her career goals without her husband's backing. Yet under the best conditions, the pressures of family life would create conflicts between work and school demands and family needs.

Another example framing black professional women's stories in terms of external enemies is one that foregrounds gender as the external threat. In the story "Hollywood Stunt Girl: Pert Peaches Jones Does Risky Work for the Stars,"[22] the physical risks Jones had to take coupled with the competitive male egos of her coworkers constituted the external obstacle she confronted. According to the article, "many a male ego has been deflated as she wound up doing a particular stunt better than he. In fact on more than one occasion the boys have nearly busted their britches trying to outdo 'the girl'" (150). Jones remarks: "They don't really like the idea of my being as proficient as they are, especially at something as physical as stunt work." In terms of pairing an external enemy with internal solidarity, this story portrays the familial solidarity of parental support. The dangerous activities of Peaches Jones' profession are encouraged by her father. Some of the dangers she describes include being stomped by horses or dragged by them, falling from horses or from tall buildings, and being in numerous staged fights and other risky scenarios. Because of the dangers she encountered in this profession, she indicated that she had her mother's support and cooperation but not her wholehearted encouragement. This leaves the reader to wonder about the ways the mother expressed her concerns or held them back.

Ebony's discursive practices in the 1970s left us with a glossy imprint of how black women coped with their new experiences. *Ebony* presented external enemies of race in stark relief against milder issues of gender. This move perpetuated a mythology of racism as the more formidable enemy rather than a more elaborate narrative reflecting the interlocking oppressions of race, class, and gender. Consequently, the complex and multiplicative effects of race, class, and gender in black women's lives did not become more evident through *Ebony* at that time. The inner day-to-day turmoil was more implied than apparent. In *Ebony*'s presentation of internal solidarities with respect to family relations, black community relations, cross-race work relationships, and black women's personal identity, black women were portrayed as having it all "together."

In order for *Ebony* to make a fuller contribution to black women's recovery, the voices of black women would have had to be more central to these articles. *Ebony*'s articles about black women were limited by a discursive structure that muted the vitality of their stories. In general, these articles describe black women rather than allowing self-description. Their stories are told by writers, often men, rather than self-defined and self-narrated.

This strategy of limiting black women's voice is well illustrated in a 1978 article about Faye Wattleton, the first woman and first black to be appointed president of Planned Parenthood Federation of America (PPFA).[23] The article provides a photo of a smiling Faye Wattleton seated at her office desk, presumably at PPFA headquarters in New York. Underneath the photo, the title of the article boldly announces, "Family Planning's Top Advocate: Young Ohio Mother Heads Planned Parenthood Federation." Yet in spite of the pleasantries depicted, we know that pro-choice advocates commonly receive hate mail and threats to their physical safety. Thus it is likely that Wattleton, as PPFA president, would have been the recipient of such threats. The article makes no mention of threats to her or to her husband and daughter, and so we have no way of assessing whether she faced this occupational stressor, what other kinds of stressors she faced, or their effects on her. Black women readers may have benefited in their own lives from more detail about how Wattleton handled some of the issues facing black women professionals in highly visible and controversial positions of leadership. Wattleton relates that she worked long hours, typically leaving the office at 11:00 P.M. when only she and the cleaning ladies were left in the building. The article quotes her as saying "the hours don't bother me because I love my work" (90). It would be useful for black women to know what quality of life measures Wattleton took to ensure her stamina and restore her energy in a position that by her own admission brought her face to face with tragedies and human suffering on a daily basis. *Ebony* did not utilize an opportunity to have Wattleton describe in her own words how she responded to job stress or how she managed the multiple negotiations of her personal and professional life.

Ultimately, the stories about black women generally revealed little of the process of how they survived the entry dynamics of transgressing the raced, classed, and gendered boundaries of new occupational territory or restored their sense of well-being on days when the onslaught of racism, classism, and sexism felt overpowering. The stories about black women generally mythologized them as protagonists in the collective quest of black people for the American dream of success; they did not address the multilayered issues of race, class, and gender oppression playing out in occupational settings. *Ebony* was uniquely positioned to carry forward an agenda of supplying this unarticulated text of black professional women's race, class, and gender experience in public and private life. To do this, however, black women needed to know more about how other professional women experienced these traumas and worked through them to restore wholeness.

Recovering Subjectivity

To contribute to the personal growth dimension of recovery in its articles about black women, *Ebony* had to retire from the front porch to the kitchen table. *Ebony*'s niche was the community dialogue symbolized by gathering on the front porch in full view of passers-by. It was necessary to transform the journalistic format used to chronicle the experiences of black professional women so that it included what womanist scholars call kitchen table discourse. Whereas the front porch symbolizes social interaction and the witnessing of a community in action, the kitchen table is rooted in the details of women's daily lives. The metaphor of kitchen table discourse relies on the kitchen as a site of woman-to-woman problem solving that employs a highly crafted exchange of emotional support. It is this context of safety, validation, and support that allows women to articulate the particulars of their experiences and discover the "true real" of what they feel and know.[24]

Under these conditions, black professional women could articulate the new experiences they were encountering that derived from the triple jeopardy of race, class, and gender. Here in this private, domestic sphere, woman-to-woman discourse strategically developed to undo racial trauma and women cultivated relationships and "deep talk"[25] as tools of resistance and recovery. This is the powerful link between the personal and the political. Of this relationship, hooks explains, "Our words are not without meaning. They are an action—a resistance. Language is also a place of struggle. . . . The oppressed struggle in language to read ourselves—to reunite, to reconcile, to renew.[26]

Some of the articles in *Ebony* did further the goals of recovery for black professional women by the very act of offering a more intimate conversation with the reader. Interestingly, the articles that make the most significant contribution in this regard are those that profile celebrities. When these celebrity profiles do not focus specifically on an entertainer's current fame or rise to unparalleled heights of success, they often revisit a celebrity to recount a crisis he or she has overcome. Examples of such articles are those written about actress Cicely Tyson, rhythm & blues singer Minnie Ripperton, jazz great Mary Lou Williams, and legendary gospel singer Shirley Caesar.[27]

A particularly poignant example is found in the 1979 article "Cicely

Tyson: She Can Smile Again After a Three Year Ordeal." In this article her achievements as an Emmy Award winning actor are told against the backdrop of her grief about her mother's passing. The article uses Tyson's own words to describe this experience of grief:

It took me nearly three years to get over my mother's death. I had a very, very, difficult time. I was totally wiped out by it, for it was the most devastating thing that has ever happened to me in my entire life. I never thought I'd survive it. I was broken, completely broken for *two solid years*, and only in the last year or so have I really been able to get over it.[28]

The article explains that Tyson and her mother were extremely close. They became estranged, however, after Tyson went into acting. "Mother thought that anything having to do with the theater, with entertainment period was pure sin. . . . She would tell me 'it's all a den of iniquity.'" Tyson reports that after she left her job as a secretary at the Red Cross to go into the theater her mother put her out of the house. They did not see each other again for over two years.

When they did reconcile they were able to regain their close relationship, which grew "closer and closer" until her mother's death at the age of eighty. Tyson's intense grief was a result of losing her mother so soon after reaching the pinnacle of her career:

One of my happiest moments came when I telephoned her after winning the "Emmys" and she said to me, "I am so proud of you. You make me feel so good." That's the one thing I'd always wanted to hear my mother say. A few months later, only a very few months, she was dead. I . . . took it so hard because there were so many things I wanted to do for her.

When Mrs. Tyson dies, Tyson is left to work through overwhelming feelings of loss. "I wanted to shower her with gifts . . . just give her all kinds of beautiful things since I had finally begun making some money after all those years."

Loneliness, isolation, and loss are intensely experienced among black professional women. Years of hard work to build their careers and years of sacrifice and training may find them at the height of their achievement only to encounter the loss of significant others with whom they had hoped to share their hard-won success. Cicely Tyson's story offers black women readers an opportunity to understand this pain. This allows black women to reflect on their fears that their most cherished communal and relational connections will be irreparably severed by their professional gains.

Another article that tells of a professional black woman and her route to recovery is Carolyn Craven's "A Rape Victim Strikes Back: Television Reporter Tells of Her Personal Ordeal and Resolve to Help Capture Her Brutal Attacker."[29] What is important here is that the black woman who was sexually assaulted writes the story herself and explores her feelings during and after the experience. She acknowledges, "I felt violated, furious that I had been made so powerless, outraged that a man could come into my life for three hours and change it so irrevocably"(160). She also explores the consequences of her assault on those close to her: "Men close to me, good gentlemen, suddenly found themselves filled with anger, frustration and feelings of violence and revenge. The women close to me learned, albeit vicariously, that we are all potential victims of rape. No matter how strong we are, no matter how independent, no matter how pretty or plain, we can all be victims" (159).

Her powerful conclusion to this first person narrative exemplifies the powerful connection she creates with the reader:

I . . . knew that I had not understood the nature of rape, had not understood that it is a crime of violence, had not understood the severity of rape for the victim and those around her. And if I as a reporter who had interviewed rape victims did not understand, then neither did most people. I decided to talk publicly about the experience. Because I was a reporter, newspapers, television and radio stations carried my story. It's my way of fighting back. (159)

The author helps the reader to see through her own eyes what it is that rape victims experience. Her narrative makes a significant contribution to black women's recovery because she openly discusses sexual assault. In doing so, she encourages black women to speak out on this issue and contributes to breaking the two-hundred-year silence around black women as the victims of sexual assault. By speaking so frankly about her feelings, Craven invites other women to liberate themselves from the fear, denigration, and self-recrimination the crime evokes.

Another example of recovery is found in an article about singer Minnie Ripperton, written after her diagnosis and treatment for breast cancer.[30] This 1976 article brings her voice to the issue of breast cancer in a way that offers black women readers another site of kitchen table discourse—this time they find a celebrity reassuring women that they can come to terms with breast cancer. She defies the stereotypes about cancer by indicating that in every way she maintained her strength and stamina, "There was nothing different about me except I'd had an operation. . . . I'm young and strong and I have a full life ahead of me." We are told that she and her husband still swim and are avid tennis players, and that within a week of her modified mastectomy she was back at work taping the Ebony Music Awards Show in Hollywood. But it is in *Ebony*'s use of Minnie Ripperton's voice that her feelings about this experience are shared and words of advice and encouragement are given to black women readers. In particular she puts her diagnosis of breast cancer into a larger cosmological perspective for women by saying, "God or whoever, . . . if God is a He or She or Them, I give thanks. I think He's always been right there with me. I think that what I've gone through might have been something worse. Instead, He let this happen to me. I could have had a combination of things, I could have had heart disease" (40).

Minnie also gives readers a dose of the positive thinking that characterized her ability to cope with the cancer.

I think when you're a good person, you radiate goodness and positiveness. That's not saying you're some saint or a fanatic about being positive, but just feeling good. . . . I wrote a song called "Feeling That Your Feeling's Right." It's on the *Adventures in Paradise* album. The idea is, whenever you feel yourself slipping and nothing seems to be going right, take it and just turn it around. Make things right. Push back that feeling because that's when the sun comes shining through. (41)

Finally, she encouraged women not to equate a mastectomy with loss of femininity. The loss of femininity was and is a general reaction women have when confronted with a mastectomy. A black woman celebrity at the height of her career, such as Minnie Ripperton, was uniquely situated to contradict the association of a mastectomy with defeminization. Her crossover popular appeal made her an effective spokesperson for women across race with regards to this issue. However, her message may have had special significance for African-American women's construction of femininity on their own terms.

These kinds of articles invite us into a different kind of conversation that is more intimate. When these public personalities describe personal struggles that affect them in both their personal and professional lives, they subvert the glossy narratives that depict black professional women as having it all together. Black women could turn to articles from those public personas who had elected to share their own emotional journeys and use these articles to enhance their own growth and development.

One might ask why *Ebony* took the liberty of offering readers such in-depth stories about black women celebrities while avoiding the complexity of other black women professionals' lives. It may be that the status of celebrities transformed the usual expectations and made it seem less necessary to invoke the protections of "lady" status. Or it might be that the longevity of black women in the performing arts had desensitized the black community's feelings that the women were vulnerable to defeminization in the same way as a more typical working woman. In addition, celebrity status had already placed these black women in a transgressive space vis-à-vis gender roles. Whatever the reason, these celebrity articles conveyed powerful lessons about healing to black women readers.

In conclusion, *Ebony*'s articles delineating black women in nontraditional occupations or their ascendance to new levels of authority and responsibility in traditional occupations were an effective indicator of the changing workforce in the 1970s. As a text of recovery, *Ebony* was a vehicle for the communal witnessing of black women's increasing presence in the workforce. Through the most highly visible and elite group of black professional women—celebrities—*Ebony* made space for a kitchen table discourse. In this privatized space, black women explored delicate issues of personal healing and growth. In addition, *Ebony* served as a site of black women's self-definition in which working women contributed to more expansive definitions of womanhood that subverted white middle-class norms for "real ladies."

Ultimately, *Ebony* served as a precedent for the emergence of other magazines that focused on the experiences of African Americans. Some of these, such as *Essence*, targeted black professional women as their primary audience. *Essence* picked up where *Ebony* left off by emphasizing black women's own voices in recounting the particulars of their personal and professional experiences. That both *Ebony* and *Essence* continue to enjoy widespread popularity suggests that each magazine satisfactorily witnesses black experience, albeit in different ways. Together with *JET*, *Ebony* and *Essence* are considered standard fare in many African American households because they cover the broad span of issues, events, and people of historical and contemporary significance within the culture. This communal chorus in black magazines includes what I refer to as small talk, big talk, and, with the addition of *Essence* in particular, deep talk. The overlapping discursive rhythms of these magazines expose the raced, classed, and gendered texture of society through an African American gaze.

Chapter 7

"Impress a New Love with Your Culinary Prowess"
Gender Lessons in Swinging Singles' Cookbooks

SHERRIE A. INNESS

In her *Single Girl's Cookbook* (1972), Helen Gurley Brown wrote that it contained "the recipes, simple instructions, and guiding philosophy to make you a fabulous cook and the utter darling of a lot of people."[1] Brown's words aptly described her book's goal. The cookbook was not only about preparing meals; it was also about how cooking could make a single woman more alluring, especially to men, which—at least for Brown and her fellow *Cosmo* girls—was essential. A number of other 1970s cookbooks addressed how single people should think of cooking as a way to attract mates. These works are valuable resources for exploring changing cultural attitudes toward single men and women, as well as for understanding their changing roles in American society. In the 70s, these texts served three major functions. First, they promoted the idea that cooking was a form of seduction. This made cooking more palatable to both men and women. No longer was cooking an arduous, unrewarding domestic responsibility; it was a talent that any suave single would wish to possess. Second, they encouraged single men, as well as women, to cook. This marked a change from earlier decades, when only a few men ventured into the taboo terrain of the domestic kitchen. Third, they taught men that cooking was simple, something any male could do. This was a change from previous years when cooking was often depicted as an arcane pursuit with which only women were familiar. These three messages reveal some of the ways the popular media encouraged new attitudes about the gendered task of cooking. More broadly, the media also implied that men and women should reflect on their relationship to other gendered tasks too.

If one wishes to understand the 1970s (or any decade) and its changing gender roles, a valuable source is cookbooks and other cooking-related literature. These works reveal a great deal about society's changing mores.

Cookbooks in the 1970s served up more than recipes for tofu-onion loaf or fondue; they also served up a recipe for how men and women were expected to act.

But why examine cookbooks in the first place? After all, they are a form of reading material that has been belittled in earlier eras as trivial and as something of interest only to women. Cookbooks have been considered so insignificant that some major research libraries do not include them in their collections, and in the past, few colleges and universities offered courses on the cookbook. But this situation has begun to change over the last three decades as scholars, many influenced by second-wave feminism, have written about cookbooks and analyzed their messages, recognizing the importance of such texts to generations of women and society at large. Harvard University, the University of Iowa, Indiana University, Texas Woman's University, and Smith College are a few of the institutions of higher learning that today have amassed sizable collections of cookbooks and other cooking literature. In addition, a number of colleges and universities now offer courses on cookbooks.

This increased interest arose with scholars' recognition that these texts, like other forms of literature associated primarily with women, contain important lessons about women's (and men's) lives. As one of the most gender-coded forms of literature, cookbooks play an important part in conveying messages about gendered behavior. These messages can be explicit—a cookbook named *For Girls Only* or one with photographs all featuring a woman shopping for, preparing, or serving a dish. But some messages are more implicit—the fact that a woman's cookbook features light and dainty dishes while a man's cookbook features heavy, substantial meat recipes suggesting the characteristics women and men are supposed to have. Whether explicit or implicit, messages about gender roles fill cookbooks, making them a valuable resource for anyone seeking to understand men and women in American society. Cookbooks are particularly important to study because they are such a common part of our lives. Millions of women (and some men) own them, read them, and use them, now as well as in the past. They are one of the most omnipresent forms of reading material, appearing in the homes of people of different classes, ethnicities, races, ages, and geographical regions. Visiting a home today, one is likely to find at least a few cookbooks. They might not be used very much or they might be dog-eared from repeated use, but they are present, and analyzing them reveals important lessons about cultural change.[2]

The Swinging Single

Before we delve into singles' cooking literature, we must understand singles' changing place in 1970s society. Before the 1960s and '70s, being a single woman was perceived by the majority of mainstream America as the worst of fates. Unmarried women over the age of thirty were identified by many as "old maids" who had nothing to look forward to but a lifetime of lonely spinsterhood. Society regarded unmarried women as failures, women too homely and unappealing to find men willing to marry them. Worse, such women were sometimes thought to be emotionally abnormal and even encouraged to talk with psychologists to understand the root of their "problems." In some cases, unmarried women were thought to be lesbians whom "normal" women should shun.

Unmarried men did not suffer the same stigma that unmarried women endured. Bachelors were tolerated, sometimes even envied. They were thought to lead adventurous, carefree lives, without the constraints married men faced. Being a bachelor, however, was not viewed in a completely positive fashion. Some people thought of bachelors as lonely and isolated. A cultural stereotype existed that they were emotionally immature because they had not "matured" into men by getting married and having children. Writes historian Howard P. Chudacoff about American society, "In the minds of some observers, bachelors exhibited arrogance and self-ishness because they stubbornly refused to marry."[3] Despite these societal misgivings about unmarried men, bachelorhood never had the grim, bleak image that spinsterhood did. Still, mainstream culture perceived both single women and men as less "normal" and well adjusted than their married counterparts, even though millions of singles were productive contributors to American society.

In the 1970s a major cultural shift changed how single women and men were viewed.[4] In the 1960s, forces were already gathering that would transform the presumably maladjusted spinster and bachelor into swinging singles.[5] Feminism, with its message that women should find themselves as individuals before they married, was a growing force. For feminists, being single was not a sign that a woman was a failure but that she was a success, willing to spend the time necessary to find out who she was before she married, if she ever did. The 1960s also saw a huge wave of young people graduate from colleges and universities. They did not want to follow in their parents' footsteps and get married while still young; they wanted to experience the world for themselves before "joining the establishment" and settling down. This was a remarkable change, as cultural historian Ruth Rosen points out in *The World Split Open: How the Modern Women's Movement Changed America* (2000): "Marriage—already battered by growing divorce rates, the values of the counterculture, and new ideas about sexual freedom—began to seem like just one of many lifestyles that men or women might choose. Never before in American history had such ambivalent attitudes toward fidelity and commitment entered mainstream society."[6] The 1960s sexual revolution also encouraged women and men to stay single, since they no longer had to wait for marriage to have sexual relationships.[7]

For all these reasons, being single was changing, but it took until the 1970s for this shift to have its major impact on women. Suddenly the single girl was glamorous, as cultural critic Pagan Kennedy notes: "While in the early sixties single career women like Sally on *The Dick Van Dyke Show* were objects of pity—dowdy, lonely, desperate—ten years later, it was housewives who were saddled with unflattering stereotypes. Now TV shows and movies portrayed single women as adventurers (Princess Leia, Mary Richards, Jill Clayburgh's Erica in *An Unmarried Woman*)."[8] For the first time in American history, the single woman was seen as enviable rather than pitiable.[9] This shift had a lasting impact on American culture and has permanently altered the public perception of single women.

Many factors influenced the changed attitudes in the 1970s about single women. Demographically, there were simply more of them than there had been in previous decades. In 1960, 19.0 percent of females were single; 23.4 percent were unmarried in 1977. The age women first married rose. In 1960, 28 percent of women from twenty to twenty-four had never married; in 1977, this figure had increased to 45 percent.[10] And more options existed for the 1970s single woman, as one contemporary commentator noted: "Things have drastically changed for the single girl, thanks to the birth-control pill and the Women's Movement and the tumultuous reassessments of the '60s."[11] It is hard to overestimate the power of the pill in helping create a swinging singles' culture for women and men. For the first time, women could be single and be sexually active without ruining their reputations or worrying about getting pregnant. One 1970s book, *Sex and the Single Ms.* (1974), praised the option of being a single sexually active woman: "You don't hear people speak of 'nice girls' or 'naughty girls' any more. Nobody expects you to be a virgin. Your landlord won't toss you out if he sees a man leaving your place in the early hours of the morning. . . . Your sex life needn't be controlled by what other people think."[12] Being a single woman was transformed from a sign that one was sexually inactive to a sign of exactly the opposite, and this was no longer a negative attribute for women; rather, it was a positive sign that they were living life to its fullest, fulfilling their potential as sexual beings, and casting aside old-fashioned notions about acceptable female sexual expression.

Across the United States, women discovered that they did not need to get married right after graduating from high school or college. They found that they could survive by themselves and even do more than survive; they could thrive and enjoy some of the many services that cropped up for singles.[13] Singles cruises and singles' weekends at hotels were popular.[14] Discos appeared across the nation, appealing to fashionable singles who did not have to worry about having to take care of little Junior when they shuffled home at 3 A.M. Social clubs also sprung up to cater to the specific needs of singles. Outfitted with "swimming pools, tennis courts, party houses, restaurants, and organized activities," apartment complexes for singles popped up in cities from New York to Los Angeles.[15] And bars across the United States catered to singles' wishes by sponsoring singles' nights. All of these activities and services for singles helped to make the 1970s into the singles' decade. Who wouldn't want to be single when such a multitude of businesses were willing to cater to one's needs?

The media also played important roles in affirming that being single was "hot" for men and women. The 1970s singles' culture resulted in a flowering of books and articles. Everyone, it seemed, wanted to jump on the bandwagon. Psychologists and psychiatrists wrote self-help books that addressed singles' problems. Women's and men's magazines described the best cities for singles to live in and discussed the best clubs, bars, and restaurants to find dates. Single men and women wrote guides to help other singles survive in many cities, including San Francisco, Los Angeles, Boston, Chicago, and New York. Countless articles in popular magazines from *Cosmopolitan* to *Playboy* touted the single life as something that any daring man or woman would want to experience.

The popular media raved about the delights of being a single woman—a remarkable change from previous decades. One 1970s author wrote that single girls "these days are admired and praised for their independent lives, instead of being pitied and scorned."[16] Similarly, Stanlee Miller Coy enthused in *The Single Girl's Book: Making It in the Big City* (1971) about the pleasures of being single: "Congratulations on being single in a big city. . . . In a city a person can explore and experiment until she finds what suits her best. . . . What do you really want? The standard American ideal be damned, who are you? Find it and face it. And enjoy!"[17] Helen Gurley Brown was also enthusiastic about the pleasures of being single: "You, my friend, if you work at it, can be envied the rich, full life possible for the single woman today. It's a good show. . . . Enjoy it from wherever you are, whether it's two in the balcony or one on the aisle—don't miss any of it."[18] "The single woman," she continued, "is emerging as the newest glamour girl of our times. She is engaging because she lives by her wits. She supports herself. . . . She is a giver, not a taker, a winner and not a loser" (13). Like Brown, novelist Rona Jaffe was enamored of the single life. She wrote in a 1977 *Harper's Bazaar* article, "Today, being single is . . . an enjoyable, often exciting alternate lifestyle for many women."[19] She went on, "The best part about being single is that you don't have to ask anyone for permission. Permission to buy something, to go on a trip, quit your job, get a job, move, go to a party . . . , bring home a pet, see your women friends, work late at the office, neglect the housework."[20]

These writers and others helped change the image of what it meant to be a single woman. No longer was it a sign of being loveless, empty, and forlorn; it was now a sign that a woman was confident, independent, and secure. Being single also connoted being modern and up-to-date. The modern woman no long needed to wait for a man to protect her; she could do it herself very nicely.

For the first time, being single was trendy and hip, and the media wanted to profit from this situation. One genre that rushed to address the needs of single people was the singles' cookbook. Numerous writers published them, hoping to profit from the booming market for singles.[21] Articles in popular magazines also focused on cooking for single men and women.[22] As I mentioned earlier, such literature provided lessons not only about how to grill a steak or bake a cake but also about how to be a man or woman. During the upheaval of the feminist movement, cooking literature depicted men's and women's changing roles and also suggested what gender roles men and women, including single ones, should adopt.

"Women Are like Street Cars": Cookbooks for the 1970s Single

Len O'Dell's book, *The Naked Chef: A Survival Plan for the Single Man* (1978), included a section called the "Hunter's Guide," which focused on how to pick up a woman. It provided a number of tips for the man seeking to find a woman, such as "Male fragrances turn many women off" and "Laundromats are a good place to meet women." O'Dell closed his book with the observation, "Women are like street cars—when you miss one, another will come along. When you find the woman who is the exception to this, your hunting days are over."[23] This was one of many cookbooks for singles that conveyed messages to readers not only about how to cook but also about how to interact with the opposite sex. These books passed on messages about changing gender roles and changing relationships between men, women, and cooking. As we shall find, this cooking literature delineated roles for both single men and women. In addition, singles' cooking literature played a part in challenging gender stereotypes by suggesting that men might find it as important and necessary to cook as women had done traditionally.

In short, singles' cookbooks were not only trying to convey lessons about cooking; they frequently commented about the joys of being single, presenting it as an exciting time when people could start over and begin a new life that was more in accordance with what they desired. One cookbook declared about single bliss for men: "Now that you're living alone, you can start a whole new social life. You can select new friends that only you like. You can meet lots of new women, many of whom you will enjoy and will enjoy you. . . . You're freer than you've been in years. Free to set a life-style that's strictly yours."[24] This book was one of many that touted the advantages of the single life. But not all were equally as ebullient. O'Dell wrote in *The Naked Chef* about his anxiety when he first had to cook without a woman's help: "I wake up one morning to find I'm alone. After having had a woman around all my life, first mother, then wife, I realize there is now no one to care for me, cook for me or minister to my special needs. Without her familiar presence, I suddenly feel naked."[25] Cookbooks were a site where anxious writers like O'Dell could discuss what it meant to live in a society where gender roles were changing dramatically. He expressed the fears of many other 1970s men who felt "naked" when women refused to cater to their needs.

As mentioned earlier, singles' cookbooks also addressed changing relationships between men, women, and cooking. These books taught that good cooking was a way to seduce a mate. Cookbooks for single women stressed that cooking was the best way to gain lovers and friends. Helen Gurley Brown observed in her *Single Girl's Cookbook*, "You want to be a good cook not only because it's creative but because cooking is a way to please friends and solidify lovers. . . . Well, to accomplish this, your cooking must have a little style—yes, a little chic" (85). For Brown, good food was an important element of seducing a man: "Let's say you've met someone dishy, dined with him several times in a restaurant, and the friendship is taking. Last night you even talked vacations together—the Costa Brava where you've always wanted to go. I'd say it's time to invite him home" (254). Food was not only a way to appeal to a man; it also served as a way to make sure of his ability to savor life to its fullest. Brown cautioned, "You're drugged, bedazzled, bewitched, and bestirred. It's love beyond any shadow of a doubt. . . . Food, of course, is part of any love relationship worth having—yet another way of pleasing the senses. Never trust a man who isn't interested in food. . . . If a man isn't capable of savoring the thrills of fine food, he can never truly savor all the marvels of a woman" (263). For Brown's single girl, a man's appreciation of good food was a sign of his appreciation of women and other sensual pleasures.

The question was, what food would tantalize men? Brown was full of ideas. To attract a man, she suggested recipes such as Shrimp with Anchovy Butter, Chicken Kiev, Strawberries with Kirsch, and Italian Broiled Shrimp. Food could be a tool even for the woman who was bored with an affair and wanted her man to leave. Brown suggested that the "trick is to shock him away with unfamiliar foods" (299). "Put together foods that are sure to offend your man," she urged. Her recipes to make a lover lose interest included Stuffed Baked Eggplant, Pimientos and Anchovies on Black-bread Squares, Liederkranz and Apples, Camembert Cheese in White Wine, Roquefort-wine Burgers, Ghastly Eggs, and Exotic Sardines. Such unappetizing dishes were sure to make the most ardent swain lose his appetite. For Brown and other authors, cooking was part of a single woman's best strategy when it came to getting, keeping, and getting rid of a man. Brown worked to perpetuate the old notion, which still exists in the twenty-first century, that cooking was the best way to a man's heart, but her book also encouraged women to be independent and have careers. However, she steered clear of telling them that it was positive to remain single forever; she also affirmed that women, no matter how successful, needed to be concerned about how to attract men.

Cookbooks for single men also emphasized that good cooking was one of the best strategies for a man seeking to seduce a woman. Nigel Napier-Andrews wrote in *How to Eat Well and Stay Single* (1974), "Whatever your reasons for wanting to cook, the first ingredient you need to put into the pot is style. . . . Conversation and lovemaking are far more important ingredients in let's say, a seduction dinner, than the dinner itself. But it's the style with which the whole package is presented that counts."[26] He went on to describe all the details of cooking a seductive dinner, from using the right color of table linen ("get her hormones tingling with red place mats, napkins and tablecloths" [4]) to the right wine ("invest in a good French wine" since "the label adds atmosphere" [3]). He cautioned his readers about trying any experimental dishes on women whom they wished to seduce, observing, "save . . . real experiments for occasions when you are entertaining very, very good friends. . . . Don't try them when you're trying to impress a new love with your culinary prowess, because if you get uptight, you'll only divert your attention from the real purpose of the evening, presuming that the meal is only a means to an end" (73). Cory Kilvert emphasized the importance of cooking in *The Male Chauvinist's Cookbook* (1974): "The rewards . . . are unlimited, and if you think you're lucky with women now, you haven't seen the half of it. . . . Women are impressionable. Unlike men, they feel instead of think. Furthermore, they basically want to be conquered—not only on the couch but in the kitchen, too."[27] This entire book was based on cooking as a form of seduction. Its back cover even had a scorecard with lines for the menu, guest, and comments. Julian G. Richter wrote in *The Single Man's Guide to Fun and Games Cookbook* (1977):

Come on, guys, you can really make it if you have the desire. We may try to excel in many of the so-called manly areas of life. Some make it and some don't. If you have those great big bulging biceps—great—but what else can you do? If you are a wizard at business—terrific—but what else can you do? . . . But if you can cook, you are a prince of the universe. . . . It's a difficult thing to try to explain why many women feel closer to a man who is just a little domestic.[28]

Napier-Andrews, Kilvert, Richter, and other male cookbook authors urged single men to cook in order to seduce women—a suitably masculine occupation.[29] In this fashion, the authors defused the femininity of cooking. They also supported traditional stereotypes of women as not as intelligent as men, who were depicted as easily seducing females simply by the right choice of wine or table cloth.

It was not sufficient for a single man in the 1970s to learn how to cook in order to attract women; he needed to learn how to be a gourmet chef, making himself seem even more desirable to the opposite sex. For a man, being a single chef was frequently presented as glamorous. For example, the dust jacket for *The Single Chef's Cookbook* (1970) read, "No one has more culinary freedom than the adventurous single chef."[30] This book included simple dishes: Pork and Bean Sandwiches, Creamed Spinach, Savory Hot Dogs, Roast Beef Hash, Basic Coleslaw, and French-Fried Beer Rings. But its main emphasis was on more elaborate ones: Psychedelic Bananas (four bananas cooked with butter, brown sugar, lemon juice, two shots of rum, and half a pint of heavy cream 75), Fondue Bourguignon, Tournedos Creole Style, Steak Diane, Veal Cutlet Cordon Bleu, Filet of Veal Oscar, Stuffed Quail, King-Crab-Stuffed Artichokes, Lobster Thermidor, Abalone Macao, Asparagus Polonaise, and Double-Frosted Bourbon Brownies. These gourmet recipes lay at the heart of *The Single Chef's Cookbook*. The recipes transformed a humdrum chef into a true gourmet. This book was not just selling recipes; it was also selling an image of masculinity, one of a man who was so debonair that he could easily handle the demands of preparing a gourmet meal, a man perhaps very much like the author of *The Single Chef's Cookbook*, Sandy Lesberg, was described on the book's dust jacket as "a man of many and varied talents. . . . He reviews on a daily basis theatre, films, music, and dance. He travels a good deal. . . . An accredited diplomatic correspondent to the United Nations, he has interviewed many chiefs of state." It was exactly this man-of-the-world image that this cookbook, and other 1970s cookbooks for single men, promoted. After reading such a book, what man would not want to cook? Lesberg made cooking seem as though it was an essential skill for any worldly man.

But where were the women in this cosmopolitan world of gourmet cooking? They were not entirely excluded; cookbooks for single women also discussed the importance of gourmet cooking. "Cooking gourmetishly is a particularly impressive skill for a career woman," Brown wrote, "put on an organdy apron, retire to the kitchen and come back with impeccable Eggs Benedict. Then listen to the purrs and praise" (145). For Brown and Lesberg, "cooking gourmetishly" was a surefire way to appear more alluring. Singles' cookbooks played a role in changing gender roles by urging men, as well as women, into the kitchen to cook gourmet meals. Singles' cookbooks also challenged the notion that a woman had to cook only for children and family; in these books, women were often portrayed as enjoying cooking the most when seduction was a possibility.

But while singles' cookbooks for men and women agreed on the need to cook gourmet meals to seduce the opposite sex, they did not always agree about other issues. The books became a battleground for fighting over which gender was the superior one. In cookbooks, men (and women) could proclaim their overall superiority by arguing for it in the kitchen. Cookbooks aimed at single men touted the superiority of males as cooks. In *Suddenly Single: A Survival Kit for the Single Man* (1973), Edwin Greenblatt proclaimed, "Despite all those colorful pictures of fluted vegetables found in the women's magazines, the best chefs are usually men."[31] Another male writer declared, "Men are usually portrayed as endearing but bumbling oafs in the kitchen. Let's lay that dreary old ghost once and for all."[32] But Cory Kilvert was the most outspoken about male superiority. The dust jacket of *The Male Chauvinist's Cookbook* stated, "Have you ever stopped to wonder why, with all the millions of practicing housewives in the world, the best kitchens have always been run by men? Well, it's simple. Men are better—on the job, in the bedroom, and in the kitchen." Kilvert wrote:

Women of the world, take heed—men have arrived in the kitchen. . . . Somewhat like Caesar, we have come, we have seen, and we are about to conquer—you. While we recognize the fact that your meat loaf isn't bad, we're pretty sure that we can do better. . . . Just go into any French or Italian or Greek or German restaurant—when you step into the kitchen to compliment the chef, whom do you find yourself addressing? A woman? Certainly not. You find a man, a chef. . . . Cooks, on the other hand, are women, and this title never had—nor will it ever have—the prestige or panache of "chef." (vii–viii)

Greenblatt and Kilvert were not only giving men a few recipes; they were also carefully supporting men's egos by stressing that males, not females, were really the best chefs. These books (and similar ones) were involved in perpetuating the male cooking mystique, one element of which is that men are *always* superior chefs.

Cookbooks of the 1970s for single men emphasized that men were not only superior cooks, but could easily cook anything. For men, cooking was child's play, something that was as easy as reading a recipe. At first, of course, the kitchen and its mysteries would seem arcane to men, since in the past women had not let them enter that space. But men would quickly set aside their worries once they tackled cooking. In *Suddenly Single*, Greenblatt reassured his male readers, "If you're like most men, you find that the kitchen has all the familiarity of a neighborhood in Antarctica. The only reason you know which appliance is the refrigerator is because that's where you keep the beer and ice."[33] But he promised the worried male, "There's no mystery to a kitchen. . . . Any man can learn to manage well in a kitchen. Just arm yourself with a good cookbook, a small assortment of pots and pans, some miscellaneous equipment, and you're ready to attack." Words such as "manage" and "attack" combined imagery of office management and warfare, both suitably male venues. Using such language, the author converted the kitchen from a feminine place to a masculine realm—a place where any man would be comfortable and not have to fear that working there could damage his masculine image. "There are literally hundreds of recipes which require little preparation and cooking time," Greenblatt assured men. "Anybody who can read can cook" (101). Like Greenblatt, Napier-Andrews thought the kitchen held few fears for men. He stated, "This book has all the things which you need to get you off on the right track, and once you understand the basic rules of the game you should be able to open it at any page and cook up a success at your first try."[34]

Cookbooks for single men argued that the reason men were not already filling America's kitchens was that, supposedly, women had unfairly kept the kitchen to themselves by claiming that cooking was more difficult than it actually was. In *Pots and Pans* (1974), Donald Kilbourn commented about how a man should approach learning to cook: "Throw your wife or girlfriend out of the kitchen and pack her off to her mother for the day. She'll probably threaten to go there, anyway, once she realizes that you intend to solve all these womanly mysteries in your own way."[35] He went on to describe cooking as a simple and straightforward scientific process that anyone could accomplish:

> Cooking is basically scientific. Women have, however, cashed in on the lack of standardization and on the variations in natural food as well as in individual tastes, and they have blown it all up into an esoteric art form which relies for its continuation on a pinch of this, a dab of that, and a load of jargon. . . . Cooking is basically a production job that is concerned with converting raw materials into a finished product. (1)

All three of these male writers insisted that cooking was easy. This suggested that women's domestic tasks were simpler than men's and that even when a woman complained that a task was particularly arduous she could not be believed. In the context of second-wave feminism and the 1970s being an era when many women spoke up against the dual responsibilities they held in the home and the workplace, authors of cookbooks for single men suggested that such complaints were exaggerated. In this fashion, singles' cookbooks were a space in which to address the much larger debates about gender roles going on in the United States.

Cookbooks as Barometers of Change

In the 1970s, singles' cookbooks served as barometers of change. They helped create new ideas about the relationship between men, women, and food. They demonstrated to men and women that cooking to seduce a member of the opposite sex was acceptable, especially when in pursuit of a mate. The books helped spread the notion that gourmet cooking was a way to make a cook, whether male or female, appear more worldly. In these ways, these cookbooks suggested ways to change who did the cooking and for whom they cooked.

These books were also part of a much larger media culture that altered how society thought about single people. Not only cookbooks but television shows, films, books, and magazine articles helped build the image of the single person as sophisticated and sexually successful. This image has had a lasting influence on American culture, and although society no longer might view singles in the same light as in the 1970s, our perception of them has altered permanently. Now single women and men are perceived more positively and not viewed by the majority as social rejects, and the 1970s popular media, including singles' cookbooks, played major roles in this shift.

It is important not to view singles' cookbooks as being too revolutionary. They did support societal change by showing both men and women cooking and by suggesting that cooking was something that any man (or woman) of the world would wish to learn, but, at the same time, the books also perpetuated traditional ideas about gender divisions. As we have seen, cookbooks were part of the war between the sexes, with each side vying for superiority. Male and female writers in the 1970s used cookbooks not only to teach about cooking but also as a platform to debate other gender issues, such as whether men or women should do domestic work.

Although I have focused on singles' cookbooks in the 1970s, it is important to recognize the role of other cookbooks as well. This was a period when the publishing industry produced thousands of cookbooks for a myriad of different tastes, and those other books, like singles' cookbooks, provide valuable lessons about cultural change. Numerous cookbooks helped to create the natural foods movement. Countless others helped to spread the gourmet foods movement. Others helped spread the culinary heritage of different groups, including Asian Americans, Hispanics, and African Americans. Despite the prevalence of 1970s cookbooks, they have been little studied by scholars, who, when they address cookbooks, tend to focus largely on earlier works—after all, a cookbook written in the 1850s seems more "weighty" and significant than one published in the 1970s, an era that many have termed "a joke." Thus, 1970s cookbooks have not been studied in great depth, except for a few rare academic forays. We need to recognize that such recent cooking literature has as much to suggest about cultural change as earlier works. After all, the 1970s was a time that directly influenced and shaped how gender roles are constructed today, and one way the period shaped gender roles was through cookbooks and other cooking literature. By analyzing such works, we will come to a better understanding about how cooking roles have changed and also how they have resisted change. Our work has only begun.

Chapter 8

Soap Spin

Changing Female Images in American Soap Operas

THOMAS D. PETITJEAN, JR.

In the anything but static popular culture of the 1970s, daytime drama found itself at odds with both the place of women in contemporary, real-world situations and the contextualized, melodramatic world of females in soap operas. While much has been written on feminist engagement with the soap opera genre[1] and the historical development of the serials' narrative structures,[2] little research has focused on female characters during the 1970s, a period when soaps flourished and audiences grew to numbers never to be reached again.

From their inception in the 1930s, daytime serials have long served as confidence builders for their female audience by presenting positive images of women who worked outside the home. Still, the central figure on most daytime dramas until the 1970s was the stay-at-home mother, generally a warm, loving matriarchal figure. Even the characters who were written as career women mirrored, to a great extent, contemporaneous female listeners and, later, viewers, most of whom were anything but confident career women. However, as the women's movement blossomed and more females began to enter the workforce, soap opera writers were forced to reconsider and reconstitute the female characters who populated the serials for which they wrote. Not only did the writers have to consider the effects of the women's movement, they also had to weigh the needs of the changing audience of daytime viewers—younger viewers of both sexes, especially of college age. To reflect the times of the turbulent 1970s, soap opera writers had to reexamine how they represented contemporary society's values. Such a reexamination led them to put a new spin on the way they wrote female characters. While soaps had always been home to strong, independent female characters, writers had to reconceptualize the way these female characters were written to better reflect the reality of the times. As viewers' lifestyles changed, so did the concept of the female soap opera character and her milieu. While the serials had always empowered females, the 1970s presented a new charge to the writers, who had to mirror the times and find a new way to show women entering the workforce.

A 1974 exchange on CBS-TV's long-running serial *As the World Turns*, between Hughes family matriarch Nancy Hughes and her son Dr. Bob Hughes, demonstrates the dilemma faced by daytime writers—and by extension, daytime characters—when serials realistically attempted to focus on the role of women in '70s society:

NANCY: I never really thought Jennifer would choose her career over her baby.
BOB: Mom, it's not just a job—just any job. It's one that she's vitally interested in.
NANCY: More so than Frannie?
BOB: Jennifer would never put a job before her child. And she'd never neglect her in any way. She loves her too much.
NANCY: I always thought she did.
BOB: She does. The problem is, she can't understand why she can't have a child and a fulfilling career, too.
NANCY: Oh, Bob! Whoever heard of a thing like that?[3]

In 1974, many women had never "heard of a thing like that" (although most had thought of the concept, and female soap opera characters, for the most part unencumbered by a spouse or children, as already living such a lifestyle). In the years that followed, soap operas would be the first among the genres in broadcasting to embrace "a thing like that," forever changing the way female characters would be presented on daytime television serials. No longer would female characters be presented as entirely good ("Saints") or entirely bad ("Sinners"); instead, female characters would be multitoned and presented in shades of gray.

Female characters would also be presented in more modern terms that were reflective of the women's movement. Soap operas had always attempted to present working women who privileged the workplace over the home and the traditional role of mother. In fact, they had championed female independence since their beginnings on radio.

The daytime soaps were important ego-builders for women long before anyone ever heard of women's liberation and even before the appearance of books like *The Second Sex* or *The Feminine Mystique*, which supposedly began the Movement. Women on serials have always been portrayed as doctors, nurses, lawyers, judges, teachers, social workers, and even a senator once. The serials have helped fight the trend of putting down women in movies and especially on nighttime television, where women are portrayed as having little effect on the social order, outside of their sexual role.[4]

This, of course, is not to say that a woman's sexual role was not incorporated into daytime drama. Her role as a sexual rival or an antagonist was important to the drama played out on television, and her role in the work-place was given secondary status until the 1970s.

Soap Opera's Inventor Reinvents the Female Character

Irna Phillips, often cited as the inventor of the American daytime serial on both radio and television, worked on her creation, *As the World Turns*, in 1972 with a new sense of defining the female in a way that was different from any type of characterization she had previously approached. Prior to 1972, Phillips's characters "were not like ordinary people, but were either Saints or Sinners. . . . They represented traditional American values: loy-alty to family, country, and friends, fidelity to marriage vows, and gen-erosity to those less fortunate than themselves."[5] By extension, these characters, first drawn in the late 1930s and still representative of a 1950s mindset, expressed traditional female roles in a society that was making strides away from the home and hearth. On daytime dramas, a woman's place was in the home, subservient to her husband (whether he was faith-ful or not) and, in a sense, to her children as caretaker. This highly moral-istic depiction of what it meant to be female on soap operas was at variance with the creator of the genre's own ideology. In fact, Phillips's own life proved paradoxical in respect to the characters she initially cre-ated for soap operas. "Although she never married, the core of her writ-ing was always the family, the rearing of children, and, ironically, the fulfillment of women through marriage."[6] As the women's movement grew, so did the number of career women on daytime dramas. Phillips's creation of Kim Reynolds served as the template for the majority of these ambivalent divas of duality. Kim, who was a divorcee, was not a "Saint," nor was she a "Sinner"; in essence, she was a reflection of her creator, who often referred to the character as "the lady in the mirror."

Phillips said of Kim Reynolds in an interview,

Everyone asks me how I got the idea of Kim Reynolds on [*As the World Turns*], because she certainly is an unusual character. She's really me—at a much younger age. She's fiercely independent, as I was, and she won't settle for second best. She looks in the mirror and refers to herself as "the lady in the mirror." Well, that was her other self, which no one knew about: the true me, the person that I always hid from the world. She's having a child out of wedlock, which will be only hers. I adopted two children—Kathy and Tommy—without having a husband. We're both the same. And she' s going to have that child to prove that a woman can do it alone.[7]

Unfortunately, Phillips's plans for this character—"to prove that a woman can do it alone"—never came to fruition. Kim Reynolds had an affair with and became pregnant by a "Saint," Dr. Bob Hughes, who was married to Kim's sister (see Figure 1). This, along with other story changes that

Figure 1. Two women who changed the way the world turns: rivals, sisters, and women in search of independence Jennifer Hughes (left, Gillian Spencer) and Kim Reynolds (right, Kathryn Hays). CBS-TV/Irv Haberman.

Phillips made in her last run as the show's head writer, was met with viewer disapproval. "Many fans were turned off by the entire scenario, seeing the doctor they had respected for so many years not only cheat on his wife but with her own sister. Rather than boost the show's ratings, the storyline sent them falling even further. Procter and Gamble responded by firing Phillips."[8] The audience's response to such a socially relevant story line—one that encompassed one of the basic tenets of the women's movement, personal independence—suggests that the audience (and, more important, the show's sponsors) were not yet ready to embrace the societal changes of the 1970s.

Phillips's last and perhaps most poignant creation—a woman who was reflective of the times in which she lived, as well as a character who embodied the idea of an independent, spirited woman—was denuded by the next team of head writers. To repair the damage to the soap's ratings, the writers toyed with the idea of writing Kim off the show, but chose instead to punish "Saint" Bob by having his wife, Jennifer, die in an automobile accident. Nonetheless, the writers were afraid to develop a romance between Bob and Kim. "One might add that Kim, as Irna delineated her, was aloof, almost cold, in her intelligent selfishness. . . . It was clear from the start that Kim was much too liberated (in the most modern sense of the word) to marry except for love—the kind of love that comes only rarely to any person's life."[9] Phillips herself had been involved with one man for years but could not or would not marry him, like Kim, who planned to raise the child independently. In the 1970s, unwed mother-hood was a taboo, even on daytime television. While story lines were writ-ten to show the trials an unmarried mother endured, they all ended with the woman marrying a man who, if not the actual father of the child, took the child in as his own and gave the baby "a name." Privately and publicly, Phillips viewed herself as a career woman but not a feminist. Nonetheless, her final creation was a reflection of her own need—and by extension, her audience's need—for female independence.

Young Love and Relevancy: A Historical Perspective

To understand the role of female characters on daytime drama in the 1970s, one must look to the launching of two serial dramas in the late 1960s: CBS-TV's 1967 Irna Phillips creation, *Love Is a Many Splendored Thing*, and Agnes Nixon's 1968 soap opera, *One Life to Live*. Phillips wanted to write a show about interracial love. Fan reaction was hostile, and the network forced her to abort the interracial love affair. Phillips immedi-ately quit writing the show, and the new writers focused on the remaining, peripheral characters who were in their late teens to mid-twenties. The show's ratings began to climb. The instantaneous popularity of the show unhinged the prevailing theory that viewers—considered to be house-wives in their thirties—wanted to see daytime dramas populated with peo-ple of their own age groups or older. On closer examination, the driving force behind the growing interest in young love was the notion that younger female characters, written with psychological grounding based in part on the women's movement of the 1970s, had more freedom to embrace societal changes. In short, the female audience could embrace the ideas and ideals of the women's movement when they were presented through characters on a daytime drama. The viewers then had role mod-els to emulate—women who delineated a new concept of what it meant to be female in the 1970s.

Similarly, Nixon's *One Life to Live* shattered programming executives' notions that the audience wanted serials populated with white Anglo-Saxon Protestant characters. Instead, Nixon chose to create a "relevant" soap opera—one that was topical and dealt with contemporary life. *One Life to Live* "had various ethnic types—Jews, blacks, Poles, Irish—struggling for identity in a WASP-dominated culture. In addition, her highly publi-cized story lines dealt with drug addiction, VD, sexual repression, prejudice, and child abuse."[10] With the premiere of *One Life to Live* came the birth of the cult of relevancy. "So relevancy gave the serials notoriety, while young love continued to gain higher ratings" (81). These two themes— relevancy and young love—would forever alter the way stories were told on daytime drama as both captured the *zeitgeist* of the 1970s inclusionary racial and ethnic movements that ran parallel to the burgeoning women's movement.

Phillips made attempts at relevancy early in the 1960s on *As the World Turns* by having the character the show's audience loved to hate, Lisa Miller Hughes Shea Eldridge, kidnapped and raped by two men in the back of their truck. "In addition to simply shocking the audience, the rape story line served to win some sympathy for the much-hated Lisa."[11] Fans wanted to see "Sinner" Lisa punished for cheating on "Saint" Dr. Bob, they but did not react as expected. Phillips gave women a means of expressing themselves, if only by extension, in their reaction to Lisa's situation. The audience knew that no woman should be raped, and they let the show know so through fan mail. "Even fans who wanted to see her punished for cheating on Bob didn't feel that she deserved what happened to her." By gaining sympathy for Lisa, Phillips began to move away from her black-and-white concept of saints and sinners, exploring the gray areas of characterization. This tendency toward multitoned characters would carry over and evolve as the soaps and women's notions about themselves as expressed in daytime drama moved into the 1970s.

During the 1969–70 broadcast season, nineteen soap operas were broadcast on the three major American networks; this was the largest number of daytime dramas to run concurrently in any broadcast year. During this time, three head writers were at work on daytime dramas: Irna Phillips, Phillips's protégée Agnes Nixon, and another Phillips-trained writer, William J. Bell, who during a stint as head writer of *Days of Our Lives* created *The Young and the Restless*. Nixon, after making her mark with the cult of relevancy, first scored with the cult of young love on January 5, 1970 when her brainchild, *All My Children*, premiered on ABC-TV.

All My Children was "the first daytime serial geared specifically toward a college-age viewing audience. . . . [T]he show's mature and intelligent handling of serious subjects, such as child abuse, abortion, cosmetic surgery, and prostitution . . . attracted a nationwide audience as diverse as the people who share such dilemmas."[12] The character who made *All My Children* a fan favorite was Erica Kane. Headstrong and impetuous, she moved through a series of love affairs with men and a variety of professions outside the home, never finding the fulfillment for which she searched. This search for fulfillment reflected the search embraced by women in the 1970s for fuller lives through careers outside home and marriage.

With Nixon hard at work on *One Life to Live* and *All My Children*, Procter and Gamble decided to take a chance in 1972 on an ex-publishing executive, Harding Lemay, who was recruited as head writer on NBC-TV's *Another World*, with Irna Phillips serving as his consultant. Lemay added shades of gray (if not depth and dimension) to archetypal characters he considered bland and one-dimensional. Lemay questioned why women were locked into a pattern of saints and sinners. As a playwright, he knew that the female characters on *Another World* lacked dimension and psychological complexity. This one-dimensional approach to characterization was basic to the soap opera genre, partly because of the industry's need to mass-produce romantic fantasies on a daily basis. If the characters were archetypal in nature—the nurturing mother, the dark villain, and the benevolent matriarch, among others—the audience could easily identify with them, given the short duration of the programs, since soap operas initially lasted only fifteen minutes.

In the late 1950s, most serials expanded to a half-hour format, but the characterization of female characters did not undergo a change. Not content to write about characters who were one-dimensional, Lemay took it upon himself to transform the way characters (particularly females) were portrayed in daytime drama: "I slowly realigned other elements of the story and character to extend the social and economic classes depicted within the story."[13] Lemay recognized that the dissatisfaction that characters, particularly females, expressed on the serials drew an audience of females who were increasingly younger and who found their own dissatisfactions with life reflected in the characters they watched daily on the soap operas. To this end, he "threw out *Another World*'s crazy melodrama and replaced it with domestic drama, class conflict, and tension created by highly complex characters falling in and out of love."[14] His concept was a success, and *Another World*'s ratings skyrocketed as its story lines aligned with the female audience's needs and desires to change their lives to match societal changes that offered independence, freedom, and fulfillment for women.

William J. Bell, another of Phillips's protégés, was hard at work writing *Days of Our Lives* and simultaneously developing, along with his wife, Lee Phillip Bell, a serial that would change forever the look of daytime drama, *The Young and the Restless*, which premiered on March 26, 1973. Bell was aware of what the audience wanted and produced a soap that featured couples who did more than simply profess undying love for each other. Soap fans wanted to see couples, even teenage couples, discuss real topics, such as whether to sleep together before getting married. Tackling social issues including obesity, mastectomy, father-daughter incest, euthanasia, alcoholism, bulimia, and the "new" sexual freedom of the 1970s seriously, Bell broke one daytime taboo after another with a cast of characters who drove the fledgling soap's story lines and captured a large viewing public.

Women in particular were fascinated by the psychologically complex, liberated female characters who advanced the drama's stories. The Brooks sisters were created from one-dimensional soap opera archetypes (the rival, the artist, the vulnerable and moralistic heroine, and the younger sister), but Bell fleshed out the characters to create women who were very much a part of the 1970s mindset as they searched for fulfillment in love and at work.

The eldest of the Brooks sisters, Leslie, was an artist—a shy introvert who blossomed as her career took center stage; despite her successes on stage as a concert pianist, she still searched for fulfillment in love. Lori, the second sister, was liberated in every sense of the word, freed from the constraints of conventional morality. Having traveled Europe and tasted all the world had to offer, she returned to the midwestern United States and attempted to settle for a career in journalism, working at her father's newspaper. Chris, the third sister, was a college student whose sense of morality was not in sync with her older sister Lori's or with the women's movement. She believed in sex only after marriage, refusing to relinquish her virginity to her true love, which led him to the bed of another woman (and led the audience to see the double standard at play in the mid-1970s: what was "right" for a man was not considered "right" for a woman). Last, Peggy was a first-year college student. Unsure of what would lead to fulfillment, Peggy was the character on *The Young and the Restless* who was the ripest for character development in terms of 1970s societal change. Early story lines had Peggy involved with an older professor who had turned away from his wife because she had become overweight; this story line also addressed the double standards females faced in the 1970s.

Eventually, three of the four Brooks sisters would be raped. However, these rapes were not perceived by the audience or the writers as punishment for some trespass the character might have committed. Instead, the rapes were "message" story lines that showed rape for what it is: a crime against women. Bell utilized the four Brooks sisters in a way no soap opera writer before him had done. The characters were young, smart women in search of fulfillment as codified by the women's movement and their own sense of free will. Bell's story lines reflected the basic tenets of women's struggle for liberation from the sort of 1950s morality that was still entrenched in most daytime dramas and in the lives of most of the women who viewed his show.

With such innovators at work during the early years of the seventies, daytime drama began to reflect the trend for women to move out of the home and into the office. However, given the nature of soap opera viewers and their tendency to react strongly in a negative fashion to change, this trend had to be gradually integrated into story lines, with women entering the workforce in traditionally female jobs. Only at the decade's

end would women on soap operas be portrayed as bosses rather than secretaries or workers in other subordinate roles.

Toward a New Female Image

To understand how the role of female characters underwent a transformation in the 1970s, one must look to the mediated image of soap opera
women from the perspective of the daytime viewing audience and fans.
One fan-turned-writer, Manuela Soares, fashioned a schema of female
soap opera archetypes in 1978, looking past the vaunted notion that soap
opera characters were either good or bad and noting, "There are certain
archetypal characters in the soaps, but they are characters of depth and
individuality."[15] Academic studies were performed in the 1970s, among
them one by Mary Cassata, Michelle Lynn Rondina, and Thomas Skill, in
which characters were "typed" according to demographics, with such categories as Chic Suburbanite, Subtle Single, Traditional Family Person,
Successful Professional, Elegant Socialite, Self-Made Business Person (no
women here), Contented Youth, Troubled Teen, Dissatisfied Homemaker, Frustrated Laborer, Happy Homemaker, and Retiring Home-
body.[16] While demographics and lifestyle certainly play a part in
fashioning a psychologically complex character, Soares's move toward
archetypes seems more fitting for an analysis of women in 1970s serials
because she bases her character evaluations on the generic archetypes ger-
mane to soap opera from its inception.

Among the archetypes Soares patterns are the young and vulnerable
romantic heroine, the old-fashioned villain, the rival, the suffering antagonist, the meddlesome and villainous mother/grandmother, the benevolent mother/grandmother, and the career woman. In defining her
archetypes, Soares finds that female characters are more fully fleshed out
than their male counterparts: "Soap opera characters are never merely
Good or Bad. Though some male characters are superficial, females
almost never are. Most display the depth, contradictions and growth that
we associate with human behavior."[17] While the females were perhaps not
superficial, in most cases they did not have lives that were necessarily
aligned with the upheaval of roles that defined what it was to be a woman
in the 1970s.

Soares listed only one 1970s female character in the archetype of the
old-fashioned villain, the type of character who allows the audience to vicariously hate him or her without the usual guilt one would feel in real life.
This is generally a male figure. Soares included *One Life to Live*'s Dorian
Cramer Lord as the lone female character who intentionally hurts people,
playing on the vulnerable with lies and blackmail. One must question
why only one female character was listed in Soares's archetype of the old-

Figure 2. *Another World*'s villainess Iris Cory Carrington (Beverlee McKinsey) lost a potential husband wooing "Saint" Dr. Russ Matthews (David Bailey). Globe Photos/NBC-TV.

fashioned villain. The answer seems to indicate that soap operas were very much a part of the social double standard, where men were able to divide and conquer but women were expected to nurture.

Another World's Iris Carrington belongs to Soares's archetype of the rival (see Figure 2). Often referred to as a "bitch goddess" (a term not used in a derogatory sense, as these women are characters the audience loves to hate, that could be considered derogatory given its antifeminist implications), the rival is generally beautiful and clothed accordingly. Natural rivals to "good" female characters, these women are generally in devious pursuit of good characters. "Too often they create misunderstanding and misfortune for purely selfish reasons; too often they oppose the true love relationship [the audience wishes] to see fulfilled. Generally the Rival is a woman who is not completely comfortable with her environment or its prevailing values" (63). Given the nature of serial story lines, the rival poses a danger in the immediate future, but the audience know she is the character who will be unhappy in the end. Soares describes *Another World*'s Iris Carrington and *All My Children*'s Erica Kane Brent as "overdrawn neurotic types" who fit the archetypal pattern of the rival (50). The rival, as drawn by Lemay and other head writers, generally serves as a show's antagonist and story line catalyst.

However, Soares does not consider the rival an antagonist. In fact, Soares codified a category for the suffering antagonist in and of itself. She defines the character as "not quite villains, these ladies may properly be called antagonists. They create trouble for our favorite characters, and very often display selfishness, jealousy, and other unattractive traits. Nonetheless, they are among the most popular and durable soap opera characters" (63). Among these characters is *As the World Turns*'s Dr. Susan Stewart. A talented professional, she demonstrated that a woman could not have it all. Thwarted in love, Susan attempted to do the same to her ex-husband, who romanced Kim Reynolds. However, Susan, like Kim, proved vulnerable. She provoked complicated, emotional responses from the audience, ranging from momentary annoyance to deep empathy, because the audience shared in her pain at the loss of not only her husband but also her daughter's father. The viewers also sympathized (if not empathized) as Susan spiraled downward into alcoholism, a fate that seemed to make her pay for her mistakes. A liberated character, Dr. Susan Stewart was the first in a line of career women who had to make a choice between career and love to find happiness, only to find herself overwhelmed by the emotional baggage that came with options.

As the World Turns's Dr. Susan Stewart became an important character in terms of the struggles women were facing in the 1970s. In their attempts to break the mold of what it meant to be female, many of the characters on soap operas were faced with overwhelming choices, and some broke under the strain. Others, like Kim Reynolds, did not. Both Kim and Susan's struggles to deal with societal changes met with equal measures of small successes and small defeats, and their search for fulfillment mirrored the lives of many of *As the World Turns*'s female viewers. The audience tuned in and learned from these contemporary morality plays that were based on issues women faced as the women's movement took root.

The most varied of Manuela Soares's soap opera archetypes is the career woman, who may be sympathetic or unsympathetic. More often than not, this character is drawn with ambiguity, straddling the line between antagonist and protagonist. As the 1970s moved onward and more women entered the workplace, the serials' head writers drew increasingly complex characters who mixed love with work and childrearing. "The career woman is not so much an archetype as a role model" (70). Indeed, career women have always been a character-type on soaps, but their jobs were generally subservient to the men for whom they worked, unless the character was a professional, such as a physician. The career woman "is strong willed but feminine; successful in her work, but pleasingly vulnerable in love and family life. Although most of the career women are, like their male counterparts, doctors or lawyers, there are novelists, architects, executives, and secretaries as well." The retention of the feminine side of the character was important in 1970s daytime dramas.

Most of the audience had preconceived notions of the outward appearance of a liberated woman; they believed her to be less than what was considered conventionally attractive and, because she had made incursions into what were considered male roles, mannish in both manner and appearance. Therefore daytime writers were careful to write career women who retained their femininity so as not to offend, and by extension lose, viewers.

However, to integrate working women into the narrative was often a difficult task. Such was the case with *Another World*'s Lenore Curtin, wife of murderer Walter Curtin, who was going to allow her be convicted for a crime he had committed. To create a more substantive story line, Lemay widowed the character of Lenore and made her a working woman to "find more intriguing stories for her than that of a woman saddled with a guilt-ridden husband."[18] Like his mentor and consultant, Lemay attempted to write Lenore as a character who was not unlike the original version of Phillips's Kim Reynolds on *As the World Turns*. He met the same opposition that Phillips met from the sponsor, Procter and Gamble. "I suggested that [Lenore] not marry again, but fall in love and have another child, this one out of wedlock. A shout of disbelief brought the sponsor's man to his feet as he demanded to know what kind of slut would do such a thing" (80). Instead, Lemay had Lenore go the traditional route of moving from home to office. "After Walter's death, Lenore was hired by Steve Frame to work in his office" (81). By moving Lenore to the workplace, Lemay was able to allow women an acceptable means of support outside marriage.

By the mid-1970s women had indeed moved into the workplace, which provided a viable backdrop for stories that were driven by complicated character needs. Still there was a tendency to portray unmarried female characters who earned their living as one-dimensional and stereotypical. Eventually, such one-dimensional characters would rarely surface in a soap opera, except as short-term characters.

These career-oriented females also had to deal with husbands, mothers-in-law, or other meddlesome females and authoritative male figures such as the aforementioned Nancy Hughes and Dr. Bob Hughes. "After Frannie was born, Jennifer began spending more time building her nursing career, to the consternation of Bob, who wanted a traditional, 'stay-at-home' wife, a sentiment seconded by Nancy."[19] As the 1970s moved to a close, more soap operas were using the workplace as a backdrop for romantic entanglements complicated by complex, psychologically motivated, *zeitgeist*-driven characters who were, for the most part, female.

When Female Characters Take Control

As the 1970s drew to a close, Mary Cassata and Thomas Skill, in a 1979 national survey published for distribution in *Soap Opera Digest*, posed questions about the role of the female character: "How does the daytime serial viewer see her favorite female character: as a model of today's contemporary women, or a throwback to the traditional housewife of years past? What lessons can we learn from her portrayal? Is she presenting women as they should be, or as they should not be?"[20] Cassata and Skill raise questions that are rooted in soap opera tradition extending back to the first serial drama Irna Phillips created on radio. Of the top nineteen characters in the poll, *Another World*'s Rachel Cory represented one of the three most popular characters, *As the World Turns*'s Kim Reynolds Stewart represented one of the three most "good" characters, and *Another World*'s Iris Carrington Bancroft represented one of the two most "bad" characters.

Rachel Cory was perceived as being "aggressive," "ambitious," and "powerful," with her most outstanding trait being her "jealous tendency." Rachel was also interpreted as being "extremely intelligent" and "independent." "Her overall character can be described as combining both good and bad elements in a somewhat realistic portrayal, with [two-thirds] of the respondents seeing her as presenting women 'as they should be'" (34). Interestingly, at the decade's end, women had come to identify with characters who were written in a manner that was far different from the way they were written in the early 1970s. Rachel had developed from an antagonistic agitator in 1967 to a beloved, independent heroine in 1979. Much of Rachel's transformation had to do with Harding Lemay's vision of the character. He noted that in Rachel he had inherited from Agnes Nixon and the writers who followed her on *Another World*, "an 'utterly worthless girl' and subtly transformed her into a girl who had certain drives and needs and was very dissatisfied with life" (see Figure 3).[21] By taking great care to present a full psychological picture, Lemay transformed a once-villainess into a fully realized individual with needs—an individual with whom the audience identified as a presentation of "women as they should be."

Figure 3. *Another World*'s Rachel Cory (Victoria Wyndham) worked as an artist, objectifying her husband in clay, a soap opera opposition to the conventional male objectification of females. Globe Photos/NBC-TV.

Kim Reynolds Stewart of *As the World Turns* was representative of a character the audience perceived as "good." In terms of "presenting women as they should be," the character scored very highly. Of twelve personality dimensions in the study, six showed high levels of agreement across the "most good." Of these six dimensions, Kim Stewart scored highly as "intelligent," "sensitive," and "believable," but received lower scores as "insecure," "jealous," and "aggressive." Given these scores, it would seem that the ideal female character at the end of the 1970s would be an intelligent, believable, sensitive woman who was rarely jealous, insecure, or aggressive—a realistically complicated but contradictory human being. Interestingly, Kim Stewart scored higher than average in terms of being "family oriented" but lower than average in terms of "emotion." The four remaining traits—ambition, career-orientedness, independence, and power—varied greatly. Cassata and Skill concluded, "the image of the 'most good' and the 'most appropriate model for women' that emerges is one that tends toward a rather traditional role—one that de-emphasizes the strong traits and encourages the softer traits" (34). In short, as the decade came to a close and female characters were more aligned with what it meant to be female as defined by the women's movement, characters showed their humanity through contradictory traits. The presence of contradiction implies the move towards acceptance of change. In order to compel the audience to accept change in the way women were written, daytime drama writers had to slowly realign what constituted the female on soap operas.

Finally, Cassata and Skill looked at characters the respondents judged "most bad," and *Another World*'s Iris Carrington Bancroft fit the profile. She was generally seen as "mostly bad and destructive." She portrayed women "as they should *not* be." Oddly, she was also seen by only a very small percentage of the respondents as "realistic." Cassata and Skill note that "perhaps the indication is that real people can't possibly be that bad" (35). The soap opera audience's view of Bancroft and other female antagonists as less than realistic may indicate that women's self-perceptions were changing because they viewed Iris and her lot as examples of what women should not be.

The end result of the Cassata and Skill survey is that characters depicted as "mostly good" were polite, gentle, and ladylike, while temperamental, aggressive, powerful female characters were seen as "mostly bad." For Cassata and Skill, "the question remains as to whether the women characters who are portrayed as taking control of their lives will always be interpreted as manipulative and self-indulgent" (35). Answers to this lingering question came to the fore in the decades that followed. Changing 1970s gender roles, women in the workplace, the double standard, and other issues brought to the forefront by the women's movement changed the role of women on daytime dramas. Today, female characters do not speak out against another female character's moving from home to the workplace as Nancy did on *As the World Turns* in 1974. Male characters are far more understanding of female characters' need for acceptance as peers both at home and at work. Many female characters on soap operas are now CEOs of global conglomerates with male underlings. Unwed pregnancy and illegitimate children, while still a plot point to drive stories, do not cast women in an unfavorable light. While there are still characters who are interpreted as manipulative and self-indulgent, the mix is relatively even in the writers' assignment of these traits to male and female characters. For the most part, such characters serve as antagonists to propel the story line. Ultimately, women on soap operas have taken control of their lives and are rarely interpreted as manipulative and self-indulgent; instead, these female characters are viewed as women—either fulfilled or in search of fulfillment—who manage not only their lives but also their families, homes, and businesses. Today's female characters, for the most part, represent fully realized, psychologically sound individuals undertaking diverse quests for self-fulfillment—women as they should be.

In the 1970s, intense audience involvement and interest as the daytime audience burgeoned raised questions about who the characters were, impelling writers to move the characters from polarized, cartoonish individuals to more fully fleshed-out human beings with complex personalities. Viewers initially rejected the transformation of females from one-dimensional characters to fully realized, psychologically complex women. However, as the ideology of the women's movement began to make an impact on the lives of soap opera viewers, the audience seemed more inclined to accept female characters whose lives were defined separately from husband, child, or home. When female characters on soap operas began the search for more fulfilling lives, so did real women. When female characters on soap operas encountered the stress that came with trying to have it all, so did real women. When female characters on soap operas began to juggle career, marriage, and children, so did real women. When female characters on soap operas became sexually liberated and destigmatized unwed motherhood, so did real women. In short, female soap opera characters were portrayed to fit the changing mores and ideologies of the tumultuous 1970s.

With such radical changes afoot, story lines were driven by realistic female characters who functioned as players in dramas that constituted contemporary morality plays. With a positive response from viewers, daytime dramas' audiences grew to sizes that would never be seen again. Such an expansion can be explained, in part, by the fact that the women who watched soap operas found contemporary role models who faced the same problems they did. As the characters worked through a story line, they found coping skills that viewers were also able to adapt to their own lives. The characters' worlds began to turn in ways that reflected the psychology and the ideology that was a part of the 1970s zeitgeist.

Chapter 9

Hysterical Scream or Rebel Yell?
The Politics of Teen-Idol Fandom

ILANA NASH

One autumn morning in 1978, I sat in my Santa Monica junior high school waiting for class to begin when I felt a tap on my shoulder. I turned and saw Liz, one of the hipper girls on my campus, smirking at me. The look was mirrored by the girls sitting nearby; all were watching me. "Hey Ilana," Liz said sweetly, "Do you know what 'wang dang sweet poontang' means?" Before I could answer, she and her friends erupted into laughter. This was just as well, since I had no idea what that absurd-sounding phrase meant. But I needed no instruction to know that it was probably dirty and that I was being mocked. What allowed me to know this was my preexisting reputation as a "virgin." There were many virgins at school, but I was an unusually high-profile innocent because I was an ardent and outspoken Shaun Cassidy fan. Liz and her circle, as their question proved, were Ted Nugent fans. That made all the difference.

In that time and place, girls defined their identities through one of two musical styles: "hard rock" (Nugent, Lynyrd Skynyrd, and especially Led Zeppelin), or teen-idol pop (Cassidy, Leif Garrett, and the Bay City Rollers), sometimes called "bubblegum." These were not always strict polarities—some girls enjoyed both styles, some neither—but the general consensus was that these styles formed the opposite ends of a teen-girl spectrum, and the stakes were high enough to warrant hostilities between warring camps. Hard rock was the only style granted cultural legitimacy. It represented a more "authentic" youth culture built around a philosophy of rebellion, and its code phrase was "sex, drugs, and rock 'n' roll." Rocker girls definitely took drugs; whether they actually had sex or not—at thirteen, at least a few of them did not—they were assumed to. Their reputations for being "cool" were cemented with personas that expressed disaffection and rebellion. Teenyboppers, however, listened to Top 40 music. We were well socialized and relatively wholesome; whether we actually had sex or not—some of us did—we were assumed not to. Because of our music, rockers saw teenyboppers as utter morons. Our literal virginity was less offensive than the consumption of our idols; that ingredient made our sexual innocence a sin against coolness.

This is one of several memories that resurfaced when I began analyzing teenybopper culture. There are some well-regarded essays on this topic, but none accounts fully for all the experiences that inflected my and my cohort's fandom. Idol fandom cannot be adequately analyzed with one model or with reference to one metanarrative about what sexuality and politics mean to girls; the meanings of fandom change according to time and place. Los Angeles in the late 1970s had a distinct cultural tone that affected our fan practices. In this chapter I explore some of those meanings by analyzing the two interdependent prongs of teen-idol fandom: its social enactment among peers and its representation in *16* and *Tiger Beat*, the magazines that most sustained it. Both spheres, the social and the textual, cooperated to create the central project in which some teenyboppers of my generation engaged: subjectivity formation. The Southern California lifestyle, the post-1960s fracturing of youth culture, and the popular dissemination of feminism and the sexual revolution made fandom for some of us a political statement about our roles in the world as girls.

Discovering Identity Politics: LA in the "Me Decade"

Before discussing the particulars of teenybopper fandom, I should lay some foundations of the culture in which my peers and I came to consciousness; it differed strikingly from the culture that had shaped girls a generation earlier, when the discursive rules constructing white teenage girls were more uniform. For example, the power of "Beatlemania" has been explained with reference to the sexually repressive atmosphere of the early 1960s, in which it was a revolutionary act for girls to defy "lady-like" prescriptions by screaming out their sexual feelings at a Beatles concert.[1] For fans of my generation, however, such activities were "revolutionary" only at an individual level, not a systemic one; by the late 1970s, teenage girls had been screaming and screwing for a long time (or so it seemed to us). In 1970s Los Angeles, such activities seemed the standard to which our culture asked us to conform. The sexually free girl had lost a lot of her stigma, and to girls my age she took on the prescriptive power of a role model.

If this sounds peculiar, remember that California was Ground Zero for the countercultural detonations of the late 1960s. Earlier, the prevailing image of the "teenage girl" had been a white middle-class "nice" girl locked into the double standard and expected to reproduce the patriarchy and capitalism—the girls whose Beatlemania was, according to some scholars, a cry for freedom. "Bad girls," familiar with drugs and sex and rebellious against middle-class values, were popularly assumed to be from "the wrong side of the tracks" or to be ethnic Others. During the 1960s, America's image of the teenage girl fractured. Coffee-table magazines showed that "bad" girls came from affluent white homes, too, and this discovery removed some of their stigma. Society's attitude toward this new creature was paradoxical; she was worrisome, but she also provided sexual titillation as the double standard began eroding. Patriarchy and capital did their usual sleight of hand in coopting this image, using it to criticize youth even while exploiting it as a marketing tool. The intriguing "hip girl" assumed a place in popular culture alongside her more traditional sister.

Ten years later, the image of the white middle-class girl who knows a thing or two about sex, drugs and rock 'n' roll had become so widely disseminated as to be almost normative. Her image was bolstered by the still-churning sexual revolution. One of the strongest messages girls of my generation received was that we were lucky to live in such progressive times—"You've come a long way, baby"—and the biggest sign of our new freedom was our access to sex. You couldn't pick up a magazine or turn on the television without encountering references to the (it seemed) newly discovered female orgasm. Our access to drugs was less publicly celebrated but tacitly included in the philosophy of the "Me Decade," which valued self-expression and self-indulgence. This ethos was perhaps stronger in LA than elsewhere; long fabled as a haven for lunatics and dreamers building new lives, Los Angeles is a fertile ground for youth, creativity, and hedonism, where you're never too old to act young. In my childhood it seemed that everybody, including respectable, gainfully employed adults, passed joints at backyard parties as casually as hors d'oeuvres. Sex and drugs simply did not belong to a "counter culture" any more in 1970s LA; they *were* the culture. Of course, as the 1980 election proved, disgruntled conservatives all over the land (including California) were waiting to turn the tables. But to my eyes none of them seemed to live in greater Los Angeles. Blissfully ignorant that the White House would soon prompt us to "just say no," my generation heard LA telling us to "just say yes" to everything.

This was interesting news for me and my peers, hit with surging hormones in one of the most permissive times and places in modern history. Even those of us who weren't sexually active yet (waiting for a certain age, or for "love," but rarely for marriage) benefited from the climate of sexual freedom. It guaranteed that a simple trip to the local bookstore could net treasure troves of information; thus, at the age of twelve, I read Nancy Drew and Nancy Friday with equal ease and interest. And, unlike many children of the following generation, we received accurate and detailed sex education in school. Even official institutions seemed to agree that sex was nothing to be feared or avoided. Remarkably, I was raised in almost total ignorance of the Madonna/whore dichotomy; among the kids I knew, only outcasts or Christians stayed virgins after the age of sixteen. Schooled in the muddy equations of popular culture, we saw women's sexual freedom as purely positive and intrinsically connected to feminism.

While few of us had the explicitly political consciousness of older women, none of us could escape some of feminism's influence; "women's lib" had arrived just as we were becoming socially aware. In 1972, at the age of seven, I informed the boy next door that I was a feminist (a pronouncement he did not receive with good grace). In 1974 I routinely entertained my fourth-grade classmates with an imitation of Helen Reddy singing "I am woman, hear me roar." I knew all the words by heart. By the time I reached junior high, however, I was beginning to notice some disturbing contradictions. I had heard the phrase "sex, drugs, and rock 'n' roll," and the triumvirate confused me. The public discourse surrounding sex was mostly positive (AIDS wasn't known yet, and other "venereal diseases" could be cured with penicillin), but drugs were darker; we heard they could kill you, even though I'd seen people I respected use certain drugs with no apparent damage. It seemed safer to simply avoid them—but if "sex, drugs and rock 'n' roll" went together, did that mean that you had to use drugs to be "properly" sexual? Did you have to have sex to be a rock fan? And was sexual and pharmaceutical "freedom" the same as "emancipation"?

My confusion stemmed from the radically different sources of my impressions. The rocker girl of popular culture was not the image from whom I had heard about the joys of sex. That knowledge came from adult women whose names were cultural buzzwords: Erica Jong, "J," Nancy Friday, and Helen Gurley Brown. My favorite television shows were *The Bionic Woman*, *Charlie's Angels*, and *Wonder Woman*, feminists mixed with sugar and water to be palatable for mass consumption. In the haze of the "anything goes" culture surrounding me, I had equated several different images of femininity—the rocker girl, feminist, and superheroine—because they all seemed part of the new "freedom" that everyone was so happy about. But as I entered adolescence and began viewing my culture with a more critical eye, those images were refusing to mesh comfortably.

Feminists talked about the "double standard" and the hazards of being "a sex object," lessons I learned and repeated with vehemence. But rocker girls seemed happy to be sex objects. They also showed me that I had misunderstood what was meant by "rock" in the "sex, drugs, and rock 'n' roll" mantra: they consumed "hard rock," which I found unappealingly violent. I quickly saw that I had little in common with rocker girls, but I couldn't be Erica Jong or Lindsay Wagner, my *Bionic Woman* heroine, for another fifteen years. Who was I supposed to be in the meantime? The options were limited. Pop culture told us that when little girls become teenagers, they either burst out and become rockers or else turn into "young ladies," bland creatures with frozen hair and a long life of community service ahead of them. This girl, although admired by adults, was not accorded a privileged status in popular culture; she was too dull and "uncool" to be emulated (my cohort refused to read *Seventeen,* a nauseating rag for girls obsessed with diets and sorority house values). The cool rocker image was preferred by the vast majority of our peers. We grappled with the implied command that if we didn't adopt hard-rock fandom, we would remain de facto children.

The movie *Grease,* for example, cemented this progression in my mind. The summer I turned thirteen, my friends and I saw *Grease* multiple times and delighted in singing the show's songs with each other. But one sour note marred the experience for me: I deeply resented the ending. Olivia Newton-John's innocent character, ribbed by her tough girlfriends ("Look at me, I'm Sandra Dee/Lousy with virginity"), has to abandon her good-girl image in order to keep John Travolta. She shows up in the final scene dressed in biker-black, with teased hair, hard-looking makeup, and a cigarette. She and Travolta drive off not just into the sunset but literally into the sky, borne aloft by the joy her long-overdue transformation has allowed them. This message echoed what my girlfriends and I heard at school: we had to change if we wanted to be cool and have a happy ending.

The parallels between Newton-John's character and myself did not escape my classmates, who began to call me "Sandra Dee." Even my best friend, a fellow teenybopper with some rocker girl sympathies, picked up this irritating habit—perhaps because she hoped that publicly proving her credentials as a teenybopper/rocker "amphibian" would separate her from my more innocent style and ensure her safety from the taunts I suffered. The power of the rocker image shaped all our behavior and rendered every act of stylistic display an irrevocable pledge of allegiance to one side or the other of a contested binary.

Rocker girls brought drugs to school, skipped class to watch boys surf at the beach, often went to rowdy concerts, and spoke glibly about casual sexual experiences with boys who treated them equally casually. Little sleep, sexual exploitation, and poor grades were prices they paid for "coolness." To me, none of those prices seemed worth paying. After I saw her up close, the rocker girl lost a lot of her appeal. No longer a freeing alternative from tradition, she had become a cultural dominant. And, like all dominant ideologies, she was oppressing someone: me and thirteen-year-olds like me everywhere. Being teenyboppers was how we fought back. That gave us our first taste of autonomy, strange though it may sound to link a mass-marketed, commodified activity with "autonomy." Teens' music had always been seen as oppositional to adults' standards, but the 1960s fracturing of youth-culture styles meant that by the 1970s we were rebelling as much against other teens as against adults.

When I became a teenybopper, I found a realm of experience that treated me more seriously and respectfully than I had been treated before. Fandom felt exhilaratingly progressive; the fact that I was contained within a fundamentally reactionary narrative (girls navigating their lives by the North Star of boys and romance) was mitigated by the knowledge that my choice transgressed against a dominant mode of youth culture that denied my values. My friends and I took the received narratives of teenybopper identity and unconsciously modified them, using what we knew of the sexual revolution and feminism to create what we lacked: a cultural space somewhere between reviled childhood and a style of teenhood that seemed unwelcoming, even threatening.

"Immature" Fans and "Feminine" Boys

Teen-idol fandom gave us an outlet for our romantic and sexual desires; fundamentally, fandom is about "love," although it is a type of love that many consider inauthentic. Cultural commentators have long said that teenyboppers consume idols because they aren't "ready" yet for real sex, real boys, or real masculinity. In fact, one of the most common methods of deriding teen idols, used by hard rock fans and adult critics of all kinds, is to ridicule their "pretty" or "baby" faces, their tendency to look "nonthreatening." Adults I knew teased me by saying that Shaun looked "like a girl"; kids at school, more bluntly, called him a fag. The implications here attacked both the idols (for representing a nonnormative version of masculinity) and us (for having an "immature" sexuality—because a mature girl should be attracted to manly men). Even the cultural producers who ran the teen idol machine spoke of us in terms of sexual immaturity: *16* editor Gloria Stavers imagined her average reader as "the girl who is too old for daddy's knee, but too young for the boy next door."[2] Scholars Angela McRobbie and Jenny Garber note:

for girls of this age real boys remain a threatening and unknown quantity. Sexual experience is something most girls of all social classes want to hold off for some time in the future. They know, however, that going out with boys invariably carries the possibility of being expected to kiss, or "pet." The fantasy boys of pop make no such demands. They "love" their fans without asking anything in return.[3]

While these authors accord a previously neglected respect to girls' cultural practices, they accept a hegemonic interpretation that sees traditional gender ideologies as inducting girls into patriarchy by bifurcating "romance" (girl turf) and "sex" (boy turf). But sex wasn't solely boy turf in 1977, the year I lost my heart to Shaun and also the year McRobbie and Garber first published their essay. They ignore the cultural milieu that allowed teenyboppers of that era greater participation in sexual discourses that emphasized female sexuality. Perhaps this omission reflects a geographical difference between Britain and urban America, or perhaps it simply reflects the authors' unawareness of how popular sexual narratives affected young girls. Their argument leaves insufficient room for girls' ability to alter meanings through consumption; even if the sexual discourses of our day really had been strictly bifurcated along gender lines— which they weren't—our practices would have loosened those ideological strictures. As many former teenyboppers will tell you, we were hardly "unready" for real romance or even sex. Sheryl Garratt gives a good rebuttal to this assumption when she critiques a newspaper's report of her teen idols:

"When their fans are old enough to start looking for *real* boyfriends," sneered a *Birmingham Evening Mail* review of [a 1975 Bay City Rollers concert], "the Rollers will soon be forgotten." But it's not that simple; some of us were lesbians, some of us *did* have boyfriends. In any case, girls mature earlier than boys, so it was more a question of waiting for *them* to grow up than the other way around.[4]

Of course, some girls truly did not have a sexual fantasy life. One compatriot told me that her dreams of her idol included dating, marrying, and having a baby with him—completely omitting the process by which babies are made. But "thirteen years old" does not designate a single, static developmental condition, just as "thirty" does not. My cohort, like Garratt's, included one lesbian as well as three straight girls with steady boyfriends, two of whom were already engaged in sexual activities, which for one of them included intercourse. Idol-fandom augmented their sex life, not replaced it, much as grown men will entertain fantasies about women celebrities while happily married to "real life" women. Even those of us who were physical virgins were not always mental virgins; far from nursing fears of "kissing" or "petting," as McRobbie and Garber claim, we thought about such behavior (and more) constantly. We waited only for a viable opportunity. Those of us more mature than junior-high boys had, as Garratt says, a long wait.

Boys' immaturity was not merely a matter of different tastes or worldviews; it manifested itself often in violent or humiliating acts of sexual aggression. When people say that teenyboppers aren't "ready" yet for "real" masculinity, they fail to consider what guise "real masculinity" takes when girls find themselves the object of its attention for the first time. My introduction to the imperatives of masculinity was distinctly unpleasant. A schoolmate named Matt greeted me daily with a hard punch in the notebook I carried like a shield in front of my chest, while Casey, who sat behind me in science class, devised an ingenious method of using two pencils to unhook my bra through my shirt. Those were just the regular occurrences; in any given week, I could experience a one-time assault from any of the hundreds of boys in my school. I bore these humiliations as best I could, for "snitching" to a teacher would imply that I was not as autonomous as I fancied myself and would also make my embarrassment more public.

Boys' behavior did not raise eyebrows; it was assumed that their natural "immaturity" must be borne with patience. In the 1990s America started recognizing this behavior as genuine sexual harassment. The American Association of University Women "released a study, 'Hostile Hallways,' that . . . reports that 70 percent of girls experience harassment and 50 percent experience unwanted sexual touching in their schools."[5] Those statistics might have been lower in 1977, but not by much. Many girls in my school had similar stories about harassment, which raises a crucial question: when commentators derided us by saying we weren't "ready" for "real boys," what precisely did they think we should be ready for? Abuse and assault? That is how masculinity often presents itself; as masculinity scholars have argued, physical and psychological aggression underlie many of our culture's prescriptions for male behavior.[6]

One of the most popular venues for expressing a masculinity based on dominance and aggression is the world of hard rock. So tightly intertwined are the conditions of masculinity and rock music that Simon Frith and Angela McRobbie termed this style "cock rock" because it is

an explicit, crude, and often aggressive expression of male sexuality—it's the style of rock presentation [personified by] Mick Jagger, Roger Daltry, and Robert Plant. . . . [Cock rock] lyrics are assertive and arrogant, though the exact words are less significant than the vocal styles involved, the shouting and screaming.

The cock rock image is the rampant destructive male traveler, smashing hotels and groupies alike. . . . These are the men who take to the streets, take risks, live dangerously and, most of all, swagger untrammeled by responsibility, sexual and otherwise.[7]

Other scholars of rock music might prefer to complicate this rather simplistic summary of a complex musical style,[8] but this thumbnail sketch accurately describes how teenyboppers perceived cock rock and gives a good idea of why we rejected it. We were vaguely puzzled by the rocker girls; while we envied them their social stature, we also thought of them as male-identified victims of false consciousness (although we lacked that vocabulary, of course). Today I recognize that the very "masculinity" of rock is what can make it attractive to girls fed up with the traditional imperatives of femininity. Those rocker girls I found incomprehensible were, quite possibly, making their own statement of emancipation by adopting a style that defied oppressive norms. But to me and my friends at the time, hard rock looked like another extension of the masculine aggression we detested. To be told that our aversion was "immature," and that "real" (i.e., aggressive) masculinity was something we should "grow into" liking, was disturbing.

The message that maturity equaled readiness for assault was echoed by the fact that adult males behaved the same way teen boys did. At thirteen I found myself constantly besieged by men who followed me, shouted at me, commented on my body, offered me rides, wanted to know what I was doing, what my name was, where I lived—an incessant hailstorm of unwanted attention. These would-be Humberts, determined to make me their Lolita, finally drove me away from the public spaces where I had sought recreation. I remember my friends and myself wailing that there was nothing we could do to make the bastards leave us alone. From having enjoyed the anonymity of childhood, we were plunged seemingly overnight into a hostile, male-centered sexual economy that consisted of ritual beatings and undressings at school, sandwiched between two slices of man-on-the-street aggression as we walked to and from home. Unfortunately, this experience does not change relative to race, class, or geographic location: teen girls everywhere, not just in LA, live with very real sexual threats. These threats can have an even more debilitating effect on young girls than they do on women, for girls often lack the inner resources that can help an adult weather assaults with her dignity intact.

How cruel, then, and how very stupid, to ridicule girls for liking "nonthreatening" or "feminine" teen idols. When we consider how masculinity presents itself to girls and the power of the threats it poses, teenybopper fandom looks less like immaturity and more like sound common sense. Shaun Cassidy did not punch our breasts or publicly unharness them, as our classmates did, nor did he shriek about "poontang," as did the performers whose rock was considered more cool. He sang of walking girls home or asking them to "come out tonight" to look at the stars. Even when he celebrated sex, which he did, the veiled lyrics suggested mutual participation instead of subject/object tension ("This will be our night / And I know that we can do it / Do it till we get it right"). Call me crazy, but that sounded more girl-friendly to me than the hunger for power demonstrated by the males around me and represented in hard rock. Teen idol fandom offered me the sole venue in which I could live the feminist promise to control my sexuality, free from the hostile aggression that made female initiative impossible or dangerous in the real world.

Sex and the Single Teenybopper

The magazines we read played an important role in our romantic and sexual fantasy lives. I want to turn briefly to an examination of the sexual ideology of these magazines, which will suggest how important it is to consider change over time in any discussion of teenybopper commodities.

From its inception and for decades thereafter, *16* Magazine maintained a consistent editorial tone that reflected editor Gloria Stavers's respect for, and commitment to, the emotional concerns of her readership:

> [Girls] were too easily led into feeling they had to change themselves to "get" a boy. . . *16*'s editors, whether it was Gloria or any of her successors, tried mightily to infuse whatever self-esteem we could into those readers. "Every girl needs to feel she is worthy, desirable, and has a shot at the object of her affections," Gloria would tell us. She believed that and, to an editor, so did we.[9]

Not merely self-flattery, this statement accurately describes *16*'s editorial practices. *Tiger Beat*, however, had no such commitment. It began as a strictly commercial proposition (from its beginning it accepted outside advertising, which *16* did not), merely one in a stable of glossy teen magazines published by the Laufer company. Its early editors, far from protecting their readership's self-respect, printed some of the ugliest statements about women and romantic relationships I have ever seen in a publication for girls. Consider this description of the marriage of Chad, half of the pop duo Chad and Jeremy, to his bride Jill:

> Jill Stuart is just a little bit of a witch . . . a beautiful witch . . . but a witch at any rate. Chad is just the right husband for Jill and she knows it. He's calm, mature, well organized, and always able to put Jill in her place. . . . Jill gets angry sometimes and pouts like a little girl. When this happens Chad simply treats her like a child until she gets over what's bothering her. He always passes judgment on her clothes and Jill wouldn't think of wearing anything Chad didn't approve of. [Chad gives her] little "love gifts" just for no reason at all. When this happens, Jill purrs like a kitten.[10]

By the early 1970s, *Tiger Beat* had a different editorial team and no longer published such insulting portraits of women and marriage—but at the same time marriage had become a more pervasive feature of the magazine's content. Issues from 1973 reveal an almost total preoccupation with marriage: descriptions of what kind of husband Donny Osmond or David Cassidy would be and what they "looked for in a wife," articles that carried prescriptions for proper feminine behavior but were nonetheless kinder than the offensive description of Jill Stuart.

Tiger Beat's romance orientation in this era was underscored by its utter lack of coverage of female personalities, except for two purposes: either to write monthly columns featuring these stars "squealing on" the boys they worked with (Brady girls squealed on Brady boys; Marie Osmond squealed on Donny and the other Osmond brothers) or to offer beauty and dating advice to readers (in 1972, *Tiger Beat* offered, through mail-order, three separate self-help booklets "by" Susan Dey of *The Partridge Family*). Very rarely did an article discuss a female star's work. This presentation implied that women's careers mattered little and that a girl's only legitimate concern is boys and how to "catch" them.

A sea change had occurred by the late 1970s, however. Aspects of popular feminism had filtered into *Tiger Beat* via its (again) different editorial staff. While boys remained the center of the magazine's project, coverage had increased for female stars, whose activities and personalities received substantial and regular attention. One pictorial piece about actress Valerie Bertinelli took readers on a tour of her home—precisely the same treatment the magazine routinely gave male stars. A photo of Bertinelli in her bedroom, proudly displaying her vast collection of Elton John posters, is captioned: "I think I'm one of the biggest Elton fans in town!"[11] She was a teenybopper just like us, which not only increased a feeling of identification with her but further validated our fandom.

Other female stars received coverage that spoke enthusiastically about their ambitions and talents. Readers were treated to a discussion of how Jaclyn Smith enjoyed investing and managing her finances, concluding with a direct exhortation: "So, the next time you're moaning over your own budget, think of Jackie—she's a super money-manager (and she has fun, too!)"[12] To readers of my generation, girls were boys' equals in the *Tiger Beat* universe; we adored our male idols but, because of the editors' frequent efforts to present female stars as role models, we were also encouraged to see ourselves as able to become competent professionals someday, with or without a man (though "with" was preferable, of course).

At the same time that *Tiger Beat* revised its vision of femininity, it expanded its notions of masculinity, too. In one case, gender distinctions were completely exploded when an advice column—a type of article that had previously always carried a female byline—was done in the voice of boy-idol Robby Benson, thus turning him into the magazine's first male sob sister. Every month he solved readers' "hassles" with school, family, friends, and "boy trouble."[13] This gesture enlisted a boy into the emotional and confessional realms traditionally designated as girl turf, encouraging girls to see male idols as allies, equals, and companions, not merely love objects to be worshiped or "caught." Couched in this context, the somewhat androgynous appearance of teen idols took on another positive signification; it signaled that they were "just like us," our equals in appearance as well as in relationships. Our similarities with them opened new opportunities for identity formation that sidestepped the dangers of "ladyhood" and cock rock alike; we could be something in between by emulating males with a more androgynous aesthetic. That, coupled with the magazine's increasing emphasis on girls' professionalism, taught us a version of the "unisex" philosophy so popular in the 1970s, which implied equality between the sexes.

Old-fashioned romance did not disappear, however. Both *Tiger Beat* and *16* traded regularly in the world of romantic fantasy. A common feature in *16* was a fiction piece that narrated a chance encounter (or some other fantasy scenario) between an idol and an average girl. Meanwhile, *Tiger Beat* and its sister publications told readers what life would be like "If Shaun Were Your Boyfriend." Such an event would guarantee that "he'd ask your opinion when he had an important decision to make. . . . You'd have to be independent at times—Shaun doesn't go for girls who constantly 'cling' to him."[14] While the general tone of such articles trained girls' imaginations along traditionally heterosexual, romantic lines, the inclusion of such feminist-friendly principles as "independence" created a welcoming space for readers like me, for whom feminism was part of the cultural landscape.

Our consumption practices, which were fueled but not limited by what the magazines offered, further militated against strictly traditional interpretations of romance. While *16* and *Tiger Beat* never discussed sex explicitly, the hints were sufficient to justify our assumption of sex as a central element of fandom. Color photographs, which the magazines always called "kissable color pin-ups," often showed idols shirtless or posed in bathing suits. One friend recently told me that, when his older sister read *Tiger Beat*, he and his friends used to flip through issues and laughingly call it "Tiger Beat-Off" because of its display of pretty boys' bodies. The magazine's lack of explicit sex clearly did not impede anyone from understanding what was implicitly being offered. In some regards, *16* and *Tiger Beat* served a similar function for us that *Playboy* did for boys, including the fact that the most privileged photographic space was the centerfold. While any idol might merit a half-page color photo or a one-page pin-up, only the true favorite of the day occupied the centerfold poster. We especially liked those posters because their larger size allowed for more coverage; they often showed the boy's body from head to toe, or head to knee, which placed his crotch at the center. The tightly packed jeans fashionable in the 1970s turned such posters into a banquet of delights, giving us fodder for countless hours of happy ponderings.

Scholars have not yet explored this connection between soft-core pornography and celebrity teen magazines as "his and her" versions of the same phenomenon, although it has always seemed obvious to me. I cannot believe that my friends and I were the only girls in the history of the world to react as we did; surely thousands of teenyboppers, particularly in the sex-drenched 1970s, found themselves similarly aroused while gazing at (slightly) suggestive images of their idols. The failure of adults to recognize this likelihood speaks less to the real meanings of such magazines than it does to our cultural myths about male and female sexuality. When "Junior" starts stashing *Playboy* under his bed, we generally accept that moment as an initiation, signaling the boy's arrival at a mature level of sexuality. But when girls the same age read *Tiger Beat* and plaster their bedrooms with posters of boys they find "sexy," conventional wisdom interprets this as signaling girls' lack of maturity. Thus we see how a powerful ideology (young girls' supposed asexuality) can obscure what should be obvious evidence to the contrary. The construction of "girlish innocence" is at once dangerous and insulting; it is dangerous because teen girls' innocence is highly fetishized by our culture, and the construction of that fetish leads often to males' feeling entitled to scrutinize and consume our "budding" sexuality (as did the Humberts who harassed me). It is insulting because it simultaneously implies that girls' sexuality is merely an adorable, miniature facsimile of the real thing—a cherry tomato, as it were.

In fact, much of the bonding among my cohort was achieved through sexually inflected forms of communication. The girl-meets-idol fiction printed in *16* prompted us to start writing stories for each other, which we called "funnies." The idea was to concoct a story about Shaun and your friend (not yourself—the stories were social acts, not merely self-serving fantasies). Each funny was highly pornographic in nature. Borrowing the conventions of plot and pacing that we found in *16*'s squeaky-clean stories, we turned ours into riots of good-spirited filth and presented them to each other as gifts. Mindful of snooping parents who might see our typewriters or listen to our phone conversations, we crafted a secret code with which to communicate our funnies with discretion. Named "Mercedes," after the make of car Shaun drove, our code assigned unrelated sexual meanings to regular words ("smoking," for example, meant having intercourse). We could thus speak and write sentences that had an innocent surface meaning and a sexual hidden one.

Dating and marriage had no part in these funnies—we wanted to sleep with Shaun but didn't care whether or not we married him. Yet the inspiration for our masterpieces derived entirely from images and stories in our magazines, which, though less acutely than in earlier years, still oriented themselves toward a conventionally "romantic" worldview. Through our creative practices we read against the grain, transforming the largely innocent tone of these publications into a safe setting for expressing a sexual interest as gritty as any boy's. Thus we could avoid the definitions of sexuality offered in the cock-rock world, where our rocker-girl classmates were used and abused while "Dazed and Confused." What girl in her right mind, we wondered, would want sex while practically unconscious, with brutal and idiotic boys who might not talk to her later? We built a space where we could be sexual on our terms, with no expectations that we leave our cultural turf and turn ourselves over to someone else. The promises of feminism came true for us only within this milieu of fandom.

"Inferior" Rebels with a Cause

A chain of associations links derogation of teen idols themselves, their music, and their fans. The music itself is worth considering, since this was the second line of attack—after idols' facial "prettiness"—that everyone employed in their assaults on our fandom. Despite other radical differences, adults and rocker teens united in believing that teen-idol music was intrinsically bad and that our consumption of it proved our "immaturity": just as it supposedly signaled our unreadiness for real males, so it supposedly signaled our unreadiness for real music.

The reasons for such condemnation differed, however. Rockers hated teen-idol music because it opposed the style that defined their own subjectivity project. This was why girls who preferred The Who, Led Zeppelin, and Ted Nugent treated us as bugs to be crushed. Liz's catty question about "poontang" was merely the mildest form of assault; I routinely suffered far worse, including having the phrase "Shaun's a fag" scribbled on my locker, my jacket, and any other item I left unattended. Kids shouted the phrase at me as we dashed through crowded hallways. One day, fed up, I screamed back "so are you" in the general direction where a voice had come from. I learned the consequences of self-defense after school that day when an enormous, pituitarily challenged girl named Celeste identified herself as the shouter of the comment and sincerely offered to beat the crap out of me. Bathrooms, too, were dangerous places where, amid "Zep Rules!" graffiti, girls would corner and kick me, murmuring sotto voce encouragements that I commit suicide as a public service.

My teenybopper friends suffered less abuse because they took seriously the threats to their safety and reputations, allowing Idolphobia to keep them "in the closet." I resented their cowardice and insisted on wearing Shaun t-shirts and buttons to school, publicly proclaiming my identity. Living with terrorism was a small price to pay—indeed, it fired my imagination to see myself as a brave martyr for my cause. This was what my fourth grade renditions of "I Am Woman" had prepared me for, a perfect example of theory put to practice ("You can bend but never break me," Reddy sang). Nicer peers saw me in the same light: my yearbook contains some heartfelt messages from kids of both sexes, praising my fortitude in sticking up for my convictions as a Shaun fan. Of course, those convictions did not resemble the cause of feminism as adult women defined it at the time—but *I* felt that my daily drama was part of the feminist struggle, and I took solace and inspiration from the image of the feminist.

My peers' vicious treatment of me suggests just how threatened rocker girls felt by the world of teenybop. To them, I must have represented every cultural force that was trying to drag them backward into the stereotypes of "childish" femininity. I recognize that now and forgive them because all of us fought our own battles to forge identities for ourselves. But these motivations don't explain why teenyboppers received so little respect from adults, whose contempt, while less violent, was more pervasive. Adult music critics and commentators attacked our tastes for reasons inflected with the same politics as those of rocker teens; in my lifetime, cock rock has always been granted more legitimacy as an "authentic" expression of youthful angst and as an art form than teen-idol music. But another reason lurked as well: some of their attacks came simply from ageist and sexist prejudices. That condemnation continues even in today's academy, in this enlightened era of scholarly recovery of Girls' Studies and Youth Culture, where I am bemused by how often I hear savvy scholars joining the rest of the world in calling teen-idol music "bad." Although they neither realize that they are doing this nor (usually) intend to do it, such scholars and other cultural commentators are participating in an unexamined oppression of young girls.

When questioned, they might explain their judgment by saying that teen-idol music deserves derogation because it is "formulaic," "pre-packaged," and "predictable," and that its singers are "talentless pretty faces." Precisely the same charges could be leveled against decades of Hollywood "starlets" who, while not taken seriously as actresses, are not often excoriated with the same uniform and vicious degree of contempt as teen idols are. I would suggest that idols' presumed lack of talent is not the problem—their audience is. Starlets are consumed by men and boys, teen idols by young girls. Art forms and cultural products identified as "for women" have always been less respected by our society than those identified as "for men." A pin-up idol for girls, then, is reviled more than a pin-up idol for boys.

But the youth of teenyboppers matters just as much as their femininity in explaining society's contempt for them. The teenybop music that critics find so "predictable" and "commercial," and which fans are thus expected to "outgrow," is in fact quite similar to any other form of mass-marketed pop music—and yet pop, broadly defined, receives a quieter form of contempt; often it is simply ignored by commentators who vocally crack wise about teen idols. Yet the musical values of pop and teen pop are very similar: an emphasis on expressive lyrics and pleasant voices that sing tuneful melodies, often with harmonies, about emotional subjects. These aesthetic values were paramount in my own consumption of Shaun Cassidy, who had a professionally trained baritone (hardly "talentless") and whose melodic songs employed emotional or poetically-evocative lyrics. Today I still enjoy those qualities, and I'm not alone; millions of adult women consume music that structurally, lyrically, and melodically resembles what they loved as teens. These facts lay bare the absurdity of stating that teen-idol music is somehow "immature" and must be outgrown. If people resonate at forty to the same aesthetics that stirred them at fourteen, then obviously "maturity" becomes a moot factor in analyzing the music's appeal.

Moreover, some critics and commentators are reclaiming the value of "bubblegum" music (sometimes linked with teen-idol music but sometimes distinguished as even further down the ladder of cultural legitimacy) by celebrating such features as the prodigious talents of its producers and its influence on other musical forms, including punk.[15] The aesthetic and political rulebooks, which often have separated "good/authentic" youth music from "bad/commercial" youth music, have begun to disintegrate, which proves how much teen-idol derogation is a cultural construct with its own politics to hide. The claim of idol-music's inherent invalidity is merely a front for what critics really consider invalid: young girls, the single least respected group among middle-class whites. If such a statement sounds overly bold, consider this fact: Gloria Stavers, editor of *16*, was nicknamed by her colleagues in the publishing industry as "the Mother Superior of the Inferior."[16] Youth exacerbates femininity, creating a double whammy of inferiority.

In the history of the "teenage girl," her most salient feature has been manic instability. Films, radio and television programs, newspapers, magazines, and every other form of mass cultural discourse over the last seventy years have constructed young teenage girls as silly, hyperbolic creatures who don't really know their own minds (if they have any). I can state without reservation that the single worst element of being teenage girls was that nobody gave us any credit for meaning what we said, for being serious, or for having a right to our tastes. Stupid little girls liked this music; that alone explained why it had to be "bad." If girls' perspectives received any respect from their culture, this charge would not be leveled so uniformly. That is why teen-idol fandom can feel like a feminist project for its participants: it asserts the values of an oppressed group and demands that girls' subjectivities be heard. Often, adults hear without listening; they dismiss girls' impassioned cri de coeur by constructing it within the old paradigm of females and their "hysteria." As Sheryl Garratt has said, "It is the sound of young women, not 'hysterical schoolgirls' as one reporter would have it—a scream of defiance, celebration, and excitement."[17]

Garratt only quotes "one reporter" demeaning girls' so-called hysteria, but she could have quoted thousands. It is by far the most common rhetorical gesture in all adult writing about teen idols and their fans. In my scrapbook of clippings is one article I remember feeling ambivalent about including, entitled "If Only I Knew Shaun Cassidy's Favorite Color, My Life Would Be Complete." The journalist, clearly irritated by his assignment to cover a Cassidy press conference, transferred his irritation to the girls who were present:

The foolish little hearts of Sharon, 13, and Linda, 12, were beating at a furious pace. It was Shaun Cassidy time at the Capital Centre. . . . The Centre was being over-run by a little army of girls in their early teens carrying "I Love Shaun" signs and quite prepared to keel over dead at the sight of The Promised One. I could only think of acne and orthodontic braces. There were blank stares in their vacant eyes, and their lungs were full of incredible power and range, like 10 million crazed locusts settled in a patch.[18]

I preserved this article in my scrapbook, but my friends and I disliked it. Animal metaphors work both ways: the snotty writer thought girls were "locusts," but we thought he was a Male Chauvinist Pig.

Adult journalism was full of such pigs, and the sounds of their snorting and snuffling marred their coverage of our idols. That was what made *16* and *Tiger Beat* so valuable. Only in those magazines could we find our tastes and our feelings treated as "just so," as facts that required no explanation, criticism, or apology. These magazines gave us a room of our own into which we could retreat from the chorus of contempt we received from other teens and adults alike. In the pages of *16* and *Tiger Beat* we found allies who believed, just as we did, that Shaun's favorite color was a valid piece of knowledge and did not merit any mockery.

There's no denying that *16*, *Tiger Beat*, and their host of lesser imitators functioned primarily to serve and to shape traditional, heterosexual romantic fantasies among their female readerships. But the history of for-girls-only popular culture is full of such contradictions; the very first teen-girl magazines of the 1940s, the Girl-Group music of the 1960s, and the teenybopper fandom of the 1970s all divided their time between replicating the dominant gender ideology and simultaneously offering something new. One lesson this history should teach us is that girls' options have always been so limited that girls have gladly embraced any phenomenon plausibly reflecting "their" reality. Their enthusiasm bespeaks an enormous hunger for representation, to be taken seriously and to be listened to, which adult cultural producers feed by proffering compromise-meals: part nutritious, to replicate adult society's patriarchal institutions, and part delicious, to give girls the fun of seeing their perspectives represented. My friends and I surely did not escape learning the traditional imperatives of heterosexual romance that these magazines and the general practices of idol-fandom drummed into our young brains. But, at the same time, we gained something new: a safe space (the *only* safe space) in which we could express an aggressive sexuality that no one else felt we had a right to, and a means for asserting ourselves against a world that called us inferior.

The problems we faced were the problems of how to formulate a subjectivity—how to imagine ourselves, how to negotiate contradictions in received roles, how to live in the rift between self-perception and others' perceptions. These were the same problems older feminists faced, as well. For all its limitations and repetitions of patriarchal structures, fandom gave us the means to participate in a feminist struggle. Assisted by the historically and geographically specific conditions that affected us, we came to terms with a subject-position (girlhood) that was debased by our culture, learning to expand and recuperate that identity for a more satisfying existence and battling the oppressors who stood in our way. None of the adult feminists I heard of, then or later, saw these connections between their struggles and ours—but we did. And, for a little while at least, the world heard us roar.

Chapter 10

Reevaluating "Jiggle TV"
Charlie's Angels *at Twenty-Five*

W H I T N E Y W O M A C K

The year 2001 marked the twenty-fifth anniversary of the debut of *Charlie's Angels*, a show often cited as the nadir of 1970s popular culture. When the show premiered on September 22, 1976, it was an instant hit, earning an amazing 59 percent share in the Nielsen ratings, a feat now achieved only by such special events as the Super Bowl.[1] It did well with a variety of audiences, including women and college graduates, not just, in Susan Douglas's words, "slavering fourteen-year-old boys."[2] Just one month after the show's premiere, the three Angels—Kate Jackson, Jaclyn Smith, and Farrah Fawcett—graced the cover of *Time* magazine under the title "TV's Superwomen" and instantly became America's new "It" girls.[3]

In 1976 I was six years old, but even the first grade was abuzz with talk of these tough but glamorous crime fighters. Tragically for me, *Charlie's Angels* aired on Wednesdays at 9:00 P.M (CST), an hour past my bedtime on a school night. I remember begging and pleading, crying hysterically, and making endless promises to clean my room in return for the rare privilege of staying up to watch the show. Even though I was not a regular viewer, the show had a major influence on my life. My friends and I used to play *Charlie's Angels* after school, solving neighborhood and schoolyard "crimes"; I always chose to play Sabrina—the smartest and coolest of the Angels. I eventually cajoled my family into buying me *Charlie's Angels* paper dolls, action figures, and trading cards, as well as a *Charlie's Angels* lunchbox and Halloween costume (a Sabrina mask, of course). My most treasured possession was a plastic bust of Farrah Fawcett, complete with her trademark feathered hairdo and blindingly white smile.[4]

At the time, I was unaware of the cultural debates raging about *Charlie's Angels*. The Angels' often tight and skimpy outfits and the show's frequent tits-and-ass shots earned the show the infamous label "Jiggle TV." While media critics generally dismissed the show as pure schlock, many feminist critics openly attacked the series, claiming it was the ultimate example of the exploitation of women on television and a direct affront to the increasingly powerful women's liberation movement of the 1970s. By 1976 the women's movement had gained widespread acknowledgment, if not always acceptance, and the National Organization for Women and other groups were actively campaigning for ratification of the Equal Rights Amendment. Commentators like Judith Coburn believed that *Charlie's Angels*, which she described as "one of the most misogynist shows the networks have produced recently," were a backlash against feminism. She compared the relationship of Charlie Townsend, the international man of mystery who owns Townsend Investigations, and the Angels to that of a "pimp and his girls. Charlie dispatches his streetwise girls to use their sexual wiles on the world while he reaps the profits."[5] The Angels, she asserted, are being shoved back into the kind of subordinate and sexualized roles from which feminists had worked to break free. Other feminists, both in the 1970s and today, have objected to the virtually unattainable ideal of thinness and beauty that the size-four Angels represented. *Stick Figure*, Lori Gottlieb's diary account of her struggle with an eating disorder in 1978, bears this out. Gottlieb writes that watching the "skinny Angels [made] me feel fat," and tells her parents she would only stop dieting "if the Angels, instead of fat people like Dr. Katz and Dr. Gold" told her she was too thin.[6] More recently, Naomi Wolf, Bonnie Dow, and Joan Jacobs Brumberg have examined the ways that such media images increase girls' and women's anxiety and insecurity about their bodies.[7]

I don't wish to dismiss all feminist criticism of *Charlie's Angels*, but these critics largely overlook what I saw and identified with in the show as a child: images of female intelligence, strength, solidarity, and community. My mother, who was in graduate school and involved in women's liberation causes at the time, was working to instill in me many of the same feminist principles represented in the show, especially women's right to equality in school and the workplace. They may have been "Angels" (an admittedly belittling, even infantilizing label), but they were at least not Angels in the House, which was the ideal still being represented at home and in the mass media to most girls in the 1970s.[8] Sabrina Duncan (Jackson), Kelly Garrett (Smith), and Jill Munroe (Fawcett) were represented as highly trained and well-paid professionals working in a nontraditional field for women. They came to work for the disembodied patriarch Charlie in order to escape sexism at the Los Angeles Police Department. Charlie actually empowered them to use their skills as investigators and, except for his occasional speakerphone chats, left them alone to do their work. These women had to work closely and watch one another's backs, especially during their undercover missions, and did so without engaging in stereotypical "catfights." Certainly many feminists objected to the Angels' using their sex appeal as a tool to nail sexist male suspects, regularly referred to by the Angels as "male chauvinist pigs," most of whom were guilty of hurting or oppressing other women. But it should be noted that we more often witnessed the Angels employing their intelligence, physical strength, and sharpshooting expertise on the job.

Importantly, the Angels led independent lives. Kelly and Jill were unmarried and Sabrina was divorced, yet none of them seemed particularly obsessed with finding a husband or "settling down." With their own money, they bought hip clothes and fast cars, including Jill's white Cobra with black racing stripes. Despite their thinness and physical beauty, the Angels were at least real, flesh-and-blood women, unlike two other female icons of the 1970s, Wonder Woman and the Bionic Woman, both of whom had unattainable supernatural powers. Even as a child I recognized that it was unlikely that I was ever going to have bionic body parts like Jamie Sommers, though I did ask for them for Christmas one year, or magic bracelets like Diana Prince.[9]

In her study *Where the Girls Are: Growing Up Female with the Mass Media*, media scholar Susan Douglas argues that *Charlie's Angels* was so popular because "it exploited, perfectly, the tensions between antifeminism and feminism" in American culture during the mid-1970s.[10] Douglas claims that rather than deny the feminist impulses that undergird the program, we should examine why certain feminist principles were deemed safe and mainstream enough to put on the airwaves, while others were still seen as too threatening during the show's 1976–81 run. The enduring popularity of the series is witnessed by its successful syndication on the cable networks TNT and TV Land, Columbia/Tri-Star's release of a home video collection of *Charlie's Angels* "classics," the creation of dozens of fan websites, and the publication of Jack Condon and David Hofstede's *Charlie's Angels Casebook*.

The popularity of the series culminated in a big-screen version of *Charlie's Angels* in 2000. The film focuses on the lives of three new recruits at Townsend Investigations: Dylan Sanders (Drew Barrymore), Natalie Cook (Cameron Diaz), and Alex Munday (Lucy Liu). As a diehard *Charlie's Angels* fan, I rushed to see the film, despite the tag line in the trailer: "Get Some Action." I was clearly not alone in my desire to see the 1970s show resurrected; the film raked in $40.1 million its opening weekend, the second highest non-summer movie opening in box-office history.[11] But I found it was not a remake or revision of the series but an over-the-top parody. While claiming to pay homage to the original series, the film instead exaggerates and mocks the series' excesses and retains virtually none of its feminist sensibilities. Feminism is replaced with a sort of watered down, Spice Girls brand of substanceless "girl power" that in many ways promotes rather than undermines traditional gender codes. While the original series is predicated on a hard-fought challenge to the patriarchal power structure of the police department, the new Angels aren't even trained police officers. Due to actor/producer Drew Barrymore's objection to gun violence, the new Angels no longer carry weapons; they now rely on high-tech, James Bond-style gadgetry and gravity-defying martial arts. Further, the film focuses far more than the series on the Angels' private lives, especially their romantic relationships, and emphasizes their feminine attributes and even their domestic skills—returning us in many ways to the Angel in the House model of womanhood.

In this essay I examine the ways that *Charlie's Angels*—both the first season of the series with the original Angels and the 2000 feature film—engages in dialogues about women's empowerment and represents popular culture's continuing uneasy relationship with the "f" word—feminism.[12] Ironically, the original series, so reviled by feminists at the time, is much more direct in its discussions of feminist issues than the recent film. Despite its popular theme song, "Independent Women, Part 1" by girl group Destiny's Child,[13] the 2000 version of *Charlie's Angels* is part of a popular backlash against feminism. While the original series embodied cultural tensions between feminism and antifeminism, the remake reveals contemporary tensions between feminism and what is being termed "postfeminism"—the notion that the need for an activist feminist movement has passed.

"Hello, Angels": *Charlie's Angels,* 1976–77

It is fair to say that *Charlie's Angels* did not set out to raise America's feminist consciousness. The series was produced by Aaron Spelling, the man behind such other eye-candy programs as *Starsky and Hutch, The Love Boat, Fantasy Island, T. J. Hooker, Beverly Hills, 90210,* and *Melrose Place.* The original concept for *Charlie's Angels* was a show entitled *Alley Cats,* starring three female detectives named Allison (Al), Lee, and Catherine (Cat), thus the title. *Alley Cats* was meant to capitalize on the popularity of 1970s detective shows like *The Rockford Files* and the new acceptance of female action series like *Police Woman.*[14] After reading the proposal for *Alley Cats,* ABC executive and later media mogul Barry Diller complained, "three beautiful girls running around, chasing criminals . . . it's not believable. It's terrible. Forget it."[15] The show went forward, but test audiences were lukewarm about the pilot's decidedly nonfeminist depictions of the Angels and urged producers to make the women "more intelligent and capable, rather than . . . three dumb models who get themselves into trouble."[16] Hollywood had underestimated the American public's desire for depictions of strong, independent women.

The back story about the Angels' defection from the LAPD, presented over the title credits of each episode, was created in order to give the

Angels more substance and credibility as crime fighters. Ironically, though, the story is presented like a child's fairy tale, a perfect example of feminism and antifeminism being presented simultaneously to the audience. The Angels sound as if they are simply Cinderella figures who had been awaiting male rescue: "Once upon a time, there were three little girls who went to the police academy, and they were each assigned very hazardous duties. But I took them away from all that, and now they work for me. My name is Charlie." But the visual images complicate this condescending voiceover spoken by Charlie, played by actor John Forsythe of *Dynasty* fame. They may be called "little girls" and look like Barbie dolls, but we are presented with visual images of tough women: Sabrina (the intelligent Angel) performs expertly at target practice; Jill (the athletic Angel) breezes through rigorous, military-style physical training; and Kelly (the streetwise Angel) dominates a male officer in self-defense class. Of course, to make sure that they don't look too masculine, the police rookies inexplicably have carefully coifed hair, manicures, and full makeup during these activities, thus underlining the tension between feminism and antifeminism that Douglas describes.

The reference in the title credits to "hazardous duties" is sarcastic, since the only jobs the police department gives them are menial, subordinate, and traditionally feminine ones: Jill has a desk job as a typist; Kelly is a crossing guard at a school crosswalk; Sabrina is a meter maid giving out parking tickets. The message to women is clear: even if you have excellent training and job skills, you still won't be given the opportunity to advance to senior or management positions. This representation of the "glass ceiling" must have struck a chord with women, who in the 1970s were joining or returning to the workforce in record numbers. Ironically, in the final episode of the first season, entitled "The Blue Angels," Chief Fenton, the same police chief who "detested the idea of police academy rookies [of the] feminine gender," hires the Angels to investigate a case of police corruption in the vice squad. Charlie announces that perhaps their work on the case can end this "bastion of sexism."

Admittedly, it is problematic that the Angels have to be rescued from this drudgery by a man, with Charlie cast in the role of fairy godmother to our Cinderellas. It would have made for a very different show if these three women had decided to sue the LAPD for gender discrimination or had created a detective agency on their own. Presumably Charlie is more progressive and enlightened than the police bureaucracy. Yet at the same time Charlie is a jet-setting millionaire and Hugh Hefner-ish playboy who is too busy globetrotting and chasing beautiful women to visit his office or meet his Angels face to face. Susan Douglas claims that Charlie embodies a traditional father figure, "commanding, unseen, permeating everything." He is also, in Douglas's words, "a complete lech, a trait we're supposed to find endearing."[17] He doesn't pursue the Angels sexually, since he's never there in person, but his dialogue is full of sexual references and innuendoes. Most episodes end with a glimpse of Charlie (or, usually, just the back of his head or his hand) offering his excuses for not joining the Angels to celebrate solving their most recent case; he is inevitably in an exotic, sun-drenched locale with a beautiful woman nearby. His dialogue is full of double entendres; in one episode a buxom woman climbs out of the pool and Charlie quips, "something just came up," while in another episode a sexy woman wearing a pair of plumber's coveralls leads him to comment that someone is "cleaning my pipes."

Even so, Charlie does enable the Angels to use their police training and grants them autonomy to do their work, although he does choose which cases they will take. The one man physically among them, Bosley, played by David Doyle, is an avuncular figure; Douglas claims he is the "eunuch" watching over Charlie's harem.[18] In the guidelines given to the series writers, the producers are insistent that Bosley be given only a supporting role: the Angels, they note, are "capable of doing practically everything a man can do (and *more*)"—a sharp contrast to the assumptions that the LAPD makes about women's crime-fighting abilities.[19] Bosley is bumbling and ineffectual, a source of comic relief and the butt of the jokes of the obviously smarter and savvier women in the office. For example, even at the end of the episode "Night of the Strangler," Bosley is still baffled about the identity of the "rag-doll killer." The women shoot each other sly glances and explain the whole case to him again slowly, as if speaking to a child. Unlike Pepper Anderson in *Police Woman*, who was regularly saved by her male partner, the Angels had to cooperate and depend on one another for assistance in emergencies, which, of course, happened every week. During the "Night of the Strangler" case, for instance, Sabrina finds herself in real danger of being raped by the fashion photographer/pornographer she suspects of being the "strangler"; it is Kelly, not Bosley or Charlie, who bursts in to help her. Sabrina comments that if Kelly had been "a few minutes later, I might have been defiled by that creep."

This scene of attempted rape is interesting for several reasons. It confronts head-on what would have been one of the LAPD's justifications for keeping women cops out of the field—their vulnerability to rape—and shows how Sabrina, with the help of Kelly, effectively handles the situation. Yet the scene could also be read as a sort of backlash against the Angels and their use of sex appeal on the job. In her discussion of *Police Woman*, Douglas notes that the rape victims on the show were inevitably depicted as somehow "asking for it" by their occupation (stripper, nude model) or by their sexy appearance.[20] All too many police officers and prosecutors in the 1970s did treat rape victims in just this way, leading feminists to make rape prevention a vital issue in the women's rights movement; indeed,

Susan Brownmiller's groundbreaking feminist work *Against Our Will: Men, Women, and Rape* was published in 1975, just a year before *Charlie's Angels* premiered. Although Sabrina does flirt with the photographer and go back to his bachelor pad, her unequivocal reaction to his unwanted advances, I believe, ultimately works to counteract the notion that rape victims somehow "ask for it" and reinforces Brownmiller's argument that rape is about "the perpetuation of male domination over women by force."[21]

In many ways the standard *Charlie's Angels* episode plot is a feminist fantasy of female community and sisterhood, of women helping other women to defy patriarchal oppression. The Angels are hired to rescue or vindicate a woman who has been in some way oppressed by a male villain. The victimized woman is usually lower class or in some other way marginalized or voiceless; the Angels, then, act as advocates for these women, whose cases, we are led to believe, would otherwise be ignored or left unsolved by a police department that doesn't take women's lives and concerns seriously. According to Douglas, these plots "suggested a female bond across class barriers that many feminists were trying to achieve in real life" and ultimately "affirmed the importance of sisterly love."[22] In her study *Tough Girls: Women Warriors and Wonder Women in Popular Culture*, Sherrie A. Inness argues, however, that these plots tend to "emphasize the weakness of women," since all women except the Angels seem "powerless in the face of a male threat."[23] In order to crack the case, the Angels would go undercover, donning new identities and, of course, new outfits that allowed them to get close to witnesses and suspects. These missions often take them into spaces and professions where their gender actually gives them an edge over male cops or detectives. In the first season alone they go undercover at a women's prison, a roller derby, a beauty pageant, several fashion shows, a massage parlor/brothel, a Playboy-like men's club, and a nursing school. It is interesting to see the empowered Angels go back into the traditionally feminine sphere and take on subservient roles during their investigations. Although they can successfully dress and act the part, they also express their frustrations about the limitations of this world as well as their desire to "free" all of the women involved (particularly in the "Angels in Chains" episode).

The label "Jiggle TV" has led to the assumption that the Angels spent most of their time running around in bathing suits or tube tops. In fact, most of their clothes are surprisingly chaste. When they are not working undercover, the Angels are far more often found in modest turtlenecks or wide-collared polyester pantsuits than in hot pants (see Figure 1). One of the show's promotional photos has the Angels in long-sleeved blouses, A-line skirts, simple gold jewelry, and sensible pumps, the 1970s dress-for-success uniform for women in corporate America. While I don't deny or

Figure 1. Beyond tube tops and hot pants: the Angels in their modest business attire. *Charlie's Angels*, Columbia/Tri-Star Pictures, 1976.

endorse the show's penchant for titillating outfits like Jill's satin roller derby ensemble or Kelly's itty-bitty white bikini at a fashion shoot, these outfits are nonetheless given a context and play a part in solving the mission at hand.

In one of the most damning criticisms of *Charlie's Angels*, Judith Coburn argues that the show "perpetuates the myth most damaging to women's struggle to gain professional equality: that women always use sex to get what they want, even on the job."[24] It's true that the Angels use their beauty and sex appeal (along with their wits and their guns) to help solve cases. But I don't think it is at all clear that the Angels *agree* with this practice or endorse a patriarchal society that leaves women with their sexuality as their primary weapon to get ahead. It is important to note that the men who treat them like sex objects *never* get away with it; sexism is clearly a punishable offense in the world of *Charlie's Angels*. In the episode "To Kill an Angel," for instance, Jill and Sabrina flirt with a sweaty, lascivious print shop owner in order to gain a vital piece of information about the identity of an autistic boy who has witnessed a murder. The man offers to help them in exchange for posing in a magazine he is putting together, which is not, he confesses, quite as "classy as *Playboy* or *Penthouse*." Jill cocks her head, flashes her 100-watt smile, and coyly asks if he'll provide her the information if she takes off her clothes. Just as he, and presumably the viewers, start contemplating this idea, Jill turns to Sabrina and asks whether or not they should arrest him for criminal solicitation. After he figures out that they are "some kind of policewomen or something," he is suddenly docile and cooperative, giving the crucial clue that they need. While he is not arrested (they are, after all, no longer police officers with powers of arrest), he is presumably chastened by the experience. Often these men find themselves on the wrong end of the Angels' conveniently purse-sized snub-nosed revolvers, which the Angels are not afraid to use. One of the most frequently used lines in the show is "Freeze, turkey," as the Angels corner one of the bad guys.

The fourth episode, "Angels in Chains," provides a perfect example of the emphasis in *Charlie's Angels* on exposing and destroying sexist institutions and practices. Yet it is also the most notorious episode of the show, described by *Time* magazine at the time as "raunchy" and "family-style porn."[25] After a vivid description of the episode, the writer asks "What is this? A report on the latest skin flick? A case study of the fantasy life of a troubled adolescent? Nope. Just a plot summary from the hottest new television show of the season" (67). While the media focused on the episode's titillation factor, especially a scene where the Angels are nude, they almost entirely overlook the content of the episode. It begins with the suspicious disappearance of a young, beautiful woman named Elizabeth after she was arrested on trumped-up drug charges in backwater Louisiana. The Angels' first job is to get arrested so they can go undercover in the Pine Parish Prison Farm for Women to find out what happened to her. As they drive through the town, the trio are pulled over for speeding by a leering, cigar-chomping sheriff who eyes them up and down before planting a plastic bag of marijuana in their car. Without being read their Miranda rights or being tried in a court of law, they are taken straight to the prison, where the sheriff cryptically notes to the warden that they've "hit the jackpot with these three, especially the blonde." The infamous nudity, which of course is just hinted at, not actually shown, takes the form of a strip search and delousing process conducted by a stereotypically butch prison matron named Maxine (Max), who leers at Jill and calls Sabrina "sweet cakes." What makes the scene less than titillating, though, is the fact that the Angels refuse to let this embarrass or humiliate them. They look straight ahead defiantly; Kelly even asks Maxine "when was the last time you were sprayed?"

The Angels, in drab denim prison uniforms but with their lip gloss still intact, soon learn why pretty women are arrested in record numbers in Pine Parish—a prison-run prostitution ring. Given slinky cocktail dresses and feather boas to wear, the Angels are selected to go to a "party" for prison suppliers that is hosted by the female warden/madam. Jill is able to find out from one of these men (who luckily falls asleep before anything sexual can happen) that Elizabeth had tried to escape, and that "if they caught her, she's dead." The Angels themselves soon face the same fate once the warden finds out about and eliminates their inside contact, a sympathetic deputy, and catches Sabrina trying to make a phone call; the sheriff is ordered to "take them where they won't be found." Even though they are shackled together, the Angels manage to cooperate and coordinate their movements to escape from the sheriff, wade through a swamp, and steal a potato truck, which leads to a big chase sequence—all without their weapons and without back-up, since Bosley is largely absent from this episode (see Figure 2). We learn at the end of the episode that, although the Angels were not able to save Elizabeth, their work has helped tear down this unjust and sexist system: the brutish prison officials are indicted, the falsely imprisoned women are released, and the governor of Louisiana promises a full inquiry into the state prison system and sends the Angels a commendation. The Angels also provide a helping hand to one of the former inmates (played by Kim Basinger) by hiring her as the receptionist for Townsend Investigations; she's never seen again on the series, however.

There were examples of the tension between feminism and antifeminism behind the scenes of *Charlie's Angels* as well. At the end of the first season, Farrah Fawcett demanded that the producers raise her salary to $70,000 a week and reduce her work hours to six hours a day or she would walk. Fawcett and Smith, who were relative television newcomers, were each earning only $5,000 a week, while Jackson, who had previously starred in *Dark Shadows* and *The Rookies*, was making $10,000 a week. Male action stars like Fawcett's then-husband Lee Majors, star of *The Six Million*

Figure 2. The controversial episode: the Angels escape from a corrupt, sexist jail. *Charlie's Angels*, Columbia/Tri-Star Pictures, 1976.

Dollar Man, were making over $50,000 a week.[26] Even Lindsey Wagner, star of *The Bionic Woman*, was paid an astounding $500,000 for the 1976–77 season.[27] By 1977 Fawcett was an international superstar due to her role in the series, for which she had just been given the People's Choice Award for Best Newcomer, and due to her famous red swimsuit pin-up poster, which hung on the bedroom walls of countless teenage boys during the 1970s. Her motivation for this fight with the producers was not so much a feminist battle for equal pay but a conflict with Fawcett's husband, who wanted her to be a more traditional, stay-at-home wife. Majors complained to Fawcett's agent, Jay Bernstein, that "when I get up in the morning she's already gone [and] when I get home she's still not back," and demanded that she get shorter work hours or leave the show.[28] While onscreen Fawcett may have been able to depict a liberated woman, in real life she was being pressured to conform to cultural norms of femininity and to stay in her "proper" sphere. The ensuing legal battle over breach of contract ended in a settlement that had Fawcett leave the show but return for periodic guest appearances, for which she was reportedly paid far more than her previous salary for a full season, and which led to increases in the other Angels' salaries. The next season, audiences learned that Jill had left to become a professional race car driver, another nontraditional though rather far-fetched profession for a woman, and that her younger but equally perky sister Kris (Cheryl Ladd) had taken her place at the agency. Ironically, Fawcett's and Majors's marriage ended not long after her decision to leave the show to spend more time at home, and she spent years trying to return to the level of stardom she had achieved with *Charlie's Angels*.

"Angels Forever": *Charlie's Angels* 2000

Although we often find it laughable today, *Charlie's Angels* clearly appealed to 1970s audiences and even earned the grudging respect of the industry, which nominated Kate Jackson and David Doyle for Emmy awards. Even after its cancellation in 1981, the show refused to die, gaining a whole new generation of fans through reruns that aired five days a week. Aaron Spelling made a much-hyped attempt to resurrect the show, retitled *Angels '88*. The new plot twist was that the Angels (four of them this time) weren't really detectives; they just played them on TV. When their television show is cancelled, they decide to open their own detective agency, despite a complete lack of skills, training, or police experience—the very qualities that made the original Angels' characters compelling.[29] Spelling, however, claimed that the new Angels were "more liberated" because they wouldn't take orders from Charlie: "It's an entire ladies' show without guidance. It's a young ladies' buddy-buddy show is what it is."[30] The show, however, never made it past the pilot. Exactly why viewers rejected the show is not entirely clear, though we can speculate that they were no longer interested in programs that embodied the 1970s tension between feminism and antifeminism and perhaps expected to see portrayals of truly independent, competent women.

The idea to make a silver screen version of *Charlie's Angels* was not a novel one. The 1990s were full of remakes of former television shows, including *The Fugitive, The Avengers, The Mod Squad, Lost in Space,* and *The Brady Bunch.* Studios have counted on nostalgic fans of the original shows flocking to the theaters, but most remakes have not been terribly successful at the box office or with film critics. Writers and filmmakers have had a difficult time setting the right tone for these films, which have been, variously, faithful retellings, updates, or parodies of the original series. For example, the *Brady Bunch* remake and its sequel took the parody route, providing tongue-in-cheek depictions of the wholesome Bradys, who now live in the 1990s but still dress and act as if were the '70s.

The film *Charlie's Angels,* which reportedly went through multiple revisions and as many as thirty screenwriters,[31] does update the series, setting it in the late 1990s, but also transforms it by making the Angels both more ditzy and more sexy than the original Angels. Actor and producer Drew Barrymore, the former child star largely responsible for bringing the series to the big screen, claims that the movie is not a spoof but that "we didn't want to take it too seriously."[32] J. Michael Riva, the film's production designer, notes that "we decided at the very beginning to try to hit a style that was cooler and . . . more Saturday morning cartoonish" than the original. In the DVD featurette "Welcome to Angel World," Riva also describes how he wanted to create an "Angel World," an alternative reality with its own rules and without the kinds of real-life issues (rape, exploitation of women) seen in the original series.[33]

Barrymore's vision for the film was decidedly devoid of feminism; indeed, she did everything she could to erase the feminist overtones of the original series. She explained that she was excited to make the film because the Angels "weren't feminist, male-bashing ladies. And that's refreshing."[34] In another promotional interview for the film, Barrymore proclaimed that she was "not a torch-carrying feminist" because she liked to be "sexy and fun."[35] This mistaken definition of feminism—that it is an outmoded ideology subscribed to by sexless, joyless male-bashers—is one seen repeatedly in late 1990s popular culture. In her article "Canny and Lacy," Ruth Shalit notes that contemporary pop culture, as seen in shows like *Ally McBeal,* promotes the idea that women are "savvy yet vulnerable, fallible yet likable, feminist yet not."[36] The character Ally McBeal (played by Calista Flockhart) may be a high-powered lawyer who specializes in discrimination law, but she is also fragile, anxious, and desperate to get married. Both *Ally McBeal* and the film *Charlie's Angels* are willing to depict independent women, as long as they confess their true desires to be dependent. This seems to be the crux of what is being called postfeminism; it is not an absolute rejection of feminism (in fact, postfeminists clearly have benefited from the work done by feminists) but a watering down and minimizing of it. While presumably feminism has gained enough legitimacy and support in American culture that it could be depicted in an open way, unlike the often covert way feminism was presented in the series, the filmmakers decided to put feminism back in the closet, to downplay its role rather than emphasize its possibilities.

The images during the title sequence make it clear that the new Angels will be, as Melinda Wittstock notes, less like the sleuth Nancy Drew and more like the international spy and notoriously sexist playboy James Bond.[37] In the original we saw the Angels chasing bad guys and looking around corners with their pistols drawn, while the new version showcases huge explosions and the Angels dangling from helicopters—scenes more typical of the male-dominated action-adventure genre. The title sequence pays homage to the original series, with several quick images of the Angels in action on earlier assignments: the Angels in combat gear as in "Bullseye"; the Angels shackled together in prison uniforms as in "Angels in Chains"; and Natalie on a skateboard mimicking Jill in "Consenting Adults." The frenetic pace, exemplified by the use of quick cutting and pop music in these opening shots, often makes the film seem like a music video. It comes as no surprise, then, that the director, Joseph McGinty Nichol, known simply as "McG," is a first-time movie director whose previous work includes the hip dancing Gap ads and videos for such pop bands as Smashmouth, Barenaked Ladies, and Sugar Ray. In the director's commentary on the DVD version of the film, McG outlines his vision for the film: "It's fantasy and just a bit of escape. . . . It's a fun, just ode-to-joy, kinda pop-a-wheelie kind of movie."

The opening also contains an update of the famous voice-over by Charlie, who is still unseen and voiced by John Forsythe. The story is once again a fairy tale, but no longer one with a feminist twist: "Once upon a time, there were three very different little girls who grew up to be three very different women. But they have three things in common. They're brilliant. They're beautiful. And they work for me. My name is Charlie." They may be referred to as women instead of "little girls" now, but the Angels no longer have had to fight back against a sexist law enforcement system that didn't allow them to use their talents. From the images that accompany this voice-over, it seems that the Angels have never had to face any type of gender discrimination; it has magically disappeared from our culture, making the ideology of feminism obsolete. We see Natalie (the blonde) winning $118,599 on *Jeopardy*, Alex (the brunette) walking in a space suit onto the space shuttle, and Dylan (the redhead) smoking in the girls' room as a wild-child teenager. In the Elizabeth Lenhard novelization of the screenplay, we are told that Natalie (who appears to be no older than twenty-five) has "earned her Ph.D. from MIT by correspondence" and that she has worked as a "research scientist at the Swedish National

Academy; U.S. Navy test pilot; Lincoln-Mercury spokesmodel."[38] Alex, meanwhile, spent "her teenage years abroad, learning levitation with a Tibetan guru; safecracking, and bomb defusing with a Parisian double agent; dancing for a time with the Stuttgart Ballet—the usual classical education," then worked for NASA and created the laptop computer (13). Although at first it seems positive to learn that these women have had incredible educational and career opportunities prior to becoming Angels, their resumes are so over the top and unreal (Ph.D. by correspondence?) that they are no longer meaningful.

It's not at all clear how these women are qualified to work as private investigators; the only one of the three to have any kind of police background is Dylan, who, we learn, was actually kicked out of the police academy for assaulting a sergeant. Their sole qualifications are that they are beautiful and thin, like the original Angels, and that they can somehow do just about everything: scale mountains, race formula-one cars, speak fluent Finnish, skydive, scuba dive, fly helicopters, hack into complex computer systems, defuse bombs, perform world-class gymnastics, and even (in a major plot twist) recognize bird calls. The first scene of the film has Dylan, disguised as an African American man (played by rap singer LL Cool J), parachute out of a 747 and meet up with Alex in midair. Both of them make perfect landings onto a powerboat driven by Natalie, who is wearing a gold lamé bikini. Though the series was hardly the height of realism, most of the skills the Angels had were at least marginally possible based on their police training, which is what made the Angels different from the Bionic Woman with her superhuman powers—though it is doubtful that even the Bionic Woman could pull off this stunt.

Drew Barrymore's insistence that the Angels not use guns further removes the movie from reality and again reinforces the film's connection to such fantasy shows as *The Bionic Woman* and *Wonder Woman* rather than to the original *Charlie's Angels*. Instead of guns, the Angels use their svelte bodies as weapons, with martial arts moves that break the laws of physics, employing (as well as spoofing) the kinds of action sequences used in films like *The Matrix* (1999) and *Crouching Tiger, Hidden Dragon* (2000) (see Figure 3).[39] Barrymore claimed that she chose not to give the Angels weapons because she didn't want to "make a body count movie," but it can hardly be said that the film is nonviolent.[40] The bad guys all have guns and shoot at the Angels (who luckily can dodge bullets and outrun missiles), while the Angels use martial arts to knock several people unconscious during hand-to-hand combat. The Angels, naturally, are never physically harmed in the film. When a bomb hurls them away from the Townsend Investigations building, they walk away with only a few smudges of soot on their faces.

In a promotional interview, Barrymore tried to make the no guns pol-

Figure 3. The new Angels showing off their martial arts moves. Courtesy of *Charlie's Angels*, Columbia/Tri-Star Pictures, 2000.

icy sound positively feminist: "We want to empower these women with their own strength and their own capabilities." Diaz concurred, saying, "There's something about being able to handle yourself, walk into a room when you're faced with danger and be able to take care of yourself."[41] But no real woman can possibly have these capabilities—the fight scenes, we learn on the DVD featurette, were done with the aid of wires, harnesses, and stunt doubles—and one of the points of appeal of the original series is that the Angels had genuine sharpshooting skills and basic self-defense moves that a real person could actually acquire. While, like Barrymore, I am no fan of guns or gun violence, they are realities in the world of law enforcement and private investigations. Denying the Angels their guns is yet another way to remove them from reality and place them into the Angel World, and to strip away their power and competence.

The plot of the film does not focus on saving an oppressed woman and kicking some sexist butt, as episodes in the series often did. Instead, the Angels are hired by businesswoman Vivian Wood (played by Kelly Lynch) to rescue her partner, computer wunderkind Eric Knox (played by Sam Rockwell), who has been kidnapped. It turns out, naturally, that Vivian and Eric have set up the kidnapping and are the true villains. They trick the Angels into stealing high-tech voice identification software made by rival computer company Red Star, all in a quest to find and destroy Charlie, who Eric thinks killed his father during the Vietnam War. The convoluted plot is largely an excuse for the Angels to go undercover in a variety of skimpy outfits, another self-conscious reference to the original. Their "normal" clothes are already quite sexy—midriff-baring t-shirts, sheer blouses, bustiers, hip-hugger pants—very different from the relatively modest "off-duty" clothes of the original Angels. During their first undercover mission they dress up as high-price escorts, geishas, belly dancers, Swiss Miss-clad yodelers, and race car drivers. In the racetrack scene, Dylan wears a platinum blonde wig with feathered wings, a hairstyle, she claims, in another homage to the original, that she had seen on "some TV show from the 70s."[42] To break into Red Star, Alex pretends to be a corporate efficiency expert but is dressed up like a dominatrix, complete with leather whip, with Natalie and Dylan cross-dressed as her male sidekicks. The novelization of the film comments on the extreme nature of these outfits: "no costume is too humiliating—if it gets the job done."[43] While the Angels do work together on these missions, as in the original series, their interaction resembles an adolescent slumber party more than a professional alliance. Their bonding consists of lots hugging, giggling, playing with one another's hair, and giving boyfriend advice, whereas in the series there was much more focus on work.

Perhaps the biggest change in the film is this focus on the Angels' private lives. In the original we did get glimpses of the Angels' backgrounds or lives outside work: Kelly was raised in an orphanage and had a soft spot for children in peril; Sabrina had been married to a cop who was still the love of her life; Jill loved sports and coached girls' basketball in her spare time. And there are a few occasions when the Angels refer to dates or talk about boyfriends. Inness argues that these scenes are used to undercut or lessen the Angels' toughness by focusing on their "heterosexual desirability . . . in a culture where heterosexual desirability in a woman often signifies submissiveness to a dominant man."[44] But where these scenes are relatively rare in the series, they dominate the film, and this conflation of their professional and personal lives, I believe, ultimately cheapens the claims made by Barrymore and Diaz that the film depicts female empowerment. The new Angels fear that their relationships with men—crucial, it seems, to their identities—are jeopardized by their "unfeminine" profession and take pains to hide their work from their boyfriends.

Alex, for example, dates an airhead actor but tells him that she is a bikini waxer. He becomes suspicious when she reveals that she knows how to defuse a bomb. Natalie and Dylan try to convince her to tell him the truth, but she is reluctant to because he might feel threatened:

> "Look, it's a fact," she [Alex] said. "Some men are intimidated by a strong woman—"
> "Who holds a seventh degree black belt, " Dylan pointed out.
> "And can hack through the Pentagon's firewall," Natalie piped up.
> "Yeah," Alex said with a pout. "They come on all lovey-dovey until they find out I can shatter a cinderblock with my forehead." She sighed.[45]

To compensate for being such a strong woman, Alex tries desperately to transform herself into a domestic goddess. In the novelization, Lenhard writes, "Alex sighed and glanced at her last batch of muffins, or rather, blackened, withered attempts-at-muffins. . . . She had designed the hyper-jet thruster engine for the space shuttle; she could crack any safe and translate any covert code; she could kick box any thug into oblivion. But this cooking thing? It was kicking her butt."[46] In the film we see her baking these "killer muffins" in tight black pants and a black leather bustier. Later her baking skills are again on display when she tries to make a soufle, which, of course, falls.

Natalie's radiant beauty is supposedly offset by her clumsiness and goofiness, traits that make it difficult for her to find a boyfriend. In the director's commentary, McG explains that Natalie is "Pollyannaish" and "lives in her own world," one that seems to be stuck in childhood; at one point she announces, like a five-year-old, that she needs "to go number one," and we also see her wearing a pair of little boys' Spiderman Underoos underwear. She meets her boyfriend Pete while the Angels are on an undercover assignment, taking time away from her investigative work to flirt. Alex and Dylan encourage her to go for it, advising her to "flip your goddamned hair" to get his attention. When they finally go out on a date, she gets to fulfill her dream of dancing on stage at a taping of *Soul Train*, ironically to Sir Mix-a-Lot's song "Baby Got Back," which contains the infamous line "I like big butts and I cannot lie." Natalie's butt is anything but big, but her attempts to shake it lead the all-African American crowd to chant "Go white girl." The issues of race brought up by this scene, as well as the scenes in which the Angels are disguised as Japanese geishas and Middle Eastern belly dancers, are never fully addressed in the film, or, for that matter, in the original series, in which race and racial difference are largely ignored. In Angel World, racism, like sexism, is a nonissue.

One of Natalie's greatest challenges is to juggle work and her relationship with Pete. Their first date is interrupted when she has to fight with a would-be assassin (Pete assumes she is a waitress, another stereotypically feminine job). Later, she takes a phone call from Pete right as she's about to rescue Bosley. She keeps the conversation going, apologizing that her work has kept her so busy, as she gets into, in McG's words, an "*uber* catfight" with bad girl Vivian Wood, who is presented as severe and "mannish" in comparison to the feminized Angels. The presence of a female villain in the film is interesting, since it was so rare in the original series ("Lady Killer" was the primary exception). The series focused more on women helping other women against men—not women fighting with each other. In their "catfight," Vivian breaks Natalie's Nokia cell phone (a nice bit of product placement), causing Natalie to proclaim, "Hey, I like that guy!" Natalie's anger at being cut off from Pete leads her to knock Vivian unconscious with several kicks to the head.

Finally, we learn that Dylan is notorious for attracting loser guys—the most recent of which is "The Chad," a pathetic but endearing character played by Barrymore's real-life former husband Tom Green. Dylan also falls for and sleeps with the film's major loser: Eric Knox, the client/enemy. While the original Angels often flirted and at times faced sexual pressure or threats, as in "Night of the Strangler," they never crossed this line, keeping their private and professional lives clearly divided. After Eric and Dylan sleep together, he attempt to kills her, but she miraculously ducks under the bullet and simultaneously throws herself out a window, thus making it seem as if she had been shot and allowing her to escape.

Dylan is clearly the Angel most willing to exploit her sexual wiles, to use sex appeal to get what she wants. In the racetrack scene, she has to distract a chauffeur so that Alex can plant a tracking device in a briefcase in the limo's trunk. Dylan unzips her red, white, and blue jumpsuit to her navel, then giggles to the driver "I've come undone." She proceeds to lean across him and lick the steering wheel in a provocative manner, which renders the driver speechless and deaf, since he doesn't hear Alex open or close the trunk. Later, the sadistic Eric ties Dylan to a chair, tapes her mouth shut, then turns his thugs on her, asking them "do you guys like Angel Cake?"—presumably an invitation for them to rape as well as kill her. Dylan then spreads her legs wide open, knowing that the men will be mesmerized, unable to take their eyes off her crotch. This gives her enough time to break out of the restraints and then fight and defeat all five men simultaneously.

Dylan, like the other Angels, is obsessed with male attention and approval. At the end it appears as if Dylan and the Chad as well as Natalie and Pete will live happily ever after—the ending every woman is supposed to desire. She also seeks acknowledgment from the paternal Charlie. While Alex and Natalie coo and flirt into the speakerphone with him, Dylan, for unexplained reasons, really wants a connection with this father figure. She is disappointed at the end when, as always, he announces via speakerphone that he can't join the Angels in Hawaii to celebrate, claiming he has "some precious treasures to watch over." At that moment, Dylan turns to see the silhouette of a sixty-something man talking on a cellular phone while walking down the beach—a glimpse of Charlie at last. Her secret smile reveals how much he means to her—something far more, it seems, than Charlie ever meant to the original Angels.

This focus on the private is an effort to prove the Angels' femininity and domestic skills, or at least their attempts to obtain domestic skills. While they are frustrated that men feel threatened by their skills and profession, they do nothing to educate men (instead, they keep their jobs a secret from their boyfriends) or try to break down these cultural codes. The women do work together, which is nicely displayed in some of the martial arts scenes, but the relationships with one another are overshadowed by their relationships with men. Over two decades after the premiere of the original, women are still forced to downplay or apologize for their intelligence and strength. The impulse in the original to stop sexism and nail the male chauvinist pigs is gone, as if sexism itself no longer exists. This deliberate blindness to the contemporary need for feminism as well as the assumption that its principles are outdated is at the heart of postfeminism. Ultimately I think the film aligns itself more with shows like *Ally McBeal* than with female detectives in shows like *NYPD Blue* and *CSI* or action heroes in shows like *Buffy the Vampire Slayer, Xena: Warrior Princess, Alias,* and *Dark Angel.*[47] The box office success of *Charlie's Angels* has led to plans for a *Charlie's Angels 2,* and it seems likely that the film's successful representation of strong, but ultimately soft and dependent, women will continue in the sequel.[48]

Return to Jiggle TV

I am proud to say that I am a feminist and a fan of the original *Charlie's Angels.* The series was never a perfect or uncomplicated vision of female empowerment, but it did help break new ground for women in the mass media. As Douglas, Inness, Dow, and other scholars have shown us, the mass media have a significant impact on the way that girls and women think about and imagine themselves. The *Charlie's Angels* series provided powerful images of women breaking through the glass ceiling and trying to help other women overcome oppression. As a six-year-old, I looked at the Angels as role models, as women who were not submissive or dependent on men, who were strong and capable in their own right. These images were not common in the mid-1970s, and they unfortunately are not as common today as we might hope. The film *Charlie's Angels* is yet another example of the media backlash against feminism in the late twentieth century that Susan Faludi and other critics have described.[49] While women have made great strides in education, athletics, and the workforce in the last quarter century, films like *Charlie's Angels* reveal that our culture is largely unwilling to acknowledge these advances and the work it took to achieve them. The new Angels return to, and even embrace, the very image of "Jiggle TV" from which the original Angels tried to break free.

Chapter 11

"You Probably Think This Song Is About You"

1970s Women's Music from Carole King to the Disco Divas

JUDY KUTULAS

When I was in high school in 1971, the singer whose songs dominated the AM radio that was the background noise to my life was Carole King. Like millions of other girls, I owned her *Tapestry* album, studied the lyrics that were printed on the liner, and knew all the songs by heart (Figure 1). King, the independent singer-songwriter with the wild curly hair like mine, recorded the first in a series of female singers' albums I bought in the 1970s, including Carly Simon's, Joni Mitchell's, and Joan Baez's. There was a time in my life when nearly all my favorite singers were female. But by the late 1970s, that had changed. Along came disco, which provided an array of female singers—Donna Summer, Gloria Gaynor, Evelyn "Champagne" King—but I wasn't interested. Disco didn't offer me the same connection or immediacy. It was fine for dancing, but little else. Its female performers seemed interchangeable and plastic.

While I was very conscious of the changing gender context within which I lived my life, I did not realize that I was also living through a turning point in women's music. In the early 1970s, my life as a woman stretched before me with possibilities previous generations of women could not imagine. A multipronged campaign for women's rights raged around me. Thanks to the National Organization for Women and other women's groups, the quotas and restrictions that might have kept me from law school or medical school no longer existed. My high school could no longer separate gym classes, keep girls out of auto mechanics, or fail to provide sports programs for both sexes. Abortion became legal. Radical feminists protested against the objectification of women, the assumption that wives were automatically responsible for housework, and the blame-the-victim mentality so common during rape trials. New terms like "sexual harassment" and "male chauvinism" found their way into my vocabulary

Figure 1. Carole King's 1971 release, *Tapestry*, was one of the best-selling albums of all time, suggesting its broad popularity and ability to speak to a particular generation.

and my *Webster's Dictionary*. But, by the end of the decade, while some of what the women's movement advocated had been codified, other parts had disappeared. Fading perhaps most quickly was the idea that society would have to accommodate women's equality. The consumer market appropriated liberation and turned it into a concept that could be used to sell convenience and luxury items to women as substitutes for social and economic change. The backlash against women had begun.

Music, particularly women's music, also changed in the 1970s. The early '70s were the era of singer-songwriters like Carole King. The female singer-songwriters were the first generation of women able to make it on their own in the music business. They were a musical manifestation of women's new status. Although female singers had existed before, these new women wrote their own music, played their own songs, and spoke to a new audience of post-adolescent women who had the money to buy their records and attend their concerts. Among other things, the women's movement helped to create a new market niche: the well-educated, young, single, white female consumer primed to make purchases partly predicated on "liberation" as a concept. (This market continues to exist, as do female singer-songwriters.) By the end of the 1970s, however, record producers were seeking a larger audience and music with a broader appeal. The softer, more personal style of the singer-songwriter was eclipsed by the booming beat of disco, and the assertive female singer-songwriter was replaced by the disco diva, beautiful, sexy, and emblematic of a more hedonistic, consumerist lifestyle. The female singer-songwriter gave voice to the subversive elements of the women's movement, but the disco diva helped contain the threat, offering women a seductive but narrower version of liberation as sexual liberation. Disco music was backlash music, not in the sense of Phyllis Schlafly and her images of female submissiveness and domesticity, but backlash nonetheless, limiting women's achievements and holding them back.

In the 1960s and 1970s, popular music helped express and contain some of the larger changes going on in American society. Because it was the music of youth, it reflected youth's changing experiences with the anti-war movement, the counterculture, the women's movement, and the sexual revolution. By the mid-1970s, the antiwar movement was mostly spent and the counterculture fading. But the women's movement and the sexual revolution offered competing visions of what life might be like for the next generation, especially women. Popular music captured the complexity of the times and, like other cultural forms, provided a safe space for exploring alternative possibilities. In the end, though, like movies, TV, and other market-driven mass cultural forms, it could not challenge the status quo significantly. Rather, its function was to mainstream elements of subversive ideas, to smooth out the radical edges, soften rough ideas, and package the result as hip and controversial enough to still seem like rebellion.[1] Disco, with its evocations of sex, drugs, and rock and roll, did just that, and its promise of sexual liberation offered a more immediately gratifying substitute for the broader social changes proposed by the women's movement.

"Like a Natural Woman": Gender and 1960s Rock

Rock and roll has always been a medium of expression for young people. In the 1960s, it was one of the few forms of which they felt ownership and control. Teenagers constituted a big market for music and music-related items. Even pre-teens could afford to buy 45s. Rock and roll radio stations presumed an adolescent audience and interspersed ads for acne remedies and soft drinks with the Top 40 hits. Parents quickly learned to tune out the sound but worried about its social implications, fearing that it encouraged sexuality, rebelliousness, and even interracial encounters. The fact that parents frowned on rock made it all the more attractive for teens, who saw it as rebel music. Teens expected to hear in rock music a familiar, authentic generational voice, one distinct from parents' expectations, educators' rules, or social convention. In reality, parents' opinions—or at least intolerance—also influenced musical production. Self-censorship was a common feature of the music industry. Record companies placated worried white parents by having white performers cover songs originally performed by African Americans. Radio stations refused to play songs with sexual lyrics or profanity, which meant that it was pointless to record such music since it wouldn't sell. Rock and roll was never a completely authentic teenage voice because any appeal it had for young people was tempered by what authority figures considered appropriate.[2]

Gender figured heavily into the marketing of rock and roll as well as the basic beliefs producers held about the music. Record executives assumed that males bought more records and females, especially younger ones, bought more fan-related items like magazines and posters. Boys' tastes were, thus, worth more than girls', even though girls might ultimately spend more on music-related items. When boys listened to music, they listened to the beat and fantasized about playing the music themselves. Girls listened to the lyrics and fantasized about romances with the singers.[3] Boys were the subjects and girls the objects, as in other mediums.[4] Although males performed most 1950s rock, by the early 1960s female rock stars had appeared. As Susan Douglas has argued, these female rock stars allowed teenage girls to try on a range of identities in a moral universe where there was a widening gap between parents and teenagers. From the tough-looking Ronettes to the carefully coifed, decked-out-in-formals Supremes, the "girl groups" of the early 1960s showed girls possibilities.[5]

The standard topic of nearly all girl-group songs was love and romance. Female singers helped prime their adolescent female audiences for the idea that love would be the centerpiece of their lives, the most coveted thing they could seek and the hardest to maintain. Indeed, in many songs women were incomplete without love. Female artists also emphasized a woman's relatively passive role in relationships. Women waited for love, hoped cheating boyfriends would reform, and stoically bore the pain of failed romances in songs like "You Keep Me Hanging On" and "Please Mister Postman."[6] Although the path to true love was strewn with obstacles, the progression was clear: love, relationship, and then, like the song said, "going to the chapel." Rock and roll reinforced dominant social beliefs about women's roles. As Charlotte Greig has noted, although there are exceptions, girl-group songs, most of them written by men, emphasized "true-love teen romance leading to marriage, white suburban style."[7]

The girl groups also reinforced social expectations about women in other ways. Rarely did they write their own songs or produce their own music. Occasionally female songwriters wrote songs, but they were behind-the-scenes people, women who were smart, not pretty, like Zelda Gilroy on *The Dobie Gillis Show*. Male producers more commonly shaped and influenced both the product and the look of the girl groups. Phil Spector and Barry Gordy, Jr., were, in the words of one writer, the "Svengalis" who ran the musical and in some cases the personal lives of their female singers.[8] At Motown Records, female singers were required to attend an in-house charm school so that they would comport themselves as good women.[9] This was deemed necessary because many of the girl groups were African American and poor, while their largest audience was white and middle class. For white teenage girls, the voice of African American performers added allure to the songs, providing a vicarious encounter with the "other." Still, respectability was key to most girl groups' looks. Black performers were taught to disguise racial characteristics like coarse hair by wearing wigs and were directed to wear glamorous costumes but not racy or revealing ones. The girl group look also denied women independence or individuality. Singers were almost interchangeable; indeed, in several groups singers were replaced. The members of each ensemble wore the same clothes, danced the same steps, and vocally supported one another. The girl groups offered a fantasy experience, but one that was clearly rooted in a real world where women were judged by their looks and their behavior and were not encouraged to stand out, hog the spotlight, or act independently of men.

The antiwar movement, the sexual revolution, and the counterculture changed popular music forever. Rock gained a harder edge in the late 1960s. The widening generation gap made it impossible for the music industry to balance teens' interest in rebellion with parents' concern for propriety. In the end, the industry followed the money and sided with teenagers. Artists took more control over the production process, which also made rock more rebellious. Suddenly it was possible to fill a song with drug references and sexual invitations and still get it on the air.[10] In many ways, rock's revolution was a male affair. Antiwar music, for example, was more logically performed by draft-eligible males than by females. The sexuality suddenly on display was likewise male. It was, after all, the Rolling Stones who urged "let's spend the night together," and Steppenwolf who wanted their women to "rock me, baby, rock me, baby, all night long." The strutting stage performances and machismo of guitar smashing echoed the urgency of the driving beat and explicit lyrics. Songs spoke of conquest, seduction, and male sexual success. Although some of the male singers who best represented the hippie subculture, like Donovan, presented themselves as gentle purveyors of peace and love, there was a strong current of hyper-masculinity running through much of psychedelic rock.

The ideal woman of late 1960s rock was the "rock chick,"[11] epitomized by Janis Joplin or Grace Slick. They were men's women, sexy, sexual, one of the guys. Joplin and Slick appeared hard and tough. They were liberated from the conventions that held back the girl groups; they wore what they wanted and felt no compunction to behave like ladies. They slept with all the men in their bands. Yet, according to Country Joe McDonald, one of Joplin's lovers, men imposed this image on them.[12] Indeed, the sexual revolution and the counterculture eliminated most of the reasons why women might avoid promiscuous sex. They did not, however, also offer women love on their own terms, nor did they completely eliminate the double standard. In rock music, as in so many other venues, men defined the sexual revolution. The rock chick was also white. Psychedelic rock pushed the mainly African American girl groups out of the spotlight, limiting their marketability. They became part of an increasingly racially separated music industry, one where African-American tastes were accommodated but not dominant. In either market, though, women remained the object more than the subject of popular music.

"Sweet Seasons": Early 1970s Women's Music

The women's movement of the late 1960s grew out of some of the contradictions of the changing experience of young, well-educated white women. It began with white women's complaints about sexual discrimination during the Freedom Summer of 1964, intensified in the male-dominated atmosphere of the antiwar movement, and finally exploded in 1968.[13] Like the civil rights movement before it, it first focused on ending legal discrimination and then addressed more intangible social and cultural discrimination. By the early 1970s, it was successful enough that it began to embed itself in popular culture, in television programs such as *The Mary Tyler Moore Show* and movies, including *Alice Doesn't Live Here Anymore.* By then the antiwar movement and the counterculture were both already in decline. As acid rock played itself out and two of its most masculine presences (Jimi Hendrix and Jim Morrison) died of drug overdoses, music began to find its more feminine side.

The music of the early 1970s was sweeter and more lyric-driven, appealing to a female audience in ways hard rock did not. Its new hero was the singer-songwriter, a one-man (or woman) musical machine who wrote, performed, and otherwise produced music.[14] Artists such as Paul Simon, Jackson Browne, and James Taylor were trained in the acoustical/folk style in which lyrics mattered. They sang about politics, current events, and social customs, but their real strength was in their ability to interpret their generation's experiences. They sang about young people negotiating the fallout of the '60s rebellions. Taylor's "Fire and Rain," for instance, was about the death of a woman he had met at a drug rehab facility. The new sexual openness of the late 1960s remained, but it was more self-reflective and self-deprecating in songs like "Fifty Ways to Leave Your Lover" or "How Sweet It Is to Be Loved by You." While a performer like Morrison or Mick Jagger built his reputation with female fans on his sexuality, the appeal of the singer-songwriter to female fans was more intellectual. Female fans liked the gentleness of Taylor and Simon and the respect they accorded women. The male singer-songwriters were representative of a new type identified in the popular media—the sensitive male.[15] They were the musical equivalent of television performers like Alan Alda or Phil Donahue.

The singer-songwriter phenomenon involved women as well as men. The style itself was particularly suited to female performers, who did not have to invade the more male playground of hard rock. Its roots were in folk, in which women had always been more of a presence and audience.[16] Folk, moreover, was a traditional forum for expressing difference and alternatives. Music that showcased lyrics appealed to female fans who, after all, were supposed to be the ones listening to the words. The singer-songwriter phenomenon empowered both the women who sang the songs and the women who listened to them. Both the performers and the fans owed the relationship to the changing youth culture, the sexual revolution, and, particularly, the women's movement.

The female singer-songwriter emerged at a time when there was more room in popular music for women than ever before. The Beatles broke up in 1970, ending their dominance of the youth market. No single style of music filled the void. Yet, paradoxically, the market expanded because American fans didn't stop listening as they aged.[17] Traditionally rock was the centerpiece of the youth music market. "Pop," softer and backed by a wider array of instruments, seemed less rebellious and so was less respected. Rock was allegedly the more male form, pop the purview of girls.[18] Thus the rock chick had to function in a male world. But in a world opened up by the demographic bulge of baby boomers who continued to buy albums and listened to FM radio, which first gained a mass market in the late 1960s, there was room for both pop and rock. Since female singer-songwriters didn't invade the male domain of rock and in many ways conformed to social expectations about women's musical performance style and subject matter, they weren't threatening. And because the singer-songwriter phenomenon involved both men and women, pop was legitimized in ways that benefited female performers.

At the same time, the women's movement itself helped legitimize serious female artists and generate interest in a women's music market. The first female disc jockeys emerged during the early 1970s, bringing a female voice to radio. Olivia Records, a women's music label, was founded in 1972 by Jennifer Woodul and Ginny Berson, one-time members of the feminist collective The Furies.[19] Holly Near founded Redwood Records around the same time; like Olivia it was dedicated to producing music by and for women. Both also were musical gathering places for the growing lesbian movement.[20] Lesbian performers did not achieve mainstream success in the 1970s; straight female performers, however, did enjoy popular success, enough so that they were courted by the big record companies. After years of writing music performed by others, Carole King finally got her moment in the sun, which suggests that tastes had changed. She took home four Grammies in 1971, for album of the year (*Tapestry*), song of the year ("You've Got a Friend"), record of the year ("It's Too Late"), and best female pop vocalist. The era of arena rock had not yet arrived, but female singer-songwriters could fill medium-sized venues and sell respectable numbers of albums. Young women liked their music, and young women were an increasingly important niche market once they ceased marrying at an early age and obtained jobs and disposable income.[21] The women's movement sensitized them to gender concerns and encouraged their expectations that music speak to them. With no one group or style dominating music in the early 1970s, there was room for the female singer-songwriter and her disproportionately female audience.

Female singer-songwriters sang about that staple of women's music, love and relationships, but with a more assertive female voice. Love seemed to cause the girl groups, to borrow the title of one of the Supremes' many songs of misery, "Nothing but Heartaches." Men had most of the power in '60s songs; women could only cry, beg, and mourn. The female singer-songwriters, however, didn't see women's role as passive; they knew what they wanted and said so. "I've just got to have you, baby," King sings in "I Feel the Earth Move." Janis Ian urges her lover to come home in "Jesse," telling him "there's a hole in the bed where we slept, and now it's growing cold." Joni Mitchell's "All I Want" tells a lover who's let her down that she wants love to "bring out the best in me and in you too." These singers communicated their expectations about love but were not unrealistic about what it could provide for them. "I'm not hooked on any hero from an idle dream," Carly Simon sings in "Mind on My Man." Above all, the female singer-songwriters embrace love as something that empowers them. "I haven't got time for the pain," Simon declares, "not since I found you."

These songs spoke to 1970s women's lived experiences. The women who came of age in the early '70s were more likely to be sexually active before marriage than any previous generation. Their romantic lives were complex and they expected more from their relationships than previous generations had. "For men, the point of the sexual revolution was, above all, more sex," Barbara Ehrenreich, Elizabeth Hess, and Gloria Jacobs observed. "Women's sexual revolution meant that heterosexuality itself was about to be redefined."[22] The love songs of the 1970s were one of the few popular cultural spaces where women could hear other women talking about love and sex. "Daddy, I'm no virgin," declared Simon in "Waited So Long." And that was what was so different about 1970s songs by female singers: they presupposed that women were sexually active and suggested ways of conducting adult relationships. Songs like "So Far Away" by King and "We Have No Secrets" by Simon went beyond the usual handholding, sweet kissing themes of the girl groups and dealt instead with adult issues like honesty, past lovers, and separations. "You're So Vain," by Simon, was a wonderfully sassy retort to a rich man used to having a woman as another accessory to his lifestyle. In her "Carter Family," she misses a lover who "used to make me moan in bed" but was otherwise "crude" and "rough." These songs did not impose limits on sexuality, but neither did they sexualize women. They told of situations and experiences familiar to a generation of women carefully negotiating their sexuality in an era between the sexual revolution and AIDS.

The women's movement and the sexual revolution opened up the traditional female progression from girlfriend to wife to mother. The post-World War II generation courted to "Love and Marriage," endorsing the sentiments in record numbers. But their daughters felt more ambivalent about marriage and motherhood, and female singer-songwriters captured all the complexity of their feelings. Simon's "That's the Way I've Always Heard It Should Be" juxtaposed traditional expectations about marriage with the actual experience she has observed as she debates whether to accept a proposal. Mitchell sang of the increasingly attractive option of living with a man without being married in "My Old Man": "We don't need no piece of paper, from the city hall, keeping us tied and true." "Children and All That Jazz," by Joan Baez, recounts one chaotic day in the life of a mother and child, a day the mother can't wait to see end ("You go to bed now. Oh can't you see, I'm tired, I'm tired, I'm tired"). Yet while this generation of women postponed marriage and children, fearing that they might hold them back as individuals, female singer-songwriters also acknowledged the downside of independence and freedom, loneliness and disconnectedness. In "My Old Man," Mitchell complains that when her lover is gone "the bed's too big, the frying pan's too wide." "Hey Jesse," begs Ian, "it's lonely, come home." The sexual revolution created a generation gap between mothers and daughters, leaving daughters with few cultural models for negotiating between traditional expectations and the possibilities opened up by liberation. Music written by women and expressing a modern women's perspective answered that need.

The safe shared space between tradition and modernity in women's songs was home. Domestic images are everywhere—frying pans, shoes,

Figure 2. The album cover for Joan Baez's *Diamonds and Rust* evokes new style domesticity, with its flowers and casual setting.

bedspreads, cats, chairs, and tables (see Figure 2). King confesses that "I've always wanted a real home, with flowers on the windowsill," in "Where You Lead." In Mitchell's "Carey," the singer talks of going to Amsterdam or Rome, but the first thing she plans to do when she gets there is "rent me a grand piano and put some flowers 'round my room." This domesticity helped establish the legitimacy of female singer-songwriters by blending the traditional women's sphere with the ideals of the counterculture and the women's movement. Home did not represent a June Cleaver-like domesticity. It was a haven, a stable and secure place where hippies and "libbers" might situate themselves physically and psychologically. The cozy domesticity of the songs also reflected the women's movement's claim that the personal was political; how you lived your life was a political statement. Baez, Simon, King, and Mitchell associated their songs with a particular lifestyle, one that grew out of the counterculture and that was rural and organic. They implicitly rejected the materialism and consumerism of the previous generation in favor of simplicity. The images on the album covers reinforced that simplicity, showing airy interior spaces filled with flowers. Thus, when the female singer-songwriters sang about home, they meant homes very different from those of their mothers.

The female singer-songwriters valued domesticity because home provided a space where people could come together and nurture one another. Their domesticity served as the physical focus for surrogate family because, while biological family might not understand your need for independence and self-exploration, friends would support your endeavors and be there for you. "You've Got a Friend," written by Carole King and performed by both King and James Taylor, promised that "you just call out my name, and you know wherever I am, I'll come running, to see you again." Lovers and friends offered a buffer against a world that's "just inside out and upside down," Simon promised in "Safe and Sound."

The female singer-songwriters didn't just sing about this kind of community; they lived it. Carly Simon and James Taylor's marriage stood at the center of a circle of performers with links to one another (Figure 3).[23] Taylor sang on Simon's songs; he sang with King; he played guitar on Mitchell's album *Blue*. The same drummer performed on King's *Tapestry*, Simon's *Hotcakes*, and *Blue*. Vicariously, the listener was also invited into this community, as she (or he) could make connections based on familiarity with its various parts. Supporting this intimacy was the porous bond between the singer-songwriters' public and private lives. Fans with a little knowledge could figure out that the "unwashed phenomenon, the original vagabond" in Baez's "Diamonds and Rust" was Bob Dylan, just as they knew that Simon's "You're So Vain" was about her affair with Warren Beatty. *Rolling Stone* mocked Mitchell's tendency to write about her lovers, dubbing her "Old Lady of the Year" and charting her affairs.[24] The shared experiences about which female singer-songwriters sang and the intimacy of their songs encouraged emotional bonds between performers and audiences, especially the female ones. Key to this bonding process was the lyrics, which were always printed on the album covers. Armed with the words, young white women could enter a world very different from their mothers' and relationships with performers very different from the fan worship they once had for the Beatles or the Monkees. It was not a consumer interaction filled with Carole King lunchboxes or Joan Baez bubblegum cards. Rather, it was a relationship of equals. Female singer-songwriters presented themselves as ordinary women and because their songs were autobiographical and written in the first person, it was easy for fans to see similarities between their lives and their own.[25]

Musically as well as lyrically, female singer-songwriters pushed the limits once imposed on girl groups without threatening the established rock hierarchy. They ignored the traditional association of strings with female voices, using whatever instruments they wanted. They often dispensed

Figure 3. Carly Simon was visibly pregnant when she posed for her *Hotcakes* album and her husband, singer James Taylor, performed on the popular single from the album, "Mockingbird."

with backup singers, modeling vocal independence. They explored a variety of musical styles—jazz, folk, ethnic, even doo-wop. They claimed input at every stage of the production process. They wrote their own songs and created their own arrangements. All these characteristics defined them as serious artists, female singers who were the equals of men.

Gone too were the sequined gowns and bouffants that sometimes objectified the girl groups. Female singer-songwriters wore their hair loose and natural and favored comfortable clothes and little makeup. They dressed for themselves, not to impress others or to attract men.[26] Their casual disregard for glamour visually associated them with the traditionally male-dominated genre of serious folk-rock, which included Dylan and Simon and Garfunkel. When they performed, they just sang and played; there were no dance moves or color-coordinated outfits. It was male rock stars like David Bowie and Alice Cooper who invented performing alter egos, brought in projection screens, and wore make-up and costumes. Female singer-songwriters shunned many of the trappings of wealth and fame, still identifying with the counterculture and reinforcing their status as serious artists not merely out to make a buck. King backed away from fame; Baez insisted for a long time that no ticket for her concerts be priced higher than two dollars.[27] They put music first and glamour, fame, and money second.

They did not, however, directly advocate feminism. The most explicitly feminist song of the era, Helen Reddy's 1972 single, "I Am Woman," was not identified with the singer-songwriter tradition. Reddy was part of a consciousness-raising group when she cowrote the song.[28] It was clearly shaped by a feminist consciousness, but it was not the kind of music female singer-songwriters preferred to sing. It was too feminist and too preachy. Part of the success of the female singer-songwriters was their ability to straddle the line between traditional womanliness and feminism; they were liberated but not adversarial. By establishing themselves as strong and confident women who loved men but had lives of their own, they supported feminism as an individual achievement more than as a social, political, or economic agenda.

Female singer-songwriters validated the changed female experience. Their own aspirations demonstrated the balance between tradition and rebellion. They expected to be treated as serious musical artists, but they didn't embrace a masculine style of performing or music. They were men's equals but not their exact copies. They represented an attractively modern way of life for women, a model of womanliness that was assertive without being aggressive. They contrasted with more traditional female singers like Karen Carpenter, who sold more songs than they did but seemed confined by an older model of femininity, her songs written by others, her brother-partner watching over her, her costumes virginal and constrained.[29] But they were not as threatening as performers like Patti Smith, who challenged convention musically, visually, and in other ways and who sometimes alienated listeners with her raw style and her willingness to make more direct assaults on gender assumptions in popular music. The female singer-songwriters represented a safe mainstream version of feminism, one whose central feature was the ability to fuse the independence of the women's movement with more traditional womanliness.

"The Boys Are Back in Town": The Mid-1970s Rock Revival

But even this limited version of feminism was under assault by 1976 or 1977. The high tide of the women's movement occurred in the middle 1970s; by the end of the decade a backlash had emerged. The Equal Rights Amendment that seemed a sure thing in 1972 or 1973 was dead in the water a few years later.[30] In the world of rock, a different kind of backlash existed. Harder rock enjoyed a resurgence thanks to artists like Led Zeppelin, Tom Petty and the Heartbreakers, and Bruce Springsteen. Their songs naturally focused on their lives as modern men. While some male performers (David Bowie, Elton John) flirted with elements of sexual ambiguity, men still claimed more attention and clout in the music industry. As a result, liberation and independence became increasingly male pleasures associated with hard rock and a more male voice.

Part of what changed was the economy. It worsened, something reflected more in songs by men than by women. The female singer-songwriters represented the prime beneficiaries of the women's movement: well-educated white middle-class younger women. Theirs were songs full of the optimism of people facing expanded opportunities. Even Joan Baez, who had a long history of performing political songs, specifically looked for what she called "up songs" for *Diamonds and Rust*.[31] But the rest of America wasn't so optimistic about the future, thanks to oil crises and double-digit unemployment and inflation rates. Music spotlighted those other experiences. Urban decay and pessimism were more male themes. Male singers "smoked cigarettes and stared at the moon" and drove aimlessly into the night in songs with titles like "Badlands" and "Darkness on the Edge of Town." Angst in music tends to be more powerful than happiness, and so too does social analysis—as opposed to individual problems—tend to be the purview of male singers.

While performers like Springsteen and Petty revived male alienation as a musical style, other male singers brought back the assertive maleness of late 1960s rock. Some called it "cock rock": "music making in which performance is an explicit, crude, and often aggressive expression of male sexuality," such as music by Elvis Presley, Jim Morrison, or Mick Jagger.[32] In these songs, women's sexual liberation was not positively represented. The Rolling Stones' "Short and Curlies" told of a woman so powerful that she had the singer "by the balls." Bob Seger's "Sunspot Baby" not only deserted him but also "charged up a fortune, with my credit cards." In "Cold as Ice" by Foreigner, the woman was "diggin' for gold." This attitude would find its fullest flower in the Stones' 1978 album *Some Girls*.[33] With its images of kinky sex ("When the Whip Comes Down") and songs of women in control ("Beast of Burden," "Some Girls"), it conveyed both sexual allure and contempt for women. Sex, to the Stones, was a game of control with domination as the reward and humiliation as the punishment. "I'm so hot for you," Mick Jagger sang two years later, "but you're so cold." The women in these songs were too powerful to be anything more than objects.

By the end of the decade, the female voice in music again took a back-seat to the male one. King's work never again achieved the popularity of her *Tapestry* album. Simon mainstreamed into a softer sound, performing on movie soundtracks and singing old classics. Baez and Mitchell returned to their folk roots. A new generation of female performers appeared; they were harder rocking but more dependent on producers, male bands, and looks that would appeal to men: Blondie's Debby Harry, Stevie Nicks and Christine McVie of Fleetwood Mac, and Ann and Nancy Wilson, the sisters who constituted Heart. They continued to bring female voices to music, yet they faced a different set of circumstances. The more male-defined the industry became, the more they needed to appeal to male fans. That might mean a stronger bass line or sexier costumes or more conventional ballads. Thanks to the spectacle of stage performances like David Bowie's or Elton John's, the presentation of rock increasingly mattered. For women, the quickest way to gain attention on stage was often to sexualize themselves. "I made my own image," Harry recalled of her punky/sexy look, "but then I was trapped in it."[34]

"She Works Hard for Her Money": The Disco Divas of the Late 1970s

Popular music mimicked popular culture, which in turn mimicked "real" life. In the late 1970s, television women like Farrah Fawcett, Suzanne Sommers, and Loni Anderson were both independent women and sex objects, but it was what critics called the "jiggle factor" that stood out the most. Indeed, on programs like *Rhoda*, the women's movement was reduced to not wearing a bra and phoning men to ask them out. The more sexualized the culture became, the more women's liberation became defined as lifestyle freedom: the freedom to go braless, pursue men, and do cocaine all night. The party lifestyle prevailed in popular late 1970s movies such as *Animal House* and *Saturday Night Fever*. It was at the center of the increasingly visible male gay subculture in cities like San Francisco. And it was this culture of excess that was the subject of a backlash by religious fundamentalists, conservative Republicans, and traditional housewives. When Phyllis Schlafly or Pat Robertson railed against the decadence of modern society, what they meant was that young people were too hedonistic and self-absorbed and unwilling to accept biologically and biblically determined gender roles. The louder the complaints against youth culture sounded, the more outrageous it became. Much of this energy was focused in clubs, which provided a physical space where restless young people could dance, drink, find cocaine, and hook up with others for one-night stands.

The music for the club circuit had to be loud and beat-driven. Dancers were not interested in lyrics or performers—they wanted music that got them up and moving and contributed to the general loss of inhibitions central to the club atmosphere. Disco began as an urban phenomenon, something that appealed to working-class youth, African American youth, and gay men. Disco music was heavily dependent on the producer for the sound, since so much was created in the studio by synthesizers and drum machines.[35] The musicians lost identity and power in disco; listeners were more important than the performers. As Neil Bogart, president of Casablanca Records, explained, he'd been to dance clubs and talked to the people there and "*they* wanted to be the stars."[36] Disco music catered to the "me decade" at high tide, providing the atmosphere that put skilled dancers on display. "A million lights are dancing and there you are, a shooting star," Olivia Newton John promised in "Xanadu." In a venue where artists were verging on the invisible, success often depended on creating an image consistent with the disco lifestyle, on looking the part and seeming to live the lifestyle. Disco had its own set of conventions for both male and female performers.

Disco was little respected by the artists who counted the most in the music world—white males. Its lyrics were repetitive and suggestive; its beat all important. Separated from the club scene or listened to without a cocaine or alcohol buzz, disco was not very sophisticated music. It had no message beyond "if it feels good, *use* it."[37] Bob Seger denounced it in "Old Time Rock and Roll"; Tom Petty was its ardent and vocal opponent. Bumper stickers declared, "Down with Disco." Disco seemed inauthentic; it was heavily marketed by record producers and club owners and reached the general public as a fad thanks to *Saturday Night Fever*. Like heavy metal, disco was big business, consuming some 20 percent of the singles market by 1978,[38] but it was a guilty, secret pleasure. Few professed to love disco music because those who did were regarded as having little musical taste.

Part of the disdain with which disco was regarded had to do with the image of its female performers, the disco divas. The most easily identifiable disco diva was Donna Summer, whose "Love to Love You Baby" was an eight-plus-minute song that consisted mostly of a writhing beat and orgasmic moans. The song was banned from many radio stations but was popular on dance floors, and it catapulted Summer and her producer, Giorgio Moroder, into the spotlight. In many circles, Summer was more infamous than famous. Musicians regarded her as "little more than the producer's puppet,"[39] and her blatant sexuality further undermined her musical reputation. The female singer-songwriters packaged sexuality as integral to the liberated female's experience, an expression of both independence and womanliness.

Summer presented sex as males might, as a physical release. The titles of her subsequent hits, including "I Feel Love," "She Works Hard for Her Money," "Bad Girls," and "Hot Stuff," conveyed the difference. While her background was not dissimilar from the female singer-songwriters', her race marked her as different. In the late 1970s, the women's movement

was still mostly a white movement, and Summer did not tap into or con-
nect with it even implicitly. Instead she embraced disco, a world where
men dominated the dance floor and the producer's booth. Simultaneously, in an era where black pride and black power were still rallying cries
for many African Americans, she pursued elements of whiteness but
invoked the stereotype of African Americans as more sexual and passionate. Liberated, modern women had choices to make, but hers seemed to
be all the wrong ones. Furthermore, the looming presence of Moroder as
a kind of producer-pimp consigned her to the category of musical slut.
Summer was a commodity, an object.

Disco divas made women's sexuality at once liberated and problematic.
They sang about assertive women but said little about the social or individual consequences of that assertiveness. Their songs rarely talked about
love, romance, or any of the other traditional touchstones of women's
music. In "Hot Stuff," for example, Summer complains that she is tired of
"waitin' for some lover to call." So she turns the tables and goes looking
for some "hot stuff," "a warm-blooded lover," because she wants to "bring
a wild man back home." While female singer-songwriters longed for particular men and for love that would empower and transform them, Summer simply "dialed about a hundred numbers, baby" and was "bound to
find somebody home." ABBA's "Dancing Queen" is "young and sweet,
only seventeen," but she's still "a teaser, you turn 'em on, leave them burning and then you're gone." In "More, More, More," Andrea True, whose
career began in X-rated movies, orders her partner to "get the action
going, get the camera rolling," evoking images of domination and pornography. For women, the idea that sex might be divorced from love was
alluring but also filled with many problems. Disco's version of sex gave
women the initiative, but men defined the terms and male composers and
producers shaped the images. Disco divas created a fantasy woman in
songs like "Dancing Queen" and "Hot Stuff," a woman whose desires completely coincided with men's.

Divas' clothes, hair, and presentation reinforced the fantastic and sexual elements of their reputations. They dressed like the dancers in the
clubs where their music played, in tube tops, halters, and clingy polyester
dresses. One consequence of the counterculture was that young people
grew adept at reading externals like clothes and hair and extrapolating
from them evidence of values. The disco look was apolitical, but sartorially
it rejected the women's movement and the black power movement. Its
sexiness contrasted with the "uniform" of the women's movement, work
shirts and jeans, and also with the casual hipness of the female singer-
songwriters. Few of the African American disco singers wore their hair in
Afros or natural. Most wore it long and layered, in imitation of that late

1970s white icon, Farrah Fawcett. The look was elaborate and formal, designed to attract attention and emphasize sexuality.

Divas deliberately presented themselves as spectacles. When they sang, they strutted the stage, posturing like LaBelle's "Lady Marmalade." The flamboyance of the style appealed to some in the audience but put off others. Yet most people didn't see disco divas perform live; disco was dance music, not concert music. There were no intimate concert experiences where female fans might get to know performers they felt they already knew thanks to liner notes and lyrics. Disco women were all surface glitz; they otherwise conveyed little sense of individuality or personality.

Women listened to and liked disco music and knew who the disco divas were, but they connected differently with the divas than with the female singer-songwriters. White middle-class women probably identified more with the singer-songwriters who better reflected their lived experiences, while African American and working-class women perhaps recognized more of themselves in the divas. Beyond their racial and class appeals, though, it was a dream lifestyle that the disco divas modeled. They were seductive, symbolizing sexual freedom and sexual success. Disco music was part of a culture of sexual liberation, and divas represented hedonists whose idea of a good time was dancing all night, being the center of male attention, and being in control. This image promised women the fullest possible version of the sexual revolution, but it was edged with dangers and limits. In the novel *Looking for Mr. Goodbar*, for example, a teacher who prowled the singles scene died at the hands of a man she picked up at a bar. More important, disco queen was only a temporary identity to be assumed after work or on weekends. Even Tony Manero, played by John Travolta in *Saturday Night Fever*, had to take off his dancing shoes and dazzling white suit and return to real life.

Disco diva, then, was understood to be a temporary and unreal identity, something underscored by its associations with the flamboyant gay community that emerged in the late 1970s. Divas' most enthusiastic public audience consisted of gay men,[40] many of whom read gay subtexts into the lyrics of songs like "So Many Men, So Little Time." Gay men had a history of embracing female singers like Judy Garland, Bette Midler, and Cher, singers with the same kind of cheekiness disco divas manifested. Dance clubs were a central part of the urban gay subculture. The images of sexual aggressiveness in a song like "Hot Stuff" were attractive in that venue. Disco queens served as models for cross-dressers. The sexual ambiguity and role reversals implicit in disco further distanced it from "real life," which meant that the sexual power of disco queens of either gender was somewhat illusory.

The role, or absence thereof, that female disco singers played in the production and marketing of their music likewise weakened their reputations with listeners acquainted with entertainment conventions. Thanks to the Beatles, "serious" artists wrote their own songs, played their own instruments, and had strong opinions about how their music was to be produced and packaged. The female singer-songwriters conformed to those expectations. Female disco performers, however, did not. They were dominated by managers, producers, and handlers. Like the clothing they favored, this seemed to be a political statement about who they were as women. To an audience that understood that women were capable of producing music on their own, the fact that the divas didn't do so made them appear too ambitious in relation to their talents. Since the more serious the artist, the fewer embellishments he or she included in his or her act, disco singers, with technomusic backing them, pulsing lights, and spandex costumes, seemed to be trying too hard. All the glitz must surely be hiding inadequacies. Disco divas appeared to be, in Lucy O'Brien's colorful phrase, the "equivalent of aspiring actresses who get stuck in porn movies."[41]

But, ironically, the image was an extreme version of the liberated woman of the late 1970s. By that point, the radical feminist had been socially and culturally defined as a threat. She upped the competition for good jobs during bad economic times. She expected her partner to do half the household chores. She saw no reason to primp for men, shave her legs, or wear mascara. She appeared not to need men at all; she was stereotyped as a lesbian. Popular culture lampooned and undermined the image of the feminist: she was presented as strident, mean, humorless, and unattractive, like Maude in the CBS hit series of the same name.[42] A sexually liberated woman, on the other hand, was a less threatening proposition. Her job was just a job, not a gender statement, and her free time was devoted to dates and parties rather than consciousness-raising groups and protests. She cared about how she looked; her legs were shaved and her hair blown dry. And she was not only available to men, but eagerly available to them. Like Charlie's Angels, she was beautiful, smart, athletic, and yet still willing to function within a system where women took direction from men. The fact that she was also a bit naughty added to her allure.

Additionally, the needs of the market chipped away at the image of assertive feminism. Female singer-songwriters appealed primarily to white women, a good enough market for a while, but not as big as the market for disco, which included both sexes and multiple races and involved a whole subculture of clothes, alcohol, club admissions, and cocaine.[43] Once Bowie and the Stones started filling stadiums, the smaller venues female artists could fill became distinctly second tier in the entertainment industry. Radical feminism did not make good business sense in capitalist

America; neither did the image created by Baez or King. Their natural look cost little and their songs celebrated the simple joys of home, love, and community. They might sell a few albums, but by promoting female independence they unwittingly undercut the usual marketing strategy of generating insecurity to compel women to buy things. But sexually liberated disco women were otherwise insecure and, thus, needed things: polyester dresses and platform shoes, not to mention birth-control pills, waterbeds, and scented candles. Men liked sexually liberated women. More important, women also liked the idea of sexual liberation. It didn't alienate them from men, wasn't as hard a form of liberation to earn as going to medical school, and appealed to an audience broader than white middle-class women. The fact that it outraged a significant percentage of the nation proved that it must be truly radical in nature. "You can dance, you can jive, having the time of your life," ABBA promised. The kind of liberation disco music offered women was merely an extension of that offered by *Charlie's Angels, The Sensuous Woman,* and *Roller Boogie.* Disco sat on the extreme edge of repackaged liberation, proclaiming women's independence from sexual conventions.

It was within a larger culture that simultaneously sexualized and sexually liberated women that they embraced disco music. No song better captured its essence than Gloria Gaynor's "I Will Survive." "I Will Survive," far more than "I Am Woman," expressed the new power of a generation of women. In contrast to the almost masochistic passivity of such girl group songs as "You Keep Me Hanging On" or even the wistful romanticism of King's "So Far Away," "I Will Survive" is an active song that conveys strength and control. "At first I was afraid, I was petrified," the singer confesses, but "I grew strong, and I learned how to get along." Gay men and straight women identified with the song; straight men generally did not. When the listener chimed in, as women so often did (and still do), she saw herself, to borrow Helen Reddy's line, as strong and invincible. Unlike most disco songs, "I Will Survive" talked about a common, real-life experience rather than the transient pleasures of the disco. It empowered women.

But the power women identified with in disco was a glamorous substitute for substantive economic or political power. "We Are Family," a song by Sister Sledge that appeared late in the disco period, shows how the one stood in for the other. Like "I Will Survive," it was not set on the dance floor. Its verses were empowering ("have faith in you and the things you do, you can't go wrong"); however its chorus promised fun ("get up everybody and dance"). Sister Sledge, moreover, were, like that other disco sisterhood, the Pointer Sisters, biological sisters, resituating the female singer within the traditional family structure or group and validating the traditional family over the nontraditional one. Even their self-esteem directive was couched as a "family jewel" or motto. "We Are Family" tamed the overt sexuality of the disco diva, but it offered nothing but platitudes about how women might achieve power. It was a feel-good song for the 1980s.

The disco craze died out just as Ronald Reagan was elected president. In the late 1970s, however, it helped erase or ease some of the gender cleavages and social dislocation of the women's movement. It was part of a larger popular culture that helped convert the concept of liberation, as Susan Douglas has shown, into a culture of self-help, self-esteem, and products and services that could be bought to make women's lives better.[44] This culture quickly replaced the legal assertiveness of the early 1970s with the image of the dancing queen: young, beautiful, confident, and sexually advanced. Disco was part of the trend, promising women easy, fun liberation, but liberation that made it no easier for them to coordinate the parts of their lives. Carole King and Carly Simon showed women that it was possible to have careers and still be womanly. They had public lives and private ones. The disco divas, in contrast, were a different kind of female model. They were musical babes, women who did not worry about jobs, children, or dinner. This image made it easy to dismiss full gender equality as a fantasy, while the image of sexual liberation so central to the disco diva made her a target for both moralists and misogynists. By the end of the decade, Jane Fonda, vocal antiwar activist, feminist, and trendsetter, had made the symbolic move to spandex, aerobics, and breast implants. Bob Seger acknowledged the change in a 1980 song that said of Fonda, "we do respect her, but, we love to watch her strut."

"Girls Just Wanna Have Fun": Some Final Thoughts

The two musical tendencies present at both ends of the 1970s coexist and mingle today. As is so often the case, what began as two extremes ended up somewhere in the middle. AIDS put an end to the on-the-prowl sexuality of the early 1980s, while postfeminism blunted liberation with its concerns about ticking biological clocks and toxic daycare centers. Many different female artists were popular in the 1980s: the Go Gos, the Bangles, Cyndi Lauper, Suzanne Vega, Tracy Chapman, and Madonna. Madonna perfected the art of playing with the space between women's liberation and the sexual revolution. Much of what she did in the 1980s and 1990s was about sex, yet while singing about sex and writing a book called *Sex*, Madonna believed she had outsmarted her audience by catering to their more prurient interests. We never quite knew if she was exploiting our interest in sex or if we were exploiting her sexuality. She successfully captured the traditionally male hold on the preteen girl market, selling a look, a lifestyle, and an attitude.

There remains a female voice in music and a strong and loyal adult female market for women's music, as evidenced by the popularity of Sheryl Crow, Sarah McLachlan, and Tori Amos. Lillith Fair demonstrated that a tour of female artists could fill a gap in the music business. For a while in the 1990s, women's music gained enormous respect, explicitly giving voice to women's issues like rape and domestic violence. But then the backlash began again. Alternative rock stations disappeared in a number of markets, while hard-rocking "oldies" stations with play lists of mostly male musicians and male drive-time disk jockeys who specialized in crude sexual and racial humor scored big in the ratings. At Woodstock, male fans demanded to see Sheryl Crow's breasts and cheered for groups like Limp Bizkit. Eminem sang of killing his wife and raping his mother. Still-teenage Britney Spears donned a school uniform that showed her navel and danced seductively around a high school. Was she another Madonna-wannabe or just another talentless disco-like diva overproduced by men? In the end, the musical legacy of the 1970s for women is as ambiguous as the legacy of the women's liberation movement.

Notes

Introduction

1. Articles that focus on the appeal of 1970s culture for a new era include "Bell-Bottomed Blues," *Washington Post*, March 12, 1995, W7; Diane Crispell, "Which Good Old Days?" *American Demographics* (April 1996): 35; David Teather, "It's Good to be Back—Can the 70s Brand Revival Survive the 90s?" *Marketing* (May 25, 1995): 13; "Why '70s Music Is So Popular in the '90s," *Jet*, June 17, 1996, 58–63; Karen Yates, "Revival of the 70s Ad Icons," *Campaign*, May 26, 1995, 11; and Ned Zeman et al, "Seventies Something," *Newsweek*, June 10, 1991, 62.

2. David Frum, *How We Got Here: The 70's: The Decade That Brought You Modern Life (for Better or Worse)* (New York: Basic Books, 2000), xxiii.

3. Carla Power, "Nostalgia Is Hot," *Newsweek*, December 25, 2000, 84 Herbert Muschamp concurs, arguing that the 1970s retro trend stems from "a fearful reluctance to move forward on the twentieth century's express toward the future" (154). See Herbert Muschamp, "Getting in Touch with the m'70s," *House & Garden*, April 1992, 154ff.

4. Pagan Kennedy, *Platforms: A Microwaved Cultural Chronicle of the 1970s* (New York: St Martin's, Press, 1994), 1.

5. Scott Matthews et al, *Stuck in the 1970s: 113 Things from the 1970s That Screwed Up the Twentysomething Generation* (Chicago: Bonus Books, 1991), 2. For other histories of the 1970s, see Christopher Booker, *The Seventies: The Decade That Changed the Future* (New York: Stein and Day, 1981); Peter N. Carroll, *It Seemed like Nothing Happened: The Tragedy and Promise of America in the 1970s* (New York: Holt, Rinehart, and Winston, 1982); Peter Knobler and Greg Mitchell, eds., *Very Seventies: A Cultural History of the 1970s, from the Pages of Crawdaddy* (New York: Simon and Schuster, 1995); and Bruce J. Schulman, *The Seventies: The Great Shift in American Culture, Society, and Politics* (New York: Free Press, 2001).

6. For more information about women's roles in the 1970s, see Gerri Hirshey, "The Seventies," *Rolling Stone*, November 13, 1997, 64–78.

7. Andrew J Edelstein and Kevin McDonough. *The Seventies: From Hot Pants to Hot Tubs* (New York: Dutton, 1990), 1.

8. Muschamp, "Getting in Touch," 154.

9. As a young girl growing up in the 1970s, I remember receiving frequently contradictory messages about what it meant to be female. On one hand, we were told that we had to appeal to boys and that meant purchasing a wide variety of commodities. For your lips, you bought Bonne Bell Lip Smackers; for your hair, you bought Gee, Your Hair Smells Terrific! shampoo. And you had to be concerned

with how your hair looked, preferably just like something that Farrah Fawcett might flip back from her radiant smile. You had to be concerned about how you appeared because you wanted to get a boyfriend—preferably Shaun Cassidy. On the other hand, popular culture also sent powerful messages to girls about the importance of being independent. Marlo Thomas's *Free to Be You and Me* was published in 1974 and was a tremendous popular success; it emphasized that girls could do anything that they aspired to accomplish. Being a girl in the '70s meant negotiating many different messages about what it meant to be female.

10. For information on the reemergence of disco, see Larry Flick, "Disco Nostalgia Thrives on TV, Film, and Record," *Billboard*, May 23, 1998, np.

11. Shelton Waldrep, ed, *The Seventies: The Age of Glitter in Popular Culture* (New York: Routledge, 2000), 2.

Chapter 1

1. Betty Friedan, *The Feminine Mystique* (New York: Dell, 1963).

2. Flora Davis, *Moving the Mountain: The Women's Movement in America Since 1960*, 2nd ed. (New York: Simon and Schuster, 1999), 50.

3. Friedan, *Feminine Mystique*, 218–19.

4. I have found no evidence that such a debate ever took place.

5. Walter Carlson, "Advertising: *Feminine Mystique* Under Fire," *Advertising Age*, June 30, 1965, 3.

6. Friedan, *Feminine Mystique*, 197.

7. Ibid., 219.

8. Maggie Humm, *The Dictionary of Feminist Theory*, 2nd ed. (Columbus: Ohio State University Press, 1995), 4.

9. Grace Lichtenstein, "Feminists Demand 'Liberation' in *Ladies' Home Journal* Sit-in," *New York Times*, March 19, 1970; "The New Feminism: A Special Section Prepared for *Ladies' Home Journal* by the Women's Liberation Movement," *Ladies' Home Journal*, August 1970, 64–71; Militant Femmes Shake up CBS' Annual Meeting," *Advertising Age*, April 27, 1970, 8.

10. Philip H. Dougherty, "Women's Role in Ads Upsets Feminists," *New York Times*, May 24, 1970; Don Grant, "Women's Libs Fume at 'Insulting' Ads; Ad Gals Are Unruffled," *Advertising Age*, July 27, 1970, 1, 28, 30, 32.

11. For a fuller description of how marketers and advertisers began to research and conceptualize the women's market in the early 1970s, see Rena Bartos, *The Moving Target: What Every Marketer Should Know About Women* (New York: Free Press, 1982).

12. Dougherty, "Women's Role."

13. House Special Subcommittee on Education, *Discrimination Against Women: Hearings on Section 805 of H.R. 16098*, 91st Cong., 2nd sess., 1970, 424.

14. Ibid., 428.

15. Linda Charlton, "Women Seeking Equality March on 5th Ave. Today," *New York Times*, August 26, 1970.

16. In subsequent years, NOW continued to pressure the industry with even more sophisticated actions. In 1972, for example, the New York chapter filed a petition with the Federal Communication Commission (FCC) asking that ABC's New York station WABC-TV have its broadcast license revoked. According to NOW, the action was based on the station's "discrimination against women in employment, failure to ascertain women's needs and interests in programming, and violation of the FCC's Fairness Doctrine, which requires that both sides be

presented in 'an issue of controversial public importance.'" See Judith A. Hennessee and J. Nicholson, "NOW Says: TV Commercials Insult Women," *New York Times Magazine*, May 28, 1972.

17. In 1973, for example, the *New York Times* identified seven women in New York who were heads of Madison Avenue advertising agencies. Judy Klemesrud, "On Madison Avenue, Women Take Stand in Middle of the Road," *New York Times*, July 23, 1973.

18. Linda Scott, in her critique of the feminist attack on advertising, points out that nearly all the founders of the major cosmetics companies were women and that cosmetics ads have traditionally been written by women. Linda M. Scott, "Fresh Lipstick: Rethinking Images of Women in Advertising," *Media Studies Journal* 7 (1993): 140–55.

19. Klemesrud, "On Madison Avenue."

20. For other examples of advertising women speaking out during the 1970s, see "'Admen Must Reinvent Woman; Old Fictions Flop,' Says Adwoman," *Advertising Age*, January 12, 1970, 3, 42; Henry R. Bernstein, "Ads Ignore Real Women, Use Stereotypes: Levine," *Advertising Age*, June 16, 1975, 86; "Commercials Tend to Ignore Working Women: Foster," *Advertising Age*, April 10, 1972, 44; Midge Kovacs, "Where Is Woman's Place? Home, Say Ads," *Advertising Age*, July 17, 1972, 48; Tina Santi, "Today's Woman Explodes Yesterday's Ad Dream World," *Advertising Age*, March 18, 1974, 49–53; "Savvy Marketers Will Improve Women's Ad Roles: JWT Exec," *Advertising Age*, March 3, 1975, 53; Kay Smith, "Role Still Small, But It's Growing," *Advertising Age*, June 18, 1979, S14, S16; "Working Women Market No Monolith, Admen Told," *Advertising Age*, November 3, 1975, 22–23.

21. Don Grant, "Women's Libs Fume at 'Insulting' Ads; Ad Gals Are Unruffled," *Advertising Age*, July 27, 1970, 32.

22. "The Lady of the House Is Dead," advertisement in *Advertising Age*, April 27, 1970, 86–87.

23. National Advertising Review Board, "Advertising Portraying or Directed to Women," report reprinted in *Advertising Age*, April 21, 1975, 72–75.

24. "Working Wives Becoming Major Marketing Force," *Advertising Age*, April 5, 1976, 34.

25. John Simley, "Virginia Slims," in *Encyclopedia of Consumer Brands*, vol. 1, ed. Janice Jorgensen (Detroit: St. James Press, 1994), 622–24.

26. Leonard Sloane, "Advertising: Women's Lib to Give Awards," *New York Times*, August 26, 1971.

27. Virginia Slims was successful because its makers developed a clever and popular advertising campaign that coopted the women's movement, but perhaps equally important were the subtleties of the marketing strategy. The cigarette was, in fact, physically slimmer—only 23 mm in circumference, a "full" 2 mm thinner than regular "men's" cigarettes—and it was given a white package with a series of thin vertical lines. But the significance of the "slimness" concept went beyond the dimensions of the cigarette and its packaging. Tobacco companies have historically pitched cigarettes to women based on their real or imagined weight-control properties, and the young female fashion models who appeared in Virginia Slims ads certainly suggested slimness (if not virginity). Diane Barthel describes the sordid history of tobacco advertising aimed at women and the use of the weight-control pitch during the 1920s, including Lucky Strike's campaign "Reach for a Lucky Instead of a Sweet." See Simley, "Virginia Slims" and Diane Barthel, *Putting on Appearances: Gender and Advertising* (Philadelphia: Temple University Press, 1988), 130–33.

28. William A. Robinson, "Virginia Slims Come a Long Way in 17 Years," *Advertising Age*, May 30, 1985, 30.

29. Lucy Komisar, "The Image of Woman in Advertising," in *Woman in Sexist Society: Studies in Power and Powerlessness,* ed. Vivian Gornick and Barbara K. Moran (New York: Basic Books, 1971), 216.

30. "Why Shouldn't a Woman," advertisement for Leilani Hawaiian Rum, *Ms.,* July 1972, 30–31.

31. "It's Time Women Got Their Own American Express Card and Started Taking *Me* to Dinner," advertisement for American Express, *Ms.,* December 1972, 101.

32. "Dewar's Profiles: Sheila Ann T. Long," advertisement for Dewar's Scotch Whiskey, *Ms.,* November 1972, inside front cover.

33. "The Phone Company Wants More Installers like Alana MacFarlane," advertisement for AT&T, *Ms.,* July 1972, 3.

34. "The Phone Company Wants More Operators like Rick Wehmhoefer," advertisement for AT&T. *Ms.,* August 1972, 3.

35. "Tabu by Dana," advertisement for Tabu perfume, *New Woman,* January–February 1974, 15.

36. Susan Faludi, *Backlash: The Undeclared War Against American Women* (New York: Crown, 1991), 202–3.

37. Susan Brownmiller, *Femininity* (New York: Simon and Schuster, 1984), 158.

38. For a more recent apologia for this perspective, see Scott, "Fresh Lipstick," 1993.

39. Davis, *Moving the Mountain,* 108.

40. Naomi Wolf has argued that the cosmetics and fashion industries have replaced the feminine mystique with what she terms "the beauty myth," the notion that women could only be accepted in the world of the new woman if they met rigid new standards of slimness, beauty, and fashion. See Naomi Wolf, *The Beauty Myth: How Images of Beauty Are Used Against Women* (New York: William Morrow, 1991).

41. "The American Woman Summer 1972: *Vogue*'s Point of View," *Vogue,* June 1972, 75.

42. "The Liberated Wool Sweater," advertisement for the American Wool Council, *Vogue,* August 1, 1970, 9.

43. Faludi, *Backlash,* 205.

44. "The Makeup That *Is* and *Isn't*," advertisement for Revlon cosmetics, *Vogue,* March 1, 1970, 16.

45. "Optical Illusions," advertisement for Geminesse eyelashes by Max Factor, *Vogue,* March 1, 1970, 12.

46. "If the Fine, Silky Bloom on Her Complexion," advertisement for Germaine Monteil cosmetics, *Vogue,* March 1, 1970, 122.

47. "Contents," *New Woman,* January–February 1974, 2.

48. Kathleen L. Endres and Therese L. Lueck, *Women's Periodicals in the United States* (Westport, Conn.: Greenwood Press, 1995), 236–42; Rochelle Gatlin, *American Women Since 1945* (Jackson: University of Mississippi Press, 1987), 157.

49. "Beautiful Tan Today. Young Looking Skin Tomorrow," advertisement for Coppertone, *Ms.,* July 1972, inside front cover.

50. Gloria Steinem, "Sex, Lies and Advertising," in *Gender, Race and Class in Media: A Text-Reader,* ed. Gail Dines and Jean Humez (Thousand Oaks, Calif.: Sage, 1995), 112–20. Excerpts from an article that originally appeared in *Ms.,* July–August, 1990. In 1989, after seventeen years of ideological and financial struggles, *Ms.* suspended publication. The following year, it reappeared as a bi-monthly with a hefty increase in price but without advertising. *Ms.* remains ad-free and currently sells for $5.95 an issue or $35 for a six issue subscription. Interestingly, the magazine in 2000 ran a two-page spread of Virginia Slims ads—not as paid pro-

motion of the product but to criticize the company's global campaign to sell ciga-
rettes to women. See Deirdre Carmody, "*Ms.* Magazine Returns with New Spirit,
But Without Ads," *New York Times*, July 30, 1990; and "Comments Please," *Ms.*,
June–July 2000, 96–97.

51. By 1988, Daniel J. Bretl and Joanne Cantor could report on fifteen content
analyses of gender in television commercials conducted from 1971 to 1988. See D.
J. Bretl, and J. Cantor, "The Portrayal of Men and Women in U.S. Television Commercials: A Recent Content Analysis and Trends over 15 Years," *Sex Roles* 18 (1988):
595–609. For a summary of work in both television other media, see Alice E.
Courtney and Thomas W. Whipple, *Sex Stereotyping in Advertising* (Lexington,
Mass.: Lexington Books, 1983), and Barrie Gunter, *Television and Sex Role Stereotyping* (London: John Libbey, 1986).

52. One study found that, although contemporary TV commercials do show
women in less traditional roles, these portrayals are more likely to be seen during
prime time, when women who work outside the home are in the audience. Daytime commercials still tend to portray women doing household chores, and weekend sports ads still frequently exploit images of women as objects of sexual desire.
R. S. Craig, "The Effect of Television Day Part on Gender Portrayals in Television
Commercials: A Content Analysis," *Sex Roles* 26, 5/6 (1992): 197–211.

53. Barthel, *Putting on Appearances*, 124.

Chapter 2

1. Quoted in Judy Klemesrud, "Feminists Recoil at Film Designed to Relate to
Them," *New York Times*, February 26, 1975, 28.

2. Ibid. In his review, David Bartholomew concurs with such negativity, suggesting that the film "represents a pessimistic view of the women's movement, the futil-
ity of changing lives and opposing narrow traditional ideas." Review of *The Stepford
Wives, Cinefantastique* 4, 2 (1975): 40–42.

3. Quoted in Klemesrud, "Feminists Recoil."

4. See Herbert J. Gans, "'The Stepford Wives': Killing Off Women's Liberation,"
Social Policy (May-June 1975): 59–60; Klemesrud, "Feminists Recoil," 28.

5. Judith Crist, "Of Heads and Heels," *New York*, February 17, 1975, 73–74.

6. Bartholomew, Review, 40.

7. See Gans, "Stepford Wives," 60; Molly Haskell, "The Stepford Mummies—
Taking Plastic Measures," *Village Voice*, February 24, 1975, 65–66; Pauline Kael,
"Male Revenge," *New Yorker*, February 24, 1975, 110–13; John Simon, "Better Viet-
nam Than Barbara Streisand," *Esquire*, June 1975, 62; Dorothy Somers, Review of
The Stepford Wives, Films in Review, April 25, 1975, 247–48; Richard Schickel,
"Women's Glib," *Time*, March 3, 1975, 6; Paul D. Zimmerman, "Suburban Gothic,"
Newsweek, March 3, 1975, 70.

8. See, respectively, A. D. Murphy, Review of *The Stepford Wives, Variety*, February
12, 1975, 28; Simon, "Vietnam,"62; Schickel, "Women's Glib," 6; Zimmerman,
"Gothic," 70; Haskell, "Stepford Mummies," 65; Vincent Canby, "Screen: 'Stepford
Wives' Assays Suburbia's Detergent Set," *New York Times*, February 13, 1975, 43;
Somers, Review, 248; Linda Arking quoted in Klemesrud, "Feminists Recoil," 28.

9. Murphy, Review, 28.

10. Schickel, "Women's Glib," 6. Complications emerge when critics attempt to
classify the film as well. Labels include satire (Bartholomew, Review, 40; Schickel,
"Women's Glib," 6; Canby, "Screen," 43; Kael, "Male Revenge,"110; Stephen King,
Danse Macabre [New York: Berkley/Penguin, 1981], 165; Somers, Review, 248; Zim-

merman, "Gothic," 70); black comedy (Murphy, Review, 28); parable (Review of *The Stepford Wives, Independent Film Journal*, February 19, 1975, 19; Kael, "Male Revenge," 112; Schickel, "Women's Glib," 6); fairy tale (*Independent Film Journal*, 19), horror/thriller (Bartholomew, Review, 40; Gans, "Stepford Wives," 60; Kael, "Male Revenge," 110; Simon, "Vietnam," 62; Somers, Review, 248; Zimmerman, "Gothic," 70); and science fiction (Bartholomew, Review, 40; *Independent Film Journal*, 19, Kael, "Male Revenge,"110).

11. Canby, "Screen," 43.

12. Kael, "Male Revenge," 112.

13. Bonnie Dow, *Prime-Time Feminism: Television, Media Culture, and the Women's Movement Since 1970* (Philadelphia: University of Pennsylvania Press, 1996), xv.

14. The goals of 1970s feminism included equality in education and the workplace, contraception and the right to abortion, and changes in laws governing domestic violence, rape, and divorce. Within the movement there were conflicts over class and race differences as well as the issue of sexual orientation. For those seeking a more thorough introduction to second-wave feminism in the context of discussions of media culture, see Joanne Hollows, *Feminism, Femininity, and Popular Culture* (Manchester: Manchester University Press, 2000).

15. For more on these media constructions, see Susan Douglas, "Genies and Witches," in her *Where the Girls Are: Growing Up Female with the Mass Media* (New York: Random House, 1994) and Bonnie Dow, "1970s Lifestyle Feminism, the Single Woman, and *The Mary Tyler Moore Show*," in *Prime-Time Feminism*.

16. Susan Brownmiller, "The Boston Women's Health Book Collective" (1998), in *Women: Images and Realities: A Multicultural Anthology*, ed. Amy Kesselman, Lily D. McNair, and Nancy Schniedewind (Mountain View, Calif.: Mayfield, 2000), 490.

17. For an entertaining overview of the cultural significance of the catfight to 1970s feminism in the U.S., see Susan J. Douglas, "The ERA as Catfight," in *Where the Girls Are*.

18. Gans, "Stepford Wives," 60.

19. Bartholomew, Review, 42.

20. Haskell, "Stepford Mummies," 66.

21. Gans, "Stepford Wives," 59.

22. "Dare to Compete: The Struggle of Women in Sports," HBO, 1999.

23. Lynn Spigel, *Make Room for TV: Television and the Family Ideal in Postwar America* (Chicago: University of Chicago Press, 1992), 33.

24. Ibid., 100.

25. Betty Friedan, *The Feminine Mystique* (New York: Dell, 1963), 296–97.

26. In a delightfully direct reference, Hollows describes Friedan's conclusions as follows: "Attempting to conform to the feminine ideal promoted by media forms such as women's magazines and advertising, it was argued, caused these Stepford Wives of the 1950s incredible psychological harm by making them deny their minds" (*Feminism*, 11). Intriguingly, the cover of Hollows's book features a promotional still from *The Stepford Wives* as its central image, though the author does not otherwise discuss the film.

27. Kathie Sarachild, "Consciousness Raising: A Radical Weapon," in *Women: Images and Realities*, 488–90.

28. Spigel, *Room for TV*, 128.

29. See Hollows, *Feminism*, 13.

30. Alice Embree, "Media Images I: Madison Avenue Brainwashing—The Facts," in *Sisterhood Is Powerful: An Anthology of Writings from the Women's Liberation Movement*, ed. Robin Morgan (New York: Vintage, 1970), 196–201.

31. Combahee River Collective, "A Black Feminist Statement" (1978), in *Mod-

ern Feminisms: Political, Literary, Cultural, ed. Maggie Humm (New York: Columbia University Press, 1992), 134–36.

32. Of course we learn that this is not the case if we simply watch 1981's *Revenge of the Stepford Wives*, in which a white middle-class female reporter, played by Sharon Gless (of *Cagney and Lacey* fame), brings down the town, with a little help from (pre-*Miami Vice* era) Don Johnson.

33. Gans finds their motivation even less empowering. He argues, "Bobbie and Joanna turned to consciousness raising as much out of isolation as liberationist fervor; it was their way of reestablishing a bit of New York City culture in an alien milieu" ("Stepford Wives," 59).

34. "Mo More Miss America!" in Morgan, *Sisterhood Is Powerful*, 585.

35. Douglas, *Where the Girls Are*, 160.

36. Kevin Thomas, "'The Stepford Wives—Glassy-Eyed in Suburbia," *Los Angeles Times*, February 13, 1975, Sec. IV, 15.

37. Schickel, "Women's Glib," 6.

38. Featuring young, braless women in hot pants is not only about beauty but about sex, of course. Alongside the film's messages about second-wave feminism, *The Stepford Wives* actively titillates via constant closeups of two braless women in tight, revealing clothing. Therefore, the statement the film makes on what middle-class men want in a wife is worthy of exploration. In contrast to Joanna and Bobbie, the robot wives all sport conservative fashions. They wear full-length (maxi) dresses, frilly aprons, and wide-brimmed straw hats. Yet the prudish fashions disguise the sexual fantasy girls beneath. Early in the film, Joanna catches Ted Van Sant groping his wife in their garden. A bit later, Joanna and Bobbie overhear another couple having intense sex in their home in the middle of the day. The seemingly puritanical Stepford women are actually far from prudish. The image the film offers is of men whose ideal women straddle the virgin/whore dichotomy in typically sexist fashion: they are virginal in public, whorish in private. The film argues that men desire above all to control women's sexuality. Female sexuality, when controlled by the woman herself, may appear out of control and frightening to men. Nevertheless, it is also exciting. So the men of Stepford create their ideal compromise: to the rest of the world, their wives' sexuality appears under control, even absent; at home, by contrast, it can be unleashed in the exclusive service of arousing and pleasing her man.

39. Available at <amc.thoughtbubble.com/about/stepfordwives2.html>

40. I teach the movie in my Science Fiction, Introduction to Women's Studies, and Women in the Media classes. Via the web, I have learned that professors from Clemson, Princeton, and the University of Nevada-Las Vegas also teach the film in courses on Science Fiction Film; Human Genetics, Reproduction and Public Policy; and Gender and Social Interaction (respectively). I am certain this sample is far from exhaustive.

41. Gans, "Stepford Wives," 60.

Chapter 3

1. See, for example, National Council for Research on Women, *Sexual Harassment: Research and Resources*, 3rd ed. (Washington, D.C.: National Council for Research on Women, 1995), 2, 50.

2. David Brock, "The Real Anita Hill," *American Spectator*, March 1992, 27.

3. Carrie N. Baker, "Sex, Power, and Politics: The Origins of Sexual Harassment Policy in the United States" (Ph.D. dissertation, Emory University, 2001), 4–6.

4. Helen Gurley Brown, *Sex and the Single Girl* (New York: Bernard Geis, 1962); see also Helen Gurley Brown, *Sex and the Office* (New York: Bernard Geis, 1964).

5. Enid Nemy, "Women Begin to Speak Out Against Sexual Harassment at Work," *New York Times*, August 19, 1975, 38.

6. Susan Brownmiller and Dolores Alexander, "From Carmita Wood to Anita Hill," *Ms.*, January–February 1992, 70–71.

7. On October 17, 1975, sexual harassment was mentioned again, but only briefly, in an article about a speakout on workplace issues sponsored by Women Office Workers in New York City. Nadine Brozen, "A Demand to Be More Than Just 'Office Girls,'" *New York Times*, October17, 1975, 45.

8. Mary Bralove, "A Cold Shoulder: Career Women Decry Sexual Harassment by Bosses and Clients," *Wall Street Journal*, January 19, 1976, 1.

9. "A *Redbook* Questionnaire: How Do You Handle Sex on the Job?" *Redbook*, January 1976, 74–75.

10. Rhoda Koenig, "The Persons in the Office: An Ardent Plea for Sexual Harassment," *Harper's*, February 1976, 87–88, 90.

11. Katie Roiphe, *The Morning After: Sex, Fear, and Feminism* (London: Hamish Hamilton, 1994); Camille Paglia, "The MIT Lecture: Crisis in the American Universities," in her *Sex, Art and American Culture: Essays* (New York: Vintage Books), 249–98.

12. Judge Charles R. Richey Papers, news articles, 1971 March 3–1996 May 13, Index, at 262–67, Ohio Wesleyan University Manuscript Collection #2.

13. *Williams v. Saxbe*, 413 F. Supp. 654, 657 (D.D.C. 1976).

14. Richey Papers, news articles, 1971 March 3–1996 May 13, Index, at 268–75.

15. Art Buchwald, "Those Are Stunning Socks You're Wearing, Callihan," *Washington Post*, April 27, 1976, B1.

16. "Sex Rears Its Mixed-Up Head," *Los Angeles Times*, April 26, 1976.

17. "The Law and Threats to Virtue," *Wall Street Journal*, April 27, 1976, 22; Richey Papers, news articles, 1971 March 3–1996 May 13, Index at 273, 275.

18. Dick Hitt, "One More Rule to Remember," *Dallas Times Herald*, April 22, 1976.

19. Jim Wright, "Now, Guidelines for That, Too," *Dallas Morning News*, May 4, 1976, D1; see also Ralph de Toledano, Editorial, *Naugatuck Daily News* (Connecticut), May 18, 1976.

20. "Sex and Judicial Progress," *National Review*, March 3, 1978, 299. The case was *Barnes v. Costle*, 561 F.2d 983 (D.C. Cir. 1977).

21. The case was *Alexander v. Yale*, 459 F. Supp. 1 (D. Conn. 1977). For the remainder of the essay, I will give citations for articles discussed specifically. For other citations, see C. N. Baker, "Sex, Power, and Politics," 285–301.

22. Russell Baker, "The Courts of First Resort," *New York Times*, July 26, 1977, A29.

23. Diane Henry, "Yale Faculty Members Charged with Sexual Harassment," *New York Times*, August 22, 1977, 30.

24. "Bod and Man at Yale," *Time*, August 8, 1977, 52–53.

25. "Executive Sweet: Many Office Romeos Are Really Juliets," *Time*, October 8, 1979, 76.

26. Paula Bernstein, "Sexual Harassment on the Job," *Harper's Bazaar*, August 1976, 12.

27. Joyce Dudley Fleming, "Shop Talk About Sex," *Working Woman*, July 1979, 31–34.

28. Cheryl Bentsen, "When Men Coach Women—Do They Have to Score?" *Ms.*, August 1976, 24–31.

29. Elvia R. Arriola, "'What's the Big Deal?' Women in the New York City Construction Industry and Sexual Harassment Law, 1970–1985," *Columbia Human Rights Law Review* 22 (1990): 44–46.

30. Claire Safran, "What Men Do to Women on the Job: A Shocking Look at Sexual Harassment," *Redbook*, November 1976, 220.

31. "Sex on the Job: Where We Are Now," *Redbook*, April 1978, 38.

32. Margaret Mead, "A Proposal: We Need Taboos on Sex at Work," *Redbook*, April 1978, 31, 33, 38.

33. Letty Cottin Pogrebin, "The Working Woman: Sex Harassment," *Ladies' Home Journal*, June 1977, 24.

34. Karen Lindsey, "Sexual Harassment on the Job and How to Stop It," *Ms.*, November 1977, 47.

35. Merrill Rogers Skrocki, "Sexual Pressure on the Job," *McCall's*, March 1978, 43; "My Problem and How I Solved It: My Boss Wanted More Than a Secretary," *Good Housekeeping*, April 1978, 28; Janet Harris, "Dealing with Bosses," *Family Circle*, April 1978, 191; Marilyn Achiron, "Solving Your Problem: Sexual Harassment on the Job," *Mademoiselle*, October 1979, 116; Jane Williamson, "I'm Being Sexually Harassed: What Can I Do?" *Working Woman*, November 1979, 30; Joan Faier, "The Working Woman's 7 Biggest Problems and How to Solve Them," *Harper's Bazaar*, August 1979, 90.

36. Anne Nelson, "Sexual Harassment at Yale," *Nation*, January 14, 1978, 7–10.

37. Shelby White, "The Office Pass," *Across the Board*, April 1977, 17; see also Shelby White, "The Office Pass (Continued)," *Across the Board*, March 1978, 48–51 (reporting on *Barnes v. Costle*).

38. Georgia Dullea, "Women Win Fight for More Construction Jobs, Less Harassment," *New York Times*, August 23, 1977, 30; Easton, "Hard Hat Women Make a Dent in Jobs," *Los Angeles Times*, May 20, 1978, 1; Allanna M. Sullivan, "Women Say No to Sexual Harassment," *Coal Age*, August 1979, 74–78; Ben A. Franklin, "Women Working in Mines Assail Harassment and Unsafe Conditions," *New York Times*, November 11, 1979, 30; "Women Miners Reassured," *Washington Post*, November 13, 1979, A4; Raymond M. Lane, "A Man's World: An Update on Sexual Harassment," *Village Voice*, December 16–22, 1981, 1; Estelle Jackson, "Mother Had the Same Problem," *Richmond Times*, June 3, 1980, 1.

39. *Ms.* Press Release, "New York Women Speak-Out on Sexual Harassment at Work," 22 October 1977, Working Women's Institute Collection, Barnard Center for Research on Women, Barnard College, New York.

40. Working Women's Institute, "1979 Annual Program Report and Audited Financial Statement," Karen Sauvigné, Papers, Brooklyn, New York; "Sexual Harassment on the Job," *Phil Donahue Show* (Princeton, N.J.: Films for the Humanities and Sciences, 1988; 1977 Phil Donahue show with Susan Meyer and Karen Sauvigné); Susan Meyer, telephone interview by author, tape recording, New York, New York, February 17, 2001; Constance Backhouse and Leah Cohen, *The Secret Oppression: Sexual Harassment of Working Women* (Toronto: Macmillan of Canada, 1979), 156.

41. "Sexual Harassment Lands Companies in Court," *Business Week*, October 1, 1979, 120 (appearing in the social issues section); "How to Tame the Office Wolf—Without Getting Bitten," *Business Week*, October 1, 1979, 107–8 (in the personal business section); Freada Klein, telephone interview by author, tape recording, Berkeley, California, March 26 and April 4, 2001.

42. Gwendolyn Mink, *Hostile Environment: The Political Betrayal of Sexually Harassed Women* (Ithaca, N.Y.: Cornell University Press, 2000), 77, 115.

43. Mary F. Rogers, "Clarence Thomas, Patriarchal Discourse and Public/Pri-

vate Spheres," *Sociological Quarterly* 39 (1998): 289–308 (describing how Thomas used arguments about privacy to avoid inquiries into whether he had sexually harassed Anita Hill).

44. National Council for Research on Women, *Sexual Harassment*, 2, 50.

45. Adam Nossiter, "6–Year-Old's Sex Crime: Innocent Peck on the Cheek," *New York Times*, September 7, 1996, A14; "Kiss Leads to a Policy Revision," *New York Times*, October 9, 1996, B9; Norimitsu Onishi, "Harassment in the 2d Grade? Queens Kisser Is Pardoned," *New York Times*, October 3, 1996, A1.

46. *Disclosure*, Warner Brothers, 1994.

47. Clare Brant and Yun Lee Too, eds., *Rethinking Sexual Harassment* (Boulder, Colo.: Pluto Press, 1994), 13.

Chapter 4

1. Mariah Burton Nelson, *Embracing Victory: Life Lessons in Competition and Compassion* (New York: Morrow, 1998), 19.

2. Peebles is credited in several cheerleading manuals for bringing cheerleading from the Ivy League to the west. A history of the University of Minnesota describes Peebles as a man of "superb dignity" who came to the university to fill a teaching position in the mental and moral philosophy department. See James Gray, *The University of Minnesota* (Minneapolis: University of Minnesota Press, 1951), 542–45.

3. This first appeared in Arturo Gonzales, "The First College Cheer" printed in the *American Mercury* (November 1956) and was included in Mary Ellen Hanson's informative history of cheerleading, *Go! Fight! Win!* (Bowling Green, Ohio: Bowling Green State University Popular Press, 1995), 11.

4. Susan Cahn writes that the bicycle craze of the 1880s opened up athleticism to middle- and upper-middle-class women. By the 1890s, women were forming baseball, basketball, and crew teams, which naturally recharged debates about femininity and health. See *Coming on Strong: Gender and Sexuality in Twentieth-Century Women's Sport* (New York: Free Press, 1994), 7–30.

5. Hanson, *Go!*, 20.

6. Newt Loken and Otis Dypwick, *Cheerleading and Marching Bands* (New York: A.S. Barnes, 1945).

7. Stella S. Gilb, *Cheerleading, Pep Clubs, and Baton Twirling* (Lexington, Ky.: Hurst Printing, 1955), vi-vii.

8. Jane Flax, "The End of Innocence," in *Feminists Theorize the Political*, ed. Judith Butler and Joan W. Scott (New York: Routledge, 1992), 453.

9. Paul Fussell argues that the atmosphere of emergency during wartime and the prolonged sexual deprivation of soldiers relaxes inhibitions and promotes a kind of hedonism and lasciviousness. The homoerotic feelings of many men during World War I created what Fussell refers to as "a sublimated (i.e., chaste) form of temporary homosexuality" (272). The boy-cheering-for-boy dynamic no doubt signaled ambiguous messages after the war and could no longer be looked at as innocently as it had been before. See *The Great War and Modern Memory* (London: Oxford University Press, 1975), 270–309.

10. Taken from Karen Kahn's introduction to *Front-Line Feminism, 1975–1995: Essays from Sojourner's First Twenty Years* (San Francisco: Aunt Lute Books, 1995), 13–37.

11. Betty Friedan, *The Feminine Mystique* (New York: Dell, 1963), 20–21.

12. Quoted in Alice Echols, *Daring to Be Bad* (Minneapolis: University of Minnesota Press, 1989), 63.

13. Echols, *Daring*, 7.

14. Robin Morgan, *Sisterhood Is Powerful: An Anthology of Writings from the Women's Liberation Movement* (New York: Vintage, 1970), xvi.

15. Ibid., 537.

16. Mary-Ellen Banashek, "Memoirs of an Ex-Cheerleader," *Mademoiselle*, June 1976, 18.

17. The protest against the beauty pageant was followed by a protest of the Bridal Fair at Madison Square Garden, staged by Women's International Terrorists Conspiracy from Hell (WITCH), a group that according to Echols "Betrayed their contempt toward non-movement women" (97). They wore black veils and sang, "Here comes the slaves / off to their graves" and glued stickers across the city saying, "Confront the Whore-makers"(97). See Echols, "The Great Divide," Chapter 2 of *Daring to Be Bad*, 92–101.

18. Echols, "Great Divide," 95.

19. Laurie Johnston, "Mrs. Friedan's Essay Irks Feminists," *New York Times*, March 8, 1973, 52.

20. Neil Offen, "Thirteen Clubhouse Intellectuals," *Esquire*, October 1974, 218–21.

21. Nancy Collins, "The Girls of Autumn," *Esquire*, October 1974, 221–25.

22. Despite popular perceptions, these professional cheerleaders receive little return for the work they do to "enspirit" professional football. They are required to sign a contract that waives their right to endorse consumer products, they wash their own uniforms, they must be beautiful when they go out in public (even when they're not in uniform), and they get paid around $50 a game, with no medical insurance. See Hanson's chapter on professional cheerleading in *Go!*, 49–74.

23. Gary Alan Fine, "The Promiscuous Cheerleader," *Western Folklore* 39 (1980): 120–29.

24. Jack Heifner, *Vanities* (New York: Samuel French, 1976).

25. *Sports Illustrated* featured an article about the big and serious business of cheerleading. But what raises the hair on the backs of sports enthusiasts is the idea of cheerleading being designated a sport. See Sonja Steptoe, "The Pom-Pom Chronicles," *Sports Illustrated*, December 30, 1991, 38–44.

26. Hanson, *Go!* 90.

27. Echols, *Daring*, vii.

Chapter 5

1. See Donald Bogle's discussion of the black female model presented in movies like *Foxy Brown* and *Cleopatra Jones* (1973) in his study, *Toms, Coons, Mulattoes, Mammies, and Bucks: An Interpretative History of Blacks in American Films* (New York: Viking Press, 1973).

2. bell hooks, "Selling Hot Pussy," in her *Black Looks: Race and Representation* (Boston: South End Press, 1992), 69.

3. "Blaxploitation" has become a term used to refer to the black urban action dramas of the 1970s that followed a too often repeated plot formula: excessive sex, crime, violence, and stereotypical representations of "ghetto blackness." Blaxploitation functions as a critical term signifying the exploitation and manipulation of African American audiences as well as African American actors, who Robert

Weems points out were paid poorly for the films. See his *Desegregating the Dollar: African American Consumerism in the Twentieth Century* (New York: New York University Press, 1998), 87.

4. Jack Hill directed several exploitation movies in the 1970s, including *Switchblade Sisters* (1975) and *The Swinging Cheerleaders* (1974). He has become credited by some as a pioneer of feminist-oriented popular culture films. Notwithstanding, many of Hill's women-oriented films imitate the masculine features and situations usually found in films starring men and rely on the exploitation of women as much as they do the tough guy movie model. Hill wrote *Coffy* as a vehicle for Grier, who previously had small parts in several of his earlier films.

5. Jack Hill, interview by Nathaniel Thompson, n.d., <www.monodigital.com/hilltalk.html> 6.

6. Pam Grier, "Pam Grier: The Mocha Mogul of Hollywood," interview by Jamaica Kincaid, *Ms.*, August 1975, 2.

7. In his book *Desegregating*, Weems explains that Hollywood was in an economic slump in the very early 1970s but was revitalized by black movies. One of the reasons American International Pictures became anxious to make an action vehicle with a black woman was the Warner Bros. success with *Cleopatra Jones* (Tamara Dobson).

8. Grier, "Foxy as Ever," interview by Louis B. Hobson, *Calgary Sun*, December 13, 1997, <www.canoe.ca/ JamMovieArtistsG/grier_pam.html>, 5.

9. Weems, *Desegregating*, 84.

10. bell hooks, *Outlaw Culture: Resisting Representations* (New York: Routledge, 1994), 56.

11. Weems, *Desegregating*, 84.

12. Michelle Wallace, *Black Macho and the Myth of the Superwoman* (New York: Dial Press, 1978), 36–37.

13. Sherrie A. Inness, *Tough Girls: Women Warriors and Wonder Women in Popular Culture* (Philadelphia: University of Pennsylvania, 1999), 24–26.

14. Grier, Interview by Hobson, 5.

15. Wallace, *Black Macho*, 32.

16. Ibid., 13.

17. Jan Nederveen Pieterse, *White on Black: Images of Africa and Blacks in Western Popular Culture* (New Haven, Conn.: Yale University Press), 178.

18. Hill, Interview by Thompson, 6.

19. Grier, Interview by Kincaid, 53.

20. Hazel Carbys offers an insightful discussion of the racial politics implicit in the "cult of true womanhood" within her discussion of African American women's literature in *Reconstructing Womanhood: The Emergence of the Afro-American Woman Novelist* (New York: Oxford University Press, 1987), 20–25.

21. Wallace, *Black Macho*, 107.

22. Grier, Interview by Kincaid, 53.

23. Michelle Burford and Christopher John Farley, "Foxy's Dilemma: Dignity or Dollars," *Essence*, August 1999, 133. Reggae artist Jennifer Hylton has also performed under the name Foxy Brown.

24. Tricia Rose, *Black Noise: Rap Music and Black Culture* (Hanover, N.H.: Wesleyan University Press, 1994), 36.

25. Ibid., 76.

26. Gangsta rap or hardcore rap is a category of rap music noted for its graphic representation of anti-bourgeois black urban ghetto identity, profanity, and sexual obscenity. For further discussion, see Bukari Kitwana, *The Rap on Gangsta Rap: Who*

Run It? Gangsta Rap and Visions of Black Violence (Chicago: Third World Press, 1994).

27. Tricia Rose offers a helpful analysis of rap music and hip-hop, calling them "cultural, political, and commercial forms" that are for a number of young people "primary cultural, sonic, and linguistic windows on the world" (*Black Noise*, 19). Rose also explains that "Hip hop . . . attempts to negotiate the experiences of marginalization, brutally truncated opportunity, and oppression within the cultural imperatives of African-American and Caribbean history, identity, and community" (21).

28. For further history on hip-hop, see Nelson George, *Hip Hop America* (New York: Viking Press, 1998) and Alex Ogg with David Upshal, *The Hip Hop Years: A History of Rap* (London: Channel 4 Books, 1999).

29. Some helpful discussions about the historical roots of the sexist/racist iconography of the black female are provided in Sander L. Gilman, *Difference and Pathology: Stereotypes of Sexuality, Race, and Madness* (Ithaca, N.Y.: Cornell University Press, 1985), and Londa Schiebinger, *Nature's Body: Gender in the Making of Modern Science* (Boston: Beacon Press, 1993). Also see bell hooks, *Black Looks* and Carby, *Reconstructing Womanhood*.

30. hooks, "Selling," 65.

31. Ibid., 69.

32. Foxy Brown, "I'll Be," *Ill Na Na* (Def Jam, 1996).

33. Brown, "Saddest Day," *Broken Silence* (Def Jam, 2001).

34. Quoted in Burford and Farley, "Foxy's Dilemma," 136.

35. Brown, "Ill Na Na," *Ill Na Na*.

36. Brown, "My Life," *Chyna Doll* (Def Jam, 1998).

Chapter 6

"Who's That Lady?" is the first line and repeated refrain of a song by the Isley Brothers that topped the rhythm and blues charts in 1973.

1. Thomas A. Harris, *I'm Ok—You're Ok* (New York: Harper and Row, 1967); Manuel J. Smith, *When I Say No, I Feel Guilty* (New York: Bantam Books, 1975); Nancy Friday, *My Mother, My Self* (New York: Dell, 1977); Gail Sheehy, *Passages: Predictable Crises of Adult Life* (New York: Bantam Books, 1974).

2. Ella Bell, Toni C. Denton (a.k.a. Toni C. King), and Stella Nkomo, "Women of Color in Management: Toward an Inclusive Analysis," in *Women in Management: Trends, Issues, and Challenges in Managerial Diversity*, Women and Work: A Research and Policy Series 4 (Newbury Park, Calif.: Sage, 1993), 105–30. See also Betty Woody, *Black Women in the Workplace: Impacts of Structural Change in the Economy* (New York: Greenwood Press, 1992).

3. Ella Bell, "The Bicultural Life Experience of Career-Oriented Black Women," *Journal of Organizational Behavior* 11 (1990): 459–78.

4. Gloria T. Hull, Patricia Bell Scott, and Barbara Smith, eds. *All the Women Are White, All the Blacks Are Men, But Some of Us Are Brave: Black Women's Studies* (Old Westbury, N.Y.: Feminist Press, 1982). See also Elizabeth Spelman, *Inessential Woman: Problems of Exclusion in Feminist Thought* (Boston: Beacon Press, 1988).

5. M. B. Lykes, "Discrimination and Coping in the Lives of Black Women: Analyses of Data," *Journal of Social Issues* 39, 4 (1983): 79–100. See also A. Smith and A. J. Stewart, "Approaches to Studying Racism and Sexism in Black Women's Lives," *Journal of Social Issues* 39, 3 (1983): 1–15.

6. My review of 1970s *Ebony* articles about black professional women was aided by the efforts of Shika Harrison, my undergraduate summer research assistant at Denison University. I would like to express my appreciation for her contribution.

7. bell hooks uses the terms "self recovery" and "recovery" interchangeably. In this essay I use the term "recovery." See bell hooks, "Self-Recovery," in *Talking Back: Thinking Feminist/Thinking Black* (Boston: South End Press, 1989), 28–34.

8. *Ebony* was founded in 1945 by Johnson Publishing Company, the world's largest black-owned publishing company and home of both *Ebony* and *JET*. See the *Ebony* home page, <www.ebony.com>.

9. The phrase "can I get a witness?" is common folk vernacular in African American church contexts. The phrase is often used by ministers to invoke a call and response dynamic from their congregations. It signifies the need to have others understand one's verbal testimony and thereby indicate experiential validation.

10. Bell, Denton, and Nkomo, "Women of Color," 459–61.

11. Peter Bailey, "The Lady Takes Charge: New Hospital Director Brings Sensitive Medical Care to Harlem's Needy," *Ebony*, November 1971, 157–66. "The Drill Sergeant Is a Lady: Lady Marine Molds Lives of Young Recruits," *Ebony*, September 1972, 31–36. "Med School Mom: Colorado Woman Blends Tough Medical Studies with Child-Rearing and Housewife's Chores," *Ebony*, June 1972, 39–46. "A Together Prof at the University of Minnesota Law School," *Ebony*, May 1972, 39–43. "She Manages the Mail: Woman Runs L. A. Postal Facility with 3,500 Employees Handling 8 Million Pieces of Mail Daily," *Ebony*, March 1978, 48–54.

12. Patricia Harris served as Secretary of Housing and Urban Development during the Carter administration (Alex Poinsett, "Patricia Harris, HUD's Velvet-Gloved Iron Hand," *Ebony*, July 1979, 33–36). Pauli Murray was among the first three women ordained Episcopal priests in 1977 (Michele Burgen, "Rev. Dr. Pauli Murray," *Ebony*, September 1979, 107–12). Unita Blackwell was elected mayor of Mayersville, Mississippi in 1977 ("The Lady Mayor of Mayersville," *Ebony*, September 1977, 53–58). Ella Curry was superintendent of Manteno (Illinois) State Hospital ("A New Force in Mental Health Care," *Ebony*, September 1975, 65–68).

13. See William Julius Wilson, *When Work Disappears: The World of the Urban Poor* (New York: Random House, 1996) for a discussion of the decreasing employment opportunities for African Americans who are among the urban poor.

14. Carol A. Morton, "The Busy, Bright World of a Blind Woman: Sightless Psychologist Copes by Helping the Sighted Cope," *Ebony*, February 1975, 45–51. Shawn D. Lewis, "A World Without Sight or Sound: Cleveland Woman Leads National Organization of the Deaf-Blind," *Ebony*, October 1976, 101–10.

15. Toni C. King and S. A. Ferguson, "Ruptured Silences: Resistances to Relating Across Sexualities Between African-American Professional Women," *Women and Therapy* 21, 4 (1998): 37–52.

16 Leith Mullings, "Images, Ideology, and Women of Color," in *Women of Color in U.S. Society*, ed. Maxine Baca Zinn and Bonnie Thornton Dill (Philadelphia: Temple University Press, 1994), 265–89. Maxine Atkinson and Jacqueline Boles, "The Shaky Pedestal: Southern Ladies Yesterday and Today," *Southern Studies* 34, 4 (1985): 398–406.

17. "Black Women in Corporate America: Female Entrepreneurs Find Femininity Mixes Well with Business," *Ebony*, August 1977, 39–47. "A Very Special Volunteer: Six Years of Service Prepares Carolyn Payton for Top Peace Corps Post," *Ebony*, September 1978, 64–70. "Casey Jones Would Be Proud: Silvia Duckens, 23, Carries on in Tradition of Legendary Engineer," *Ebony*, March 1977, 53–61. "Women in the Ring: Despite Opposition, Sport Is Growing Nationwide," *Ebony*, April 1976, 83–88.

18. "Together Prof," 39.

19. Quoted in hooks, *Talking Back*, 28.

20. Frank Sikora, "Three Strikes Is Not Always Out: A Young Black Woman Fights Triple Prejudice," *Ebony*, April 1979, 44–56.

21. "Med School Mom," 39.

22. Walter Price Burrell, "Hollywood Stunt Girl: Pert Peaches Jones Does Risky Work for the Stars," *Ebony*, December 1971, 147–54, at 150.

23. Shawn D. Lewis, "Family Planning's Top Advocate: Young Ohio Mother Heads Planned Parenthood Federation," *Ebony*, September 1978, 85–90.

24. hooks, *Talking Back*, 28–29.

25. Toni C. King, L. Barnes Wright, N. Gibson, L. Johnson, V. Lee, B. Lovelace, S. Turner, and D. Wheeler, "Andrea's Third Shift: The Invisible Work of African-American Women in Higher Education," in *This Bridge We Call Home: Twenty Years Later—Enacting the Visions of Radical Women of Color*, ed. Gloria Anzaldúa and AnaLouise Keating (New York: Routledge, 2002).

26. hooks, *Talking Back*, 28.

27. Charles L. Sanders, "Cicely Tyson: She Can Smile Again After a Three Year Ordeal," *Ebony*, January 1979, 27–36; Bob Lucas, "Minnie Ripperton: Singing Star Discusses Her Recent Surgery for Breast Cancer," *Ebony*, December 1976, 33–42; Phyl Garland, "The Lady Lives Jazz: Mary Lou Williams Remains as a Leading Interpreter of the Art," *Ebony*, October 1979, 56–74; "First Lady of Gospel Shirley Caesar: New Album, New Contract, New Methods for Gospel Music Industry," *Ebony*, September 1977, 98–104.

28. Sanders, "Cicely Tyson," 30.

29. Carolyn Craven, "A Rape Victim Strikes Back: Television Reporter Tells of Her Personal Ordeal and Resolve to Help Capture Her Brutal Attacker," *Ebony*, September 1978, 153–60.

30 Bob Lucas, "Minnie Ripperton: Singing Star Discusses Her Recent Surgery for Breast Cancer," *Ebony*, December 1976, 34.

Chapter 7

1. Helen Gurley Brown, *Single Girl's Cookbook* (Greenwich, Conn.: Fawcett, 1972), 5.

2. For works that explore the importance of cookbooks and the messages they contain about American culture, see Anne Bower, ed., *Recipes for Reading: Community Cookbooks, Stories, Histories* (Amherst: University of Massachusetts Press, 1997); Sherrie A. Inness, *Dinner Roles: American Women and Culinary Culture* (Iowa City: University of Iowa Press, 2001); Inness, ed., *Kitchen Culture in America: Popular Representations of Food, Gender, and Race* (Philadelphia: University of Pennsylvania Press, 2001).

3. Howard P. Chudacoff, *The Age of the Bachelor: Creating an American Subculture* (Princeton, N.J.: Princeton University Press, 1999), 3.

4. For additional information on the changing perceptions of being single in the 1970s, see Sarah Anders, *Woman Alone: Confident and Creative* (Nashville, Tenn.: Broadman, 1976); Rex Buckman, *For Bachelors Only* (Laredo, Tex.: R.J. Erwin, 1970); Marie Edwards and Eleanor Hoover, *The Challenge of Being Single* (New York: Mason/Charter, 1977); Patricia O'Brien, *The Woman Alone* (New York: Quadrangle, 1973); Jack Olsen, *The Girls in the Office* (New York: Simon and Schuster, 1972); "The Pleasures and Perils of Being Single Today," *Mademoiselle*, October 1979, 91; David Reuben, "The Sexual Problems of Women Alone," *McCall's*, February 1971,

62; Elin Schoen, "Can a Woman like Me Live Without a Man?" *Ladies' Home Journal,* July 1979, 12; "Single Woman's Survival Guide: The Special Problems of Cooking for Yourself," *Glamour,* November 1979, 56; "What Women Should Know About Single Men," *Redbook,* November 1976, 135; and Judith Viorst, "Is Married Better?" *Redbook,* January 1978, 74.

5. For works that explore the life of the swinging single, see *Swinging Single: Representing Sexuality in the 1960s,* ed. Hillary Radner and Moya Luckett (Minneapolis: University of Minnesota Press, 1999); Paul Gillette, *The Single Man's Indispensable Guide and Handbook* (Chicago: Playboy Press, 1973).

6. Ruth Rosen, *The World Split Open: How the Modern Women's Movement Changed America* (New York: Penguin, 2000), 314. Sociologist Karla B. Hackstaff concurs with this belief: "Marrying became an 'option' as attitudinal changes provided leeway to have sex, live together, and live a singles life without the sting of stigma prominent in the 1950s." See her book, *Marriage in a Culture of Divorce* (Philadelphia: Temple University Press, 1999), 38.

7. The number of singles continued to rise throughout the 1970s. By 1980, close to a quarter of U.S. households included only a single person. David Frum, *How We Got Here: The 70s, the Decade That Brought You Modern Life (for Better or Worse)* (New York: Basic Books, 2000), 91.

8. Pagan Kennedy, *Platforms: A Microwaved Culture Chronicle of the 1970s* (New York: St. Martin's Press, 1994), 92.

9. Some 1970s articles went so far as to suggest that single women were as successful or more successful than their married peers; see, e.g., "Success and the Single Girl," *Society,* July 1973, 10.

10. Chudacoff, *Age of the Bachelor,* 331.

11. Viorst, "Is Married Better?" 74.

12. Ruth Halcomb, *Sex and the Single Ms.* (Chatsworth, Calif.: Books for Better Living, 1974), 7.

13. For more information about the vast marketplace of goods offered to singles in this era, see "Rise of the 'Singles'—40 Million Free Spenders," *U.S. News and World Report,* October 7, 1974, 54; and "The Way 'Singles' Are Changing U.S.," *U.S. News and World Report,* January 31, 1977, 59–60.

14. "Games Singles Play," *Newsweek,* July 16, 1973, 52.

15. Chudacoff, *Age of the Bachelor,* 266.

16. Viorst, "Is Married Better?" 74.

17. Stanlee Miller Coy, *The Single Girl's Book: Making it in the Big City* (Englewood Cliffs, N.J.: Prentice-Hall, 1971), 1.

18. Brown, *Single,* 12.

19. Rona Jaffe, "The Joy of Staying Single," *Harper's Bazaar,* March 1977, 92.

20. Ibid., 149. Mary-Ellen Banashek, writing for the popular magazine *Mademoiselle* in 1977, also had a positive view of what it meant to be a single woman: "Singlehood is powerful. And it can be a very positive form of selfishness. . . . Sometimes living alone can be the easiest route to self-discovery—no distractions, no acting for the benefit of others. Just a way to grow" (95).

21. Additional singles' cookbooks from different decades include Jane Doerfer, *Going Solo in the Kitchen* (New York: Knopf, 1995); George W. Jacobs, *Cooking for One* (Woods Hole, Mass.: Cromlech Books, 1992); Paulette Mitchell, *The 15–Minute Single Gourmet: 100 Deliciously Simple Recipes for One* (New York: Macmillan, 1994); Louise Pickoff, *You Can Cook for One (or Even Two)* (New York: Gramercy, 1961); June Roth, *The On-Your-Own Cookbook: Cooking for Yourself by Yourself* (New York: Dial, 1972); Pauline Tai, *The Bachelorette Cookbook: Easy Fun Ideas for the Single Chef* (Garden City, N.Y.: Doubleday, 1968); Bernard Wile, *Cooking for One and Two*

(New York: Hearthside Press, 1960); and Woman's Day, *Cooking for One*, ed. Jeri Laber (New York: Random House, 1978).

22. For other 1970s articles that focus on cooking for the single woman or man, see Bernadine Morris, "It's Not Just Women's Work: Men Who Cook," *New York Times*, April 20, 1975, 54; "Singles Cookery," *Ebony*, April 1978, 148; "Single Woman's Survival Guide: The Special Problems of Cooking for Yourself," *Glamour*, November 1979, 56; and Angela Taylor, "Now It's Men's Turn to Stand over a Hot Stove," *New York Times*, February 1, 1975, 20.

23. Len O'Dell, *The Naked Chef: A Survival Plan for the Single Man* (Cheyenne, Wyo.: Dunmore Publishing, 178), 32.

24. Edwin Greenblatt, *Suddenly Single: A Survival Kit for the Single Man* (New York: Quadrangle, 1973), 156.

25. O'Dell, *Naked Chef*, n.p.

26. Nigel Napier-Andrews, *How to Eat Well and Stay Single* (Toronto: Kakabeka, 1974), 3.

27. Cory Kilvert, *The Male Chauvinist's Cookbook* (New York: Winchester Press, 1974), ix.

28. Julian G. Richter, *The Single Man's Guide to Fun and Games Cookbook* (Plantation, Fla.: S. Arden Press, 1977), 50.

29. Other ways existed to make cooking appear more masculine to male readers. Cookbooks for men emphasized the manly nature of cooking so that men would not feel uncomfortable in the feminine world of the kitchen. For example, cookbook author Nigel Napier-Andrews described kitchen utensils as "weapons" (104) and described laying out a meal as "like a battle plan" (17–18). If cooking could be made to seem as masculine as possible by its association with warfare, cooking would its association with femininity.

30. Sandy Lesberg, *The Single Chef's Cookbook* (Englewood Cliffs, N.J.: Prentice-Hall, 1970).

31. Greenblatt, *Suddenly Single*, 3.

32. Donald Kilbourn, *Pots and Pans: Man's Answer to Women's Lib: A Cook Book for Men* (London: Luscombe, 1974), 1.

33. Greenblatt, *Suddenly Single*, 37.

34. Napier-Andrews, *Eat Well*, vii.

35. Kilbourn, *Pots and Pans*, 16.

Chapter 8

1. See Charlotte Brunsdon, *The Feminist, the Housewife, and the Soap Opera* (Oxford: Oxford University Press, 2000).

2. See Robert C. Allen, *Speaking of Soap Operas* (Chapel Hill: University of North Carolina Press, 1985).

3. *Soaps: The First 50 Years*, CBS-TV, October 24, 1994.

4. Robert LaGuardia, *The Wonderful World of TV Soap Operas* (New York: Ballantine, 1974), 5.

5. Harding Lemay, *Eight Years in* Another World: *The Inside Story of a Soap Opera* (New York: Atheneum, 1981), 37.

6. Christopher Schemering, *The Soap Opera Encyclopedia* (New York: Ballantine, 1987), 281.

7. Quoted in LaGuardia, *Wonderful World*, 198.

8. Gerard J. Waggett, *The Soap Opera Encyclopedia* (New York: HarperCollins, 1997), 57.

9. Robert LaGuardia, *Soap World* (New York, Arbor House, 1983), 109.

10. Robert LaGuardia, *From* Ma Perkins *to* Mary Hartman*: The Illustrated History of Soap Operas* (New York: Ballantine, 1977), 80.

11. Waggett, *Encyclopedia*, 54.

12. Patricia Kearney and Jane Kutler, *Super Soaps: The Complete Book of Daytime Dramas* (New York: Grosset and Dunlap, 1977), 41.

13. Lemay, *Eight Years*, 84.

14. Schemering, *Encyclopedia*, 273.

15. Manuela Soares, *The Soap Opera Book* (New York: Harmony Books, 1978), 57.

16. Mary Cassata, Michelle Lynn Rondina, and Thomas Skill, "Placing a 'Lid' on Television Serial Drama: An Analysis of the Lifestyles, Interpersonal Management Skills, and Demography of Daytime's Fictional Population," in *Life on Daytime Television: Tuning-In American Serial Drama*, ed. Cassata and Skill (Norwood, N.J.: Ablex, 1983), 12.

17. Soares, *Soap Opera Book*, 57.

18. Lemay, *Eight Years*, 65.

19. Julie Poll, As the World Turns*: The Complete Family Scrapbook* (Los Angeles: General Publishing Group, 1996), 45.

20. Mary Cassata and Thomas Skill, "Soap Opera Women: An Audience View," in *Life on Daytime Television*, 23.

21. Soares, *Soap Opera Book*, 57.

Chapter 9

1. Barbara Ehrenreich, Elizabeth Hess, and Gloria Jacobs, "Beatlemania: Girls Just Want to Have Fun," in *The Adoring Audience: Fan Culture and Popular Media*, ed. Lisa A. Lewis (New York: Routledge, 1992), 84–106.

2. Randi Reisfeld and Danny Fields, *Who's Your Fave Rave?* (New York: Boulevard Books, 1997), vii.

3. Angela McRobbie and Jenny Garber, "Girls and Subcultures," in *Feminism and Youth Culture*, ed. McRobbie (Boston: Unwin Hyman, 1991), 13.

4. Sheryl Garratt, "Teenage Dreams," in *On Record: Rock, Pop, and the Written Word*, ed. Simon Frith and Andrew Goodwin (New York: Pantheon Books, 1990), 401.

5. Mary Pipher, *Reviving Ophelia: Saving the Selves of Adolescent Girls* (New York: Ballantine Books, 1994), 69.

6. For example, see Jackson Katz's comments in the educational film *Tough Guise: Violence, Media, and the Crisis in Masculinity*, dir. Sut Jhally (Northampton, Mass.: Media Education Foundation, 2000).

7. Simon Frith and Angela McRobbie, "Rock and Sexuality," in *On Record: Rock, Pop, and the Written Word*, ed. Frith and Andrew Goodwin (New York: Pantheon, 1990), 374.

8. See, e.g., Steve Waksman's nuanced analysis of Led Zeppelin and "cock rock" in *Instruments of Desire: The Electric Guitar and the Shaping of Musical Experience* (Cambridge, Mass.: Harvard University Press, 1999), 237–76.

9. Reisfeld and Fields, *Fave Rave*, 107.

10. "Why We Luv ...!," *Tiger Beat*, December 1965, 3 (closed ellipses in original).

11. "At Home with Valerie!" *Tiger Beat*, October 1976, 8–9.

12. "Angel Jackie: Money's Her Hobby!" *Tiger Beat Star*, December 1977, 51.

13. "Dear Robby!" *Tiger Beat*, April 1977, 14.

14. "If Shaun Were Your Boyfriend," *Tiger Beat Star*, July 1977, 4.

15. Kim Cooper and David Smay, eds., *Bubblegum Music Is the Naked Truth* (Los Angeles: Feral House, 2001). For definitions of teen-idol music versus bubblegum, see Cooper and Smay's introduction, "Bubble Entendres," 1–8. For bubblegum's connections to punk, new wave, and other musical forms, see the essays in the "Unlikely Bubblegum" section, 240–50.

16. Reisfeld and Fields, *Fave Rave*, xi.

17. Garratt, "Teenage Dreams," 401.

18. John Sherwood, "If Only I Knew Shaun Cassidy's Favorite Color, My Life Would Be Complete," *Washington Star*, April 13, 1978, sec. C.

Chapter 10

1. Jack Condon and David Hofstede, *Charlie's Angels Casebook* (Los Angeles: Pomegranate, 2000), 29.

2. Susan J. Douglas, *Where the Girls Are: Growing Up Female with the Mass Media* (New York: Random House, 1994), 212–13.

3. "TV's Superwomen," *Time*, November 22, 1976, 67–71.

4. *Charlie's Angels* merchandise was big business; Hasbro Industries, for example, spent over $2.5 million to advertise its *Charlie's Angels* dolls. For a complete list of *Charlie's Angels* products, see Condon and Hofstede, *Casebook*, 275–87.

5. "TV's Superwomen," 69.

6. Lori Gottlieb, *Lori, Stick Figure: A Diary of My Former Self* (New York: Simon and Schuster, 2000), 131–32.

7. See Naomi Wolf, *The Beauty Myth: How Images of Beauty Are Used Against Women* (New York: Morrow, 1991); Bonnie Dow, *Prime-Time Feminism: Television, Media Culture, and the Women's Movement Since 1970* (Philadelphia: University of Pennsylvania Press, 1996); and Joan Jacobs Brumberg, *The Body Project: An Intimate History of American Girls* (New York: Random House, 1997).

8. The term "Angel in the House," which dates to the mid-nineteenth century, refers to the Victorian ideal of passive, domestic womanhood. In her 1942 essay "Professions for Women," feminist writer Virginia Woolf urged women to kill the "Angel in the House" in order to free themselves from this restricting icon (*Norton Anthology of Literature by Women*, ed. Sandra Gilbert and Susan Gubar [New York: Norton, 1345–48]). Yet even in the 1970s images of women as passive housewives and mothers (Carol Brady, for instance) predominated in the mass media.

9. For more complete discussions of *Wonder Woman* and *The Bionic Woman*, see Douglas, *Where the Girls Are*, 217–19, and Sherrie A. Inness, *Tough Girls: Women Warriors and Wonder Women in Popular Culture* (Philadelphia: University of Pennsylvania Press, 1999), 45–48.

10. Douglas, *Where the Girls Are*, 213.

11. Melinda Wittstock, "Charlie's Angels Ride Again," *Observer* (London), November 12, 2000, 22.

12. I am focusing on just the first season with the original cast of *Charlie's Angels*, before the departures of producer Barney Rosensweig (who went on to produce the female crime drama *Cagney and Lacey*) and Farrah Fawcett in 1977 (Fawcett's decision to leave the show is discussed later in this essay). What followed was a revolving cast of Angels, including Cheryl Ladd as Kris Munroe (1977–81), Shelly Hack as Tiffany Welles (1979–80), and Tanya Roberts as Julie Rogers (1980–81). At the show's cancellation, the only original Angel remaining was Jaclyn Smith. The later Angels lacked the chemistry of the original trio, and the writing and direction became increasingly formulaic. For details about the departures of Kate

Jackson and Shelley Hack, see Carolyn See, "'I'm Not the Difficult One'," *TV Guide*, February 18–24, 1978, 26; Megan Rosenfeld, "The 'Angel Who Flew Charlie's Coop," *Washington Post*, October 31, 1979, B1.

13. Destiny's Child, "Independent Women, Part 1," Music for *Charlie's Angels* (Sony, 2000). This song, which went to the top of the pop charts, focuses on women's economic empowerment, which is only alluded to in the film (the Angels all drive great cars, as in the original series). See the following lines: "The shoes on my feet / I bought it / The clothes I'm wearing / I bought it . . . The car I'm driving / I bought it / I depend on me."

14. For a discussion of *Police Woman* and its connection to *Charlie's Angels*, see Sumiko Higashi, "Hold It! Women in Television Adventure Series," *Journal of Popular Film and Television* 8, 3 (1980): 26–37. He refers to Pepper Anderson and the Angels as "gumshoes in drag," who take on masculine roles and behaviors but undermine or contradict them with stereotypical female behavior.

15. Condon and Hofstede, *Casebook*, 6.

16. Ibid., 25.

17. Douglas, *Where the Girls Are*, 214.

18. Ibid.

19. Condon and Hofstede, *Casebook*, 35.

20. Douglas, *Where the Girls Are*, 211–12.

21. Susan Brownmiller, *Against Our Will: Men, Women, and Rape* (New York: Bantam, 1975), selection in *Feminism in Our Time: The Essential Writings, World War II to the Present*, ed. Miriam Schneir (New York: Vintage, 1994), 282.

22. Douglas, *Where the Girls Are*, 214.

23. Inness, *Tough Girls*, 44–45. Inness argues that the show's frequent use of disguises works to undermine the Angels' power and the show's feminism: "Going undercover—masquerading as someone else—shows the constructed nature of identity. All is illusion. The constructed nature of the Angels' identities is brought into question. . . . Toughness, the show hints, is perhaps as artificial as the Angels' roles as hookers, nurses, or roller derby queens" (43).

24. "TV's Superwomen," 69.

25. Ibid., 68.

26. Condon and Hofstede, *Casebook*, 59

27. Inness, *Tough Girls*, 46.

28. Quoted in Condon and Hofstede, *Casebook*, 59.

29. D. Keith Mano, "So You Want to Be an Angel," *Life*, May 1988, 144–46.

30. Quoted in Susan Faludi, *Backlash: The Undeclared War Against American Women* (New York: Anchor, 1991), 141. Similar comments by Aaron Spelling are cited in Lynn Schurnberger, "Should Angels Fear to Retread?" *Glamour*, September 1988, 61.

31. Stephen Schaefer, "Arresting 'Angels'," *Boston Herald*, October 29, 2000, O63.

32. Quoted in Claudia Puig and Josh Chetwynd, "Three of a Heavenly Kind," *USA Today*, November 3, 2000, 1E.

33. "Welcome to Angel World" is included on the DVD version of *Charlie's Angels*, dir. Joseph McGinty Nichol (Columbia/Tri-Star, 2000).

34. Puig and Chetwynd, "Three of a Heavenly Kind," 1E.

35. Wittstock, "Charlie's Angels Ride Again," 22.

36. Ruth Shalit, "Canny and Lacy," *New Republic*, April 6, 1998, 32.

37. Wittstock, "Charlie's Angels Ride Again," 22.

38. Elizabeth Lenhard, *Charlie's Angels* (New York: Pocket Books, 2000), 12.

39. In fact, the *Charlie's Angels* fight scenes were choreographed by Cheung-Yan Yuen, who has worked on many of Jackie Chan's Hong Kong martial arts films and is the brother of the fight choreographer for *The Matrix*. The DVD contains an explanation of how several of Yeun's stunts were accomplished with the Angels on wires (which were later digitally erased from the film).

40. Jane Stevenson, "Angels with Attitude," *Toronto Sun*, October 29, 2000, S8.

41. Ibid.

42. Lenhard, *Charlie's Angels* 77–78.

43. Ibid., 93.

44. Inness, *Tough Girls*, 43.

45. Lenhard, *Charlie's Angels* 29.

46. Ibid., 19.

47. For a reading of *Xena: Warrior Princess*, see Inness, *Tough Girls*, 160–76.

48. For details about the sequel, see "Avenging Angels," *Empire Online*, May 17, 2001, <www.empireonline.co.uk/news/news.asp?3128>.

49. Faludi explains that there has been a pattern of backlashes against feminism in the twentieth century: "But if fear and loathing of feminism is a sort of perpetual viral condition in our culture, it is not always in the acute stage; its symptoms subside and resurface periodically. . . . If we trace these occurrences in American history . . . we find such flare-ups are hardly random; they have always been triggered by the perception—accurate or not—that women are making great strides" (*Backlash*, xix).

Chapter 11

I would like to thank Mark Allister, Matt Rohn, Mary Titus, and Jill Watts for reading drafts, Michael Furmanovsky for his knowledge of music trivia, Bryn Geffert for trying so hard to find statistics and photographs for me, and my husband, Michael Fitzgerald, for listening to my ideas, even if he thinks none of this is "real" history.

1. My interpretation of the function of popular culture is drawn from a feminist model, particularly Susan Douglas, *Where the Girls Are: Growing up Female with the Mass Media* (New York: Random House, 1994); Bonnie Dow, *Prime-Time Feminism: Television, Media Culture, and the Women's Movement Since 1970* (Philadelphia: University of Pennsylvania Press, 1996); and Janine Basinger, *A Woman's View: How Hollywood Spoke to Women, 1930–1960* (New York: Knopf, 1993). These authors, in turn, have drawn on Antonio Gramsci's notion of cultural hegemony and some of the cultural works of Mikhail Bakhtin.

2. Stuart Hall and Paddy Whannel, "The Young Audience, 1964" in *On Record: Rock, Pop, and the Written Word*, ed. Simon Frith and Andrew Goodwin (New York: Pantheon, 1990), 27–37.

3. Simon Frith, *Sound Effects: Youth, Leisure, and the Politics of Rock and Roll* (New York: Pantheon, 1981), 226–28.

4. See, for example, Laura Mulvey, "Visual Pleasure and Narrative Cinema," *Screen* 16 (Autumn 1975): 6–18 for a Freudian interpretation of women as objects in the movies.

5. Douglas, *Where the Girls Are*, chap. 4; Barbara Bradby, "Do-Talk and Don't-Talk: The Division of the Subject in Girl-Group Music," in Frith and Goodwin, *On Record*, 341–68 dissects song lyrics to show tensions between objectivity and passivity and fantasy and reality elements in girl group music, proving Douglas's con-

tention. Charlotte Greig's chapters on the girl groups of the 1960s are in her *Will You Still Love Me Tomorrow: Girl Groups from the 50s On* (London: Virago, 1989), 33–131.

6. On lyrics, see Donald Horton, "The Dialogue of Courtship in Popular Song," in Frith and Goodwin, *On Record,* 14–26.

7. Greig, *Will You,* 103. Greig's interpretation has considerably more subtlety than I have room for here.

8. Lucy O'Brien, *She Bop: The Definitive History of Women in Rock, Pop, and Soul* (New York: Penguin, 1995), chap. 3; Gillian G. Gaar, *She's a Rebel: The History of Women in Rock & Roll* (Seattle: Seal Press, 1992), 78–79 talks about Barry Gordy, Jr.'s control over the Supremes.

9. Gaar, *She's a Rebel,* 70–71.

10. Ed Ward, Geoffrey Stokes, and Ken Tucker, *Rock of Ages: The Rolling Stone History of Rock and Roll* (New York: Summit Books, 1986), 328–49.

11. O'Brien, *She Bop,* chap. 4.

12. Ibid., 99, or Gaar, *She's a Rebel,* 107.

13. See Sara Evans, *Personal Politics: The Roots of Women's Liberation in the Civil Rights Movement and the New Left* (New York: Vintage, 1979) and Alice Echols, *Daring to Be Bad: Radical Feminism in America, 1967–1975* (Minneapolis: University of Minnesota Press, 1989).

14. On the singer-songwriters see Ward, Stokes, and Tucker, *Rock of Ages,* chap. 27 or David Szatmary, *A Time to Rock: A Social History of Rock 'N' Roll* (New York: Schirmer Books, 1996), chap. 11.

15. See, for example, entry on Alan Alda in Jane Stern and Michael Stern, *Encyclopedia of Pop Culture* (New York: HarperPerennial, 1992), 6–8 or Bruce J. Schulman, *The Seventies: The Great Shift in American Culture, Society, and Politics* (New York: Free Press, 2001), 177–79.

16. See O'Brien, *She Bop,* 175–77.

17. Frith, *Sound Effects,* 10 and Ward, Stokes, and Tucker, *Rock of Ages,* 468–69.

18. Lisa A. Lewis, *Gender Politics, and MTV: Voicing the Difference* (Philadelphia: Temple University Press, 1990), 28–42.

19. Gaar, *She's a Rebel,* 124–26, 142.

20. Ibid., chap. 4.

21. Erik Barnouw, *Tube of Plenty: The Evolution of American Television* (New York: Oxford University Press, 1975, reprint 1982), 470, focuses on the importance of female viewers for the television networks in this same period.

22. Barbara Ehrenreich, Elizabeth Hess, and Gloria Jacobs, *Re-Making Love: The Feminization of Sex* (Garden City, N.Y.: Anchor Press, 1986), 74. See also Schulman, *The Seventies,* 174–75 and Gerri Hirshey, *We Gotta Get Out of This Place: The True, Tough Story of Women in Rock* (New York: Atlantic Monthly Press, 2001), 100–102.

23. Hirshey, *We Gotta,* 87, describes Simon as "one of rock's first hot mamas," who could be both maternal and sexy.

24. Gaar, *She's a Rebel,* 189, or Hirshey, *We Gotta,* 81.

25. When asked what one album she would take on a desert island, actress Cynthia Nixon replied *Tapestry* because "you can sing along to those songs and feel like you're singing about yourself." See *Biography,* 6/01, 38. On the autobiographical style of singer-songwriters see Ward, Stokes, and Tucker, *Rock of Ages,* 474.

26. Baez, in her autobiography *And a Voice to Sing With* (New York: Summit Books, 1987), 242, recalled that Bob Dylan told her in the mid-1970s, "I'd start selling albums again if I let my hair grow." Anne-Lise François notes in "'These Boots Were Made for Walking': Fashion as 'Compulsive Artifice,'" in *The Seventies: The Age of Glitter in Popular Culture,* ed. Shelton Waldrep (New York: Routledge, 2000),

156, that on the cover of *No Secrets* Carly Simon "dress[ed] down as the ordinary American girl, seeking to establish intimacy with everyone and anyone on the street . . . because she is like everyone else."

27. Gaar, *She's a Rebel*, 185.

28. Ibid., 121–23.

29. On Carpenter, see ibid., 60–64.

30. Winifred Wandersee, *On the Move: American Women in the 1970s* (Boston: Twayne Publishers, 1988) talks about the movement; Susan Faludi, *Backlash: The Undeclared War Against American Women* (New York: Crown, 1991), talks about the backlash.

31. Baez, *And a Voice*, 291.

32. Frith and McRobbie, "Rock and Sexuality," 374.

33. Tom Carson, "Rocket to Russia," in Frith and Goodwin, *On Record*, 445, describes *Some Girls* as a rediscovery of rock's trashy side.

34. As quoted in O'Brien, *She Bop*, 139. A poster picturing Harry and featuring the caption "wouldn't you like to rip her to shreds" was part of the marketing campaign Chrysalis Records used to promote Blondie. See Gaar, *She's a Rebel*, 260.

35. Schulman, *The Seventies*, 144–45, describes the economic climate against which disco developed. On the music, see Ward, Stokes, and Tucker, *Rock of Ages*, 527.

36. Quoted by Szatmary, *A Time to Rock*, 244. See also Iain Chambers, *Urban Rhythms: Pop Music and Popular Culture* (New York: St. Martin's Press, 1985), 187.

37. The quotation comes from Richard Dyer, "In Defense of Disco," in Frith and Goodwin, *On Record*, 418.

38. Szatmary, *A Time to Rock*, 244–46 (all the room he devotes to disco) is typical of the negative press disco gets in rock histories.

39. Quotation is from Ward, Stokes, and Tucker, *Rock of Ages*, 528; on sexuality and the disco diva see O'Brien, *She Bop*, 273.

40. O'Brien, *She Bop*, 272 sees the phenomenon extending beyond the disco era proper.

41. Ibid., 272.

42. Douglas, *Where the Girls Are*, chap. 9.

43. By 1979, disco was a five-billion-dollar industry. Steve Rubell, founder of the disco Studio 54, boasted that only the Mafia had a better profit margin. See Szatmary, *A Time to Rock*, 246.

44. See Douglas, *Where the Girls Are*, chap. 11.

Contributors

CARRIE N. BAKER is assistant professor and director of women's studies at Berry College in Mount Berry, Georgia. She specializes in women's legal history and feminist legal and political theory. She has published articles on sexual harassment in employment and education and on representations of battered women in legal discourse. Her dissertation is entitled "Sex, Power, and Politics: The Origins of Sexual Harassment Policy in the United States."

STEVE CRAIG is professor of radio, television and film at the University of North Texas. His research interests include gender images in the media and radio and television history. He is editor of *Men, Masculinity, and the Media* and coauthor of *Consuming Environments: Television and Commercial Culture.* His articles on the media have appeared in *Journalism Quarterly, Journal of Broadcasting and Electronic Media, Journal of Communication, Sex Roles,* and other scholarly journals.

STEPHANE DUNN is assistant professor of English at Ohio State University. Her research interests include representations of race, gender, and sexuality in modernism, twentieth-century American literature, popular culture, and African-American culture. She is also a creative writer of nonfiction essays, drama, and fiction.

MOLLY ENGELHARDT is a Ph.D. candidate in the English department at the University of Southern California. Her research centers primarily on Victorian popular culture, adolescence, and representations of the classed and gendered body in the nineteenth-century British novel. Her dissertation is entitled "Dancing out of Line: Ballrooms, Ballets, and Victorian Bodies in Motion."

ELYCE RAE HELFORD is professor of English and director of women's studies at Middle Tennessee State University. Her research centers in representations of gender, race, and feminism in science fiction and fantasy literature, television, and film. Helford is editor of *Fantasy Girls: Gender in* the New Universe of Science Fiction and Fantasy Television, coeditor of Enterprise Zones: Critical Positions on Star Trek, and author of articles and book chapters on Buffy the Vampire Slayer, Xena: Warrior Princess, Tank Girl, and fiction by Octavia Butler, Carol Emshwiller, Jewelle Gomez, Misha Nógha, Marge Piercy, and Stanislaw Lem. She is currently writing a book on women and anger in contemporary media culture.

SHERRIE A. INNESS is associate professor of English at Miami University. Her research interests include gender and cooking culture, girls' literature and culture, popular culture, and gender studies. She is author of Intimate Communities: Representation and Social Transformation in Women's College Fiction, 1895–1910; The Lesbian Menace: Ideology, Identity, and the Representation of Lesbian Life; Tough Girls: Women Warriors and Wonder Women in Popular Culture (University of Pennsylvania Press); and Dinner Roles: American Women and Culinary Culture, and editor of Nancy Drew and Company: Culture, Gender, and Girls' Series; Breaking Boundaries: New Perspectives on Regional Writing; Delinquents and Debutantes: Twentieth-Century American Girls' Cultures; Millennium Girls: Today's Girls Around the World; Kitchen Culture in America: Popular Representations of Food, Gender, and Race (University of Pennsylvania Press); Running for Their Lives: Girls, Cultural Identity, and Stories of Survival; Pilaf, Pozole, and Pad Thai: American Women and Ethnic Food; and Cooking Lessons: The Politics of Gender and Food.

TONI C. KING is associate professor of black studies and women's studies at Denison University. Her expertise is feminist therapy with an emphasis in relational psychology. She has published extensively in the area of Black women's adult development with a focus on issues of recovery for African American professional women. She is currently coediting a text on Black women's matrilineal traditions of leadership development. She has also coauthored a meditation book for women, Deep Woman Feelings: A Book of Contemplations, which addresses recovery issues in Black women's lives.

JUDY KUTULAS is professor of history, American studies, women's studies, and media studies and director of women's studies at St. Olaf College. Her research interests are divided between twentieth-century American liberalism/radicalism and her ongoing fascination with more recent popular culture. She is author of The Long War: The Intellectual People's Front and Anti- Stalinism, 1930–1940 and assorted articles on radical intellectuals of the 1930s, the American Civil Liberties Union, and American television. She is currently working on a manuscript on the American Civil Liberties Union and American liberalism.

ILANA NASH is a research associate at the Five College Women's Studies Center. She received a Ph.D. from the American Culture Studies program at Bowling Green State University. Her dissertation, "America's Kid Sister: Teenage Girls and Popular Culture, 1930–1965," explores the historical development of representations of adolescent femininity in popular fiction, film, radio, and television. She has published articles about Nancy Drew in *Girlhood in America* (ABC-CLIO, 2001) and *Dime Novel Round-Up*.

THOMAS D. PETITJEAN, JR. is assistant professor of English at Northwestern State University of Louisiana. His areas of research include popular culture, gender and sexuality representations, technical writing, sociolinguistics, supernatural fiction, and Edith Wharton. He has worked for *New York* magazine and written for the daytime dramas *As the World Turns* and *Another World*. Under the pseudonym Leila Bercier he has published four contemporary romance novels: *Style, Style Two, Vanities,* and *My Life to Live*. He has also published papers in academic journals, books, and encyclopedias.

WHITNEY WOMACK is Assistant Professor of English at Miami University. Her research interests include nineteenth-century British and American women's literature, gender studies, and popular culture. She has published articles on Harriet Beecher Stowe, Elizabeth Gaskell, Rebecca-Harding Davis, Elizabeth Siddal, and Margaret Sackville. Currently, she is working on a book that examines the figure of the woman reformer in nineteenth-century women's literature.

Index

Acknowledgments

I wish to thank all the people who made this book possible. My contributors have done an excellent job of keeping deadlines. I am grateful for the help of all people at Denison University who helped me when I was editing the book, including Eloise Buker, Mandy Graver, and Mae Pound. I want to thank individuals, including Hallie Bourne, Kelley Bullard, Theresa Hurst, and Whitney Womack, who read sections of the book before its publication. Robert E. Lockhart, Alison A. Anderson, Samantha Foster, Carol Ehrlich, and all the others at the University of Pennsylvania Press who made this book possible also deserve my sincere appreciation for their outstanding work, as do the reviewers for the press, Patricia Gantt and Norma Pecora. I could not expect a better group of people, professional, knowledgeable, and prompt, and I am honored to work with them.

I appreciate my friends, including Julie Hucke, Michele Lloyd, Deb Mandel, Heather Schell, Lisa Sommer, and Liz Wilson. Kelley Bullard deserves special appreciation. I cannot express how important they are to me and what encouragement they provide to me. I thank all my colleagues at Miami University for being supportive, considerate, and encouraging. They nourish my work. I especially appreciate Kathy Burton, John Krafft, Peter Martin, Diana Royer, and Whitney Womack. I am also deeply grateful to some especially important people in my life, my mother and father, Ruth and Lowell Inness, my two dearest friends; I can never thank them enough for that.

Finally, this book is dedicated to Hallie Bourne, someone whose support means a great deal to me. I admire her integrity and straightforwardness and respect her keen intelligence. Because she questions beliefs and assumptions that others take for granted, she makes me think more deeply about my writing and the world. She also has a tremendous zest for life that she shares with others; it is impossible not to be influenced by her spirit.